Praise for

MONEYHUNT

"Consider this: most large companies start small. This book is one more example of how *MoneyHunt* plays an important role in helping entrepreneurs grow their companies."
—John W. "Jay" Jordan II, chairman and CEO, Jordan Industries, Inc.

"There they go again . . . shamelessly exploiting the fact that we all harbor fantasies about starting a business—and that most of us should never act on such a foolish impulse. A very entertaining and useful guide to the perils of entrepreneurship."
—Tom Post, senior editor, *Forbes Magazine*

"Each story communicates the excitement that characterizes both the startup phase of a company and appearing on the show. This book is like the show: You're scared if you're in it, and you're offended if you're not. Read it and reap." —Guy Kawasaki, garage.com

"Entrepreneurs learn best from each other. This lively, readable book has all the war stories you'll need to avoid the pitfalls when it comes to financing your dreams."
—Jane Applegate, syndicated columnist, entrepreneur, and author of
201 Great Ideas for Your Small Business

"The hunt for money is the only hunt I know where the hunted are the predators and the hunters are the prey! *MoneyHunt* offers real protection and good advice to the courageous souls who are trying to raise money from some of the toughest people on earth."
—Reese Schonfeld, founding president and CEO, CNN

"Young entrepreneurs everywhere are starting businesses and growing them with amazing speed. The fresh perspective and real life drama of *MoneyHunt* plays an important role in teaching and entertaining this new generation. What a book!"
—Doug Mellinger, chairman, PRT Group, Inc., past president, Young
Entrepreneurs' Organization

"This book is right on the money for growing a business—MoneyHunt is great!"
                                        —Jerry Yang, cofounder, Yahoo!

"MoneyHunt is the road map to the future of American business, which will continue to be built by the risk takers. Like the turtle, entrepreneurs have to stick their necks out if they want to get anywhere."
                              —John Y. Brown, founder, Kentucky Fried Chicken,
                                        former governor, State of Kentucky

"The Internet is leveling the playing field in terms of who can start and grow a business, and yet mining the experience of others can make the difference between success and failure. Women, seniors, kids and anyone else who dreams of being an entrepreneur should clamor to read this book!"
—Candice Carpenter, cochairperson of the board and CEO, iVillage.com

"Like most entrepreneurs, we had to learn to understand and face the realities of how banks, sophisticated investors, and Wall Street look at our companies. . . . This book shares a deeper perspective on how they all think and how entrepreneurs should handle them: invaluable advice for anyone hunting for money!"
                              —Brian Maxwell, president and CEO, PowerBar, Inc.

"MoneyHunt provides a no-holds-barred telling of what being an entrepreneur is without sugarcoating. For those who want to make it—really make it—this book will be under their pillows."
     —Paul and Sarah Edwards, authors of the Working from Home series,
                              including *The Secrets of Self Employment*

"So many business books are boring how-tos that lack the drama of real entrepreneurs and their challenges. MoneyHunt's twenty-seven rules are another story altogether. When it comes to entertaining and teaching entrepreneurs, Miles and Cliff are playing a whole new tune."
                              —Jason Olim, cofounder and CEO, CDnow

MONEYHUNT

MILES SPENCER AND CLIFF ENNICO

MONEYHUNT

27 New Rules for Creating and Growing a Breakaway Business

HarperBusiness
A Division of HarperCollinsPublishers

To our wives, Karen and Dolores

HarperCollins books may be purchased for educational, business, or sales promotional use. For information please write: Special Markets Department, HarperCollins Publishers, Inc., 10 East 53rd Street, New York, NY 10022.

FIRST EDITION

Designed by Jessica Shatan

Library of Congress Cataloging-in-Publication Data

Spencer, Miles
    MoneyHunt : 27 new rules for creating and growing a breakaway business / Miles
Spencer and Cliff Ennico. — 1st ed.
        p.   cm.
    Includes index.
    ISBN 0-06-661995-5
    1. New business enterprises—United States—Management.   2. New business
enterprises—United States Case studies.   3. Corporations—United States—Growth Case
studies.   4. Success in business—United States Case studies.   5. Entrepreneurship—
United States Case studies.   I. Ennico, Cliff.   II. MoneyHunt (Television program)
III. Title.
    HD62.5.S687   1999
    659.1'1—dc21   99-31686

99 00 01 02 03 RRD/❖ 10 9 8 7 6 5 4 3 2 1

CONTENTS

ACKNOWLEDGMENTS

The building of *MoneyHunt* has involved a good deal more than two people; at various times more than a hundred people have played roles in the development of our TV show, Internet site, and other products and services for the entrepreneurial community. We cannot possibly hope to thank them all. There are a few, however, whose contribution to *MoneyHunt* can never be overlooked or underestimated:

- Special thanks to our agent, Wes Neff; our editor, David Conti; our marketing whiz, Lisa Berkowitz; and the many entrepreneurs whose stories gave us the inspiration for this book.

- Niles Cohen, Warren Struhl, and Teddy Struhl of Capital Express LLC, our initial investor.

- Joyce Fischman, our first producer in the "wild and woolly" days of public-access cable TV, and Dan Snellman, who recommended her to us.

- Steve Samuels, for inching us along the yardstick of success, and for introducing . . .

- Deborah Ely, our producer and favorite "celebuttante," for constantly raising the bar on quality.

- David Othmer of WHYY Channel 12 in Philadelphia, for thinking out of the box and doing the right thing.

- Scott Carlin of Warner Brothers, for sharing his in-depth knowledge of the television business.

- Frank Henson, affectionately known as "Bubba," whose gonzo brainstorming has led to some of our more inspired ideas.

- Wellington "Tad" Jones, the man responsible for our "energy, energy, energy."

- Margot Lee, hands down the most beautiful and charming of the MoneyHunt on-air personalities, even though she always sides with the entrepreneurs.

- Chris Ogden, for introducing us to all his friends in public television.

- Blair Tardino, the MoneyHunt office manager, who holds it all together with glue and paper clips.

- Greg Matusky and Gregory Communications, for getting the word out about MoneyHunt.

- Mitchell's of Westport, Connecticut, for consulting on our wardrobe.

- Studio 210 LLC, whose creative vision has been a keystone of our property.

- Laura Kushner and Jan Akers of Price Waterhouse Coopers, Jerry Yang and Karen Edwards of Yahoo!, Steve Abrams and Al Diamant from MasterCard International, and Jay Jordan of Jordan Industries, for their early support.

- NetScape, MoneyHunt mascot and mother of six (at last count).

- Karen Krieger, wife of Miles, for her tolerance.

- Dolores Ennico, wife of Cliff, for loving the man, not the Wall Street lawyer.

- All who have dreamed the entrepreneurial dream.

INTRODUCTION

Welcome to *MoneyHunt*

ENTREPRENEURSHIP: THE "CROSSROADS OF THE AMERICAN DREAM"

It has never been a better time to be an entrepreneur—the owner of your own business.

In the 1950s, the "American Dream" meant owning your own home along with an eight-cylinder, gas-guzzling, American-made automobile in the garage. Today, the "American Dream" means owning your own career. At least one in every five Americans today dreams of starting their own small business, turning a hobby into a moneymaking machine, getting in on the ground floor of a fast-growing entrepreneurial company, or just plain not working for somebody else anymore. Don't believe us? Go to any social function and ask people if they have ideas for a new business. We guarantee just about everyone in the room has one that they've been thinking about for quite a while.

Are you a would-be entrepreneur? Do you daydream at the office, fantasizing about telling your boss to "take this job and shove it!" and heading out to work for yourself in your spare bedroom in your bathrobe and fuzzy slippers? Have you read so many of the *Dilbert* cartoons that you are starting to identify with the animal characters? Do you look at your business card and realize you can't explain to someone else what you do for a living in less than thirty seconds? Do you stay up late on Sunday nights working on business plans, screenplays, the great American novel, whatever, telling your spouse that "this is it—this is the year I go independent." Do you moonlight, pursuing a different job or career or "testing the waters" on weekends, weekday evenings, and holidays? Do you attend adult-education classes at your local high school or community college on small-business management? Do you talk about your ideas and plans for a new business at cocktail parties and family gatherings, to anyone who will listen?

If you do, or think or dream about, any of the above, this book is for you. We want you to get off your butt, stop thinking about starting your own business, and start taking those first few baby steps toward your own American dream. In the words of the ancient Chinese philosophers, "A journey of ten thousand miles begins with a single step." Let MoneyHunt be that first step that transforms you from a "wanna-be" entrepreneur into the genuine article—one of the new American class of "self-made people" who have made millions as the owners of their own companies.

Entrepreneurs are America's heroes today just as political figures were during the postwar baby boom of the 1950s and 1960s. The reasons for the shift are many. For one thing, it is really, really hard to look up to many of the political and artistic figures making the headlines today as role models. The serial downsizings, mergers, and relocations of the large Fortune 500 corporations have convinced a majority of America's corporate executives that they cannot count on their employers for long-term job security. Americans working today are the most educated people (on average) in America's history—most have college degrees, and a large minority have at least two years of graduate school under their belts— which has made them better able than previous generations to challenge and criticize the status quo. That education has taught American workers that while working for a large company will pay the mortgage and send the kids to college, it will never make you rich (unless you are one of the senior executives whose names appear in the "executive compensation" table in the company's Annual Report to Shareholders).

There are other, largely social, factors at work here. In American industry today, frequent "job hopping" by employees actually enhances their skills and performance by showing them different ways to do the same thing (although at a cost of decreased loyalty to employers, consumer brands, marriage partners, and just about everything else). Most Americans today are reluctant to put off until tomorrow the gratification of their deepest desires, having embraced the philosophies of "live for today" (the words of a 1960s popular song by the Grass Roots), "seize the time" (the title of a 1960s book by Black Panther Bobby Seale), and "you only go around once in life so you have to go for all the gusto you can" (the words of a 1960s beer commercial). Contrast this with earlier, more patient generations who adopted the view that "there is pie in the sky by and by when you die" (the words of a 1940s swing-era dance tune).

Perhaps most importantly, the advent of modern, affordable technology—particularly the personal computer, software, the Internet, digital telecommunications, fax machines, portable phones, pagers, beepers, and multichannel cable television—has empowered people working out of their spare bedrooms to compete nose to nose with America's largest corporations.

The demographics of successful entrepreneurs are broad and shatter all traditional stereotypes you may have about the type of person that succeeds in an entrepreneurial environment. For example:

Candice Carpenter, a single mother, was concerned about the lack of child-rearing support on the Internet. She formed iVillage, an Internet networking site for parents of small children, has raised $60 million in venture capital to date, has made a public offering of her company's stock, and has one of the largest and most popular sites on the World Wide Web.

Jay Hewitt, a college student, started "Planet Symphony," a Web site consulting firm, in his college dormitory room. He built a million-dollar business within a single year, raised venture financing, and sold out to a major advertising agency, all before he graduated from college.

The late Raymond Kemp, a seventy-four-year-old retired corporate engineer, was speaking to his daughter on the telephone one night when he heard sirens in the background. Looking out the window, he saw an ambulance driving down the street. The ambulance would stop every few feet while a paramedic ran up to each house looking frantically for the house number of one of Ray's neighbors, who, it turned out, had suffered a heart attack and called 911. Realizing that the best ambulance service in the world can't save lives if they can't find people's houses in time, Ray developed, patented, and marketed the "Emergency House Alert," a strobe light that attaches to the exterior of a house and flashes a beacon that can be seen for miles when someone in the house dials 911.

Candice Carpenter, Jay Hewitt, and Raymond Kemp have only one thing in common, other than being entrepreneurs—they have all appeared on *MoneyHunt*, the television show we founded and host.

WHO ARE WE AND WHAT DO WE THINK WE KNOW?

Between Miles and Cliff, you are looking at thirty years of experience and involvement with tens of thousands of entrepreneurial companies around the world.

Miles Spencer left college at the tender age of nineteen to become a banker on Wall Street. After amassing a small war chest, he entered the investment-banking business for himself, focusing on early-stage entrepreneurial companies in the consumer-products industries. Miles has raised tens of millions of dollars for entrepreneurs and developed a keen sense for what entrepreneurs and investors need most. He is also a member of Capital Express LLC, a private investment fund, and a founder of Cove Associates, a corporate finance advisory firm, but devotes a substantially full-time commitment to *MoneyHunt*.

Cliff Ennico was a lawyer on Wall Street for fifteen years, where he specialized in securities regulation, corporate finance law, and venture-capital investments. The author or editor of eight books on the legal problems of the growing entrepreneurial company, including the New York State Bar Association's handbook on business corporation law, Cliff is also an entrepreneur, being the founder and chief executive officer of Biennix Corporation, a publisher of career management books and resources for lawyers, paralegals, and other members of the legal community.

For the past decade we have been featured speakers for entrepreneurial seminars, programs, and associations throughout the United States and Canada. As a result of *MoneyHunt* and our involvement in the venture-capital community, we review literally thousands of business plans a year and witness hundreds of entrepreneurial stories unfold before our eyes.

WHY THIS BOOK CAN HELP YOU

For all their differences, the thousands of entrepreneurs we've met all have one thing in common. Their experiences, triumphs, and failures teach profound and sometimes disturbing lessons about entrepreneurship and what it takes to succeed in business. Many of these lessons never appear in business books, and when they do they are usually so sugar-coated that they fail to provide accurate, real-world advice to the burgeoning entrepreneur.

This book is a celebration of some of the successful (and unsuccessful) entrepreneurs we have met in the course of building *MoneyHunt*—our "*MoneyHunt* Heroes" and "*MoneyHunt* Heroines." Some were guests on the TV show, some auditioned for the show but didn't make the initial cut, some were our initial mentors, one was the caterer for the production crew during one of our early seasons. These are their stories, and the lessons you can learn from them.

Be forewarned: Some of these stories are not pleasant to read, because they teach some harsh and painful truths. No one ever said the world of entrepreneurship was an easygoing, user-friendly place. It often is quite the opposite: a ruthless, cutthroat Darwinian universe where the life of poorly planned businesses is all too often (to quote the philosopher Thomas Hobbes) "nasty, brutish, and short."

We didn't make these rules; we are merely reporting our observation of thousands of entrepreneurs and what has worked for them. If you want spiritually soothing words designed to heal your entrepreneurial soul, read the other books about small business that clutter the shelves of your local bookstore. Don't get us wrong: We have nothing against inspiration and spirituality. Some of the stories in this book will make you feel really good about yourself and what you are planning to do. It's just that we believe "feel good" advice doesn't really help you kick ass in a tough and unforgiving marketplace. Some of our *MoneyHunt* Heroes and Heroines are, to but it bluntly, not very nice people, but they are successful.

If you want to know the truth about entrepreneurs and the world you will be living in once you join their ranks . . . if you want to learn the real world's secrets to successfully growing a world-class business . . . if you want to know how to beat the living crap out of the competition, feel REALLY good about yourself and grow rich as the master of your career, your life, and your destiny, this is the book for you.

HOW TO USE THIS BOOK

Each chapter of this book covers a basic rule of entrepreneurship that we call a "*MoneyHunt* Rule." In some cases, the rules will be familiar ones, but we guarantee there are at least a few that you haven't seen or heard about anywhere else. The first section of each chapter explains the rule, and its significance and value for any entrepreneur.

We have learned from our live presentations that there are two types of listeners, and we suspect there are two similar types of readers. One type likes to be lectured to and wants to know "just the facts." The other wants us to tell them stories. In this book we try to make both types of reader happy. After articulating and explaining the rule in each chapter, we then illustrate the rule by telling a story about an actual entrepreneur we knew who confronted the rule and either won by accepting and bending to it, or who flew in the face of the rule and came crashing down in flames. Regardless of the outcome of the story, we refer to these entrepreneurs as our *MoneyHunt* Heroes and Heroines because to us all entrepreneurs are heroes who swim against the stream to avoid reaching someone else's goals.

After the story, we conclude each chapter by explaining what happened to the *MoneyHunt* Hero or Heroine, how he or she handled the rule in question, and how it might have turned out differently.

We have grouped the chapters and rules into sections by topic, in roughly the order you will encounter them in your entrepreneurial business venture. We begin with rules and stories about you as an entrepreneur—your personality, background, experience, psychology, and other intangible values that you bring to the entrepreneurial world. Not everyone is cut out to be an entrepreneur. We find that when businesses fail, often the cause can be attributed to character flaws in the company's founders as much as it can to external factors such as economic downturns, lack of capital, or legal problems. The rules and stories in this section deal with the fundamental issue of an entrepreneur's character in the face of adversity. While it may be tempting to skip this section to get on to the "hard stuff" in later chapters, we strongly recommend against doing so. You will unquestionably find yourself in one of these situations during your first few years in business.

The next group of rules and stories deals with finding the right business idea at the right time. Developing an idea too far ahead or too far behind the marketplace is a common road to failure in an entrepreneurial business. Like Goldilocks, the timing must be "just right."

The next three sections deal with your marketplace and the competition you will face in the business world, finding the right people as business partners and employees, and seeking money from investors and lenders. The last section of the book deals with what we call "exit strategies"—knowing when to sell your business if things are going well, knowing when to cut your losses and close up shop if things are not going well.

Did all of these stories really happen? Do the *MoneyHunt* Heroes and Heroines really exist? You bet. Everything you read in this book actually happened to entrepreneurs we have known. Of course, it is difficult to tell *any* story without leaving out some details, emphasizing others, and streamlining the narrative so that the reader doesn't get bored with a mind-numbing chronicle of dates, places, and events that must be tied together and organized in the reader's mind. You inevitably alter a story in the process of telling it.

Although we do obtain permission from entrepreneurs to tell their stories as part of the *MoneyHunt* message, the reader must remember that these are privately owned companies whose activities are not a matter of public record, and we must be very careful to protect their confidentiality, anonymity, and trade secrets. In each story we have changed certain irrelevant details (details that don't go to the heart of the lesson the story teaches) in order to ensure that only the entrepreneurs involved (and sometimes not even they) will recognize themselves when they read these stories.

Entrepreneurs are the new American heroes. If you are thinking of joining their ranks, or if you are already struggling in the trenches trying to build a business, we're here to help improve your odds of success. Mind the rules, enjoy the stories, digest the lessons in this book, and maybe we'll be seeing you as a guest on our MoneyHunt television show.

Welcome to the "Crossroads of the American Dream," and MoneyHunt!

THE MONEYHUNT TELEVISION SHOW

What if you had an idea for a new business, and had to defend that idea before a panel of the Spanish Inquisition, knowing that:

- If you don't convince them your idea is sound and that you are the right person to build a successful business around that idea, the result is likely to be the failure of your business and extreme personal embarrassment, but

- If your presentation is successful, the result can be a successful business generating millions of dollars in revenue and recognition in the international business community.

Thousands of entrepreneurs go through this process every day when they "pitch" their business plans to customers, suppliers, investors, employees, and anyone else whose input is necessary to their success. It is the most dramatic moment by far in a small company's life—the moment that will either "make or break" the company's future. We have taken that moment and turned it into a television program—MoneyHunt—that will make you into a better, more confident entrepreneur. Our show has been aptly described as *Wall Street Week* meets *Jeopardy*.

Picture the scenario. You are kept alone in an isolated waiting room, mulling over the strengths and weaknesses of your business plan, when you are suddenly pitched through a revolving door into a brightly lit room and seated at a conference table. On the other side of the table sits (in the words of a TV critic) "America's toughest panel of business experts"—the two authors of this book and a "MoneyHunt Mentor," a leading authority in your industry who knows your industry, markets, and competition better than you probably ever will. Our *MoneyHunt* Mentors have included such luminaries of the business world as Jerry Yang, cofounder of Yahoo! Inc.; Debbie Fields, the founder of the Mrs. Fields' cookies franchise bakery chain; Stuart Hirsch, the chief operating officer of King World; and Candice Carpenter, the founder of iVillage.

In addition to the three panelists, a team of business analysts, including students in the entrepreneurship program at Yale and the Wharton School of Business at the University of Pennsylvania, has picked apart your business plan and uncovered every flaw and inconsistency. You have been researched on Lexis/Nexis, the Internet, and just about everywhere else, and the panel knows everything there is to know about you and your business.

After a brief introduction, in which you are given about sixty seconds to describe your products and services and tell how the company was started (more than you will get in an actual business meeting, by the way), the panel begins to grill you on virtually every aspect of your business plan, focusing on five general areas:

- Your products and services, and their weaknesses.

- The market for your products and services.

- Your competitors and your strategies for dealing with them.

- The strengths and weaknesses of your management team.

- Your financial condition and capitalization.

You are on the firing line for only twelve minutes, but we guarantee it will seem longer than that. The *MoneyHunt* panel comes out of the chute looking for your blood, asking the toughest questions you've ever been asked, poking holes in your business plan, pointing out inconsistencies (and, occasionally, illegalities) in what you are planning to do, and asking "off the wall" questions in the hopes that you will lose your cool on the set and demonstrate that you are not really ready to be taken seriously in the business world. All in front of an international television audience, including your friends and family, your employees, and your investors.

After you have been grilled and charbroiled to a crispy crust, the *MoneyHunt* panel analyzes what they have heard and points out areas where you can improve your business plan. Despite the tough questioning, our goal on the *MoneyHunt* show is to have each guest leave a better entrepreneur than when he or she stepped through the swinging doors.

After what is left of you has been carted off the set, the MoneyHunt panel does the same thing to another entrepreneur in your industry—perhaps one of your competitors.

At the end of the show the MoneyHunt Mentor selects one of the two guests to receive much-needed guidance and mentoring from the MoneyHunt Mentor and access to the mentor's network of business contacts—a real boon to early-stage entrepreneurs whose access to the "players" in the business world is severely limited.

Sound a little frightening? It's no more so than a business meeting in the real world. What we do on the MoneyHunt show pales in comparison to the real-world pressure of pitching your business, where walking away empty-handed can mean the death of your business and a return to the corporate cubicle. Still, as we say on the show, "It ain't easy."

We are the first to admit that the MoneyHunt panel can sometimes be wrong (or, to put it correctly, that the marketplace knows more than we do), but we're fair about it. If you lose on the MoneyHunt show but come up a winner in the real world, we will invite you back on the set to tell us how wrong we were! If you are really successful, you may even be invited back as a MoneyHunt Mentor. Similarly, if the MoneyHunt panel was right in their analysis, we hope you will want to come back on the set and tell us so. Some of the stories in this book are based on feedback we have received from former MoneyHunt guests.

If you appear on the show, we cannot promise that you will find the resources you need or that you will succeed in growing a successful business. We certainly will not recommend that our audience invest in your business or assist you in raising capital. Nonetheless, an appearance on MoneyHunt can be the first step toward national recognition and credibility for your start-up and early-stage company and may help you make the contacts and raise the money you need to keep going.

If you think you have what it takes to survive the MoneyHunt challenge, you can audition for the show on-line at www.moneyhunter.com.

Oh, and one more thing. Many of the rules in this book are based on questions the MoneyHunt panel routinely asks on the show, so you may want to hold on to this book . . . just in case.

PART ONE

Do You Have What It Takes?

MONEYHUNT
RULE #1

"The Insecure Rabbit Lives Longest"

MoneyHunt Heroine: Rosa Rodriguez

One of the great myths about entrepreneurs is that they are masters of their own destinies. When we first dream of owning our own business, how do we visualize ourselves? Usually we picture a secure, dynamic, self-confident superhero who can "leap tall buildings in a single bound" without even losing her breath—someone who never worries, never panics, never gives in to emotion, who remains cool, and who always outsmarts the bad guys.

A few years back, a popular movie named Tucker brought this vision to life. Based on a true story, Tucker was a feel-good "David and Goliath" movie about a lone entrepreneur who, tinkering in his garage on evenings and weekends, invented an automobile that ran better and lasted longer than anything Detroit was then capable of producing. Most auto entrepreneurs in such a situation today would get a patent on their invention, license the patent to a major auto company, and live the rest of their lives on the royalty income. But the movie was set in the late 1940s. People must have been different back then. Tucker girded his loins, set up his own manufacturing company with borrowed money, and took on the Big Three automakers chin to chin. Of course, he was wiped off the map, but everyone applauded Tucker at the end of the movie. Square-jawed, stoic, braving the odds no matter how much the deck was stacked against him, and holding his head up high as he strode into bankruptcy court, Tucker had unquestionably gained hero status.

We have seen tens of thousands of entrepreneurs in our careers as venture capitalist and business lawyer, and we see very few Tuckers. The few we see usually do very badly. The people we see (the successful ones, especially) will never become the subject of a Hollywood movie, except perhaps for one directed by Woody Allen. If we were to introduce to you ten of the most successful entrepreneurs we have met and gave you the chance to talk candidly with them in a soundproof room for an hour or two, we bet the first thing you would say upon leaving the room would be "My God! These are some of the most insecure, neurotic people I have ever seen in my life! I don't think they're sure of their own middle names, much less their businesses. Are you *sure* these are the good ones?"

Yes, we're sure. Contrary to the popular image, the people who succeed as entrepreneurs are extremely insecure about who they are and what they do. The minute they become as self-confident and self-assured as Tucker (the movie version), they have taken the first step toward failure.

OF RABBITS, LIONS, AND ENTREPRENEURS

Have you ever seen a rabbit up close and personal? Maybe in a pet shop, a petting zoo, or in your backyard eating your vegetable garden? If you have, the first thing—we mean the *very* first thing—you notice about the rabbit is that it is constantly in motion. The whiskers are wiggling, the ears are twitching, the teeth are constantly grinding away at something, the tail is vibrating, the haunches are thumping. You can get tired very easily looking at a rabbit. A rabbit (apologies to John Updike) is never truly at rest unless it is dead. Even when the rabbit is sleeping, parts of its body are in motion, alert, ready for anything. The rabbit is an animal that is incredibly well tuned to what's going on in its immediate environment.

Why do you think the rabbit is designed that way? Well, we are not animal experts, of course, but we think it's because the rabbit, being a highly intelligent animal, knows its place in the food chain. This is not, after all, a creature that stalks the forest, leaping and pouncing upon its helpless prey, roaring its triumph. More likely, the rabbit is on the receiving end of the Darwinian stick, and it knows this. If a rabbit is sitting in the grass munching on whatever it has found to eat, and it sees, in the distance, out of the corner of its eye, a leaf on a faraway bush start to twitch rhythmically, the rabbit (correction: the successful rabbit, the one that lives to reproduce) says to itself, "Now, that can be any of several things. It can be raindrops falling on the leaf making it twitch. It could be a gentle summer breeze. Or . . . it could be a fox behind that bush whose rhythmic breathing is making the leaf twitch. I'm not taking any chances; I am getting the hell out of here!" And the rabbit hightails it down its hole. Many times it is raindrops or a gentle summer breeze that makes the leaf twitch. But every once in a while it is a fox looking for its next meal.

Next, let's consider the lion (bet you didn't expect to read about rabbits and lions in a business book). Have you ever seen a lion in a zoo? It's a big disappointment, isn't it? You expect the lion to be ferocious, roaring every three minutes, chasing and tearing apart its prey, perched on a rock Lion King–style surveying its domain with an imperious air. Instead, what do you see? The lion is sprawled on a rock, snoozing away, occasionally twitching an ear to rid itself of an annoying housefly or scratching itself in places you have to keep the kids from staring at, and generally giving the impression that it hasn't done an honest day's work since it received its visa from the Immigration and Naturalization Service.

Why do you think the lion is designed that way? Same as the rabbit, the lion knows its place in the food chain. Except for those pesky two-legged creatures in white pith helmets, wearing designer shorts, and carrying shotguns, there really isn't much in the jungle the lion has to be afraid of. It is more often the hunter than the hunted, and it knows it. There isn't really much need for the lion to be supersensitive to its environment. If it wants to take a snooze in broad daylight, there aren't a whole lot of other animals who will wake it up and ask it politely to move.

Now here's a pop quiz. When you are starting a fast-growth company in an even faster industry, in today's "take no prisoners" competitive environment, which of the following do you more closely resemble:

A. The Lion, or

B. The Rabbit?

You get the idea. By being constantly on the "edge," questioning their own judgment, never really trusting what their eyes and ears tell them, supersensitive businesspeople pick up on new opportunities, and spot potential threats to their success, before any of their competitors do. This enables them to make the necessary adjustments in their business plan before the freight train bears down on them. Entrepreneurs usually do not have the resources to play "catch-up" if they make mistakes; errors in judgment, especially in the early years, can often prove fatal in a fast-changing marketplace. If in running your business you reach a point where you truly believe that you know what you are doing, where you are going, and what's going on around you, chances are you are over-looking something very important.

Comfort, complacency, and confidence—the "three Cs"—spell disaster for an entrepreneurial company.

So Maybe I Should Stay in the Big, Safe Corporate World?

Of course, corporate life is not the safe, secure haven of lifetime employ-ment it was in the 1950s and 1960s. With downsizings happening left and right, and political behavior the order of the day, most corporate executives and employees are running scared these days, and it may be tempting to think "Yeah, I hear what Miles and Cliff are getting at, but it can't be any worse than what I go through every day here." Perhaps.

When you start your own business, though, you are the one making all the big decisions. In a large corporation, it often doesn't matter if you're wrong once or twice, as long as there aren't serious adverse consequences to the company or your division. In your own company, every mistake is potentially fatal. In a large corporation, you can bounce ideas off of your colleagues and hold meetings to analyze data and explore alternatives. In your own company, the buck stops with you, and often there isn't the time to study situations in depth before you have to act or react to them. You have to go on your best instincts with imperfect information.

Some people conceal their insecurity under a swaggering, swashbuck-ling demeanor. We have all heard the expression "He's like a duck—calm and placid on the surface, but paddling like hell underneath." In busi-ness, however, it is difficult to keep up a facade for a long time before the cracks start showing. Psychologists tell us that if we adopt a persona that is not truly our own by maintaining a "brave face," one of two things will happen. Either (a) our true self will find a way to break through the facade sooner or later, often in the most embarrassing and damaging way, or (b) our inner self will conform to the persona and we will truly become confident, reckless, and comfortable with our business lives. Either way, the entrepreneur loses.

It's better to be a live rabbit than a dead lion.

Things to Be Insecure About

When you are growing a business, there is no shortage of things to keep you awake at night. Here are a few:

Your Products and Services. Do they work properly? Are they made of the right materials? Do we have enough quality control? Can we squeeze a few dollars from our manufacturing budget by making the stuff in China? Can we substitute plastic for metal without the stuff falling apart or melting? Are people using them the way our instructions say they should? Is the government getting ready to ban or regulate one of our key ingredients? Are people finding new uses for our products and not telling us? Is there a new technology on the horizon that will make my products and services obsolete?

Your Markets. Are people still buying our stuff? Are demographic trends moving toward or away from our products and services? Are people's attitudes and beliefs changing in a way that will require us to change our products and services? Is my geographic area growing or shrinking in population? Can I raise my prices a few pennies and get away with it without losing market share? Can I sell more stuff by expanding internationally? Can I sell more stuff by coming out with different versions or sizes of the product?

Your Competition. Do I know who all my competitors are? Have I correctly assessed their strengths and weaknesses? What are they doing that I should be doing? Are there any new players coming into my market? If so, how do their resources compare with mine? Are there any new product or service categories coming into the market that will take market share away from me? Can I find a better way to knock the legs out from under my competitor across the street? If I don't have the resources to go toe to toe with a new competitor (example: you are a small hardware store and a "Home Depot" superwarehouse moves in across the street), can I get out of its way and stay alive by focusing on a niche market?

Your Finances and Investors. Am I making enough money to keep going and grow? How can I raise revenues? Can I shave a penny off my costs here? A dollar over there? Will I be able to pay all of my bills this month? Most of them? Is there a "cash crunch" looming on the horizon? Am I paying too much in taxes? Are my investors happy? Do I have the right kind of investors?

Your Management Team. Do I have all the people I need to make this business happen? The right people? Can I afford them without giving away too much of the company? Is Joe really putting out 100 percent for us or do I have to keep a closer eye on him? Is somebody planning to leave tomorrow and start up a competing company? Should I continue as a "virtual company" where there are no employees, or should I start hiring full-time people to fill the key positions?

Your Legal Environment. Have I done enough to insulate my business from being sued? Are my personal assets at risk if somebody sues my business? Who out there is the most likely person to sue me? Are there new government regulations that impact my business? Am I in compliance with all existing government regulations that affect my business?

Your Office Environment. Am I presenting the right image for this business? Is it time to move the business from my garage to a real office location? Should I rent, or is it better to buy the building and lease out the space I don't need? Am I in the right geographic location for this business? Can I afford to be in the right location for this business? Can I reduce my costs by relocating the business to a part of the country with a lower cost of living, or will my credibility in the industry suffer because I am no longer "where the action is"?

Yourself. Do I have what it takes to be in this business? Do I have the right skills and training? Am I tough enough? Do I know the business inside and out? Is my personal style the right one for this business? Do I present the right image? Do I have the time to make this business a success? Am I willing to work seven days a week, twenty-four hours a day if necessary? Am I passionate about this business? Am I willing to put everything else in my life to one side for a while in order to be the best I can possibly be? Am I fooling myself?

The minute you have final answers to any one of these questions, start worrying, because there are no final answers to these questions. You will ask them every day of your entrepreneurial life, up to (and including) the day you retire, if you are any good.

An inside tip: If you are invited to appear as a guest on our *MoneyHunt* television show, keep this list of questions handy. The *MoneyHunt* panel has asked all of them at one time or another.

MoneyHunt Heroine: Rosa Rodriguez

When you start a business from scratch, there are certain services that are absolutely indispensable. One of these is a mailbox service: In virtually every community in America today there is at least one franchise outlet that will give you a post office–type box with a street address (i.e., "123 Main Street, Suite No. 456"), accept and sign for registered and certified mail and overnight deliveries addressed to your box, and maintain basic office equipment (copiers, fax machines, bulk printers) for your use if you are a mailbox renter. Because of the explosive growth in home-based businesses in the past few years, mailbox franchises have expanded like kudzu across the country. By using one of these mailbox franchises as your office address, you will avoid antagonizing your neighbors (who will turn you in to the local zoning authorities if their kids can't ride their bikes in the street because they're too busy dodging UPS trucks going to and from your home office), you will not be tied down to the house waiting to sign for registered mail and parcel deliveries, and any door-to-door salespeople or solicitors in the area will be surprised as hell when they show up at your corporate headquarters and it's six by twelve inches.

When we first started MoneyHunt, we ran the business out of our homes. One of our first acts in the television business was to rent a mailbox from our local mailbox franchise, and Rosa Rodriguez, the owner of the franchise, was our first real office manager. We often swore she knew as much about our business as we did, although she swore she never read our mail!

Rosa never intended to be a business owner. Born and raised in a small village in Spain, she was working as a waitress at a tapas bar near a U.S. military base in the Mediterranean when she struck up a conversation with a nice U.S. serviceman on leave who wanted to try out his high school Spanish. Six months later they were married, and twelve months later she was a U.S. citizen expecting her first child. Unfortunately, the marriage fell apart several years later, and Rosa found herself on her own with three small children. While her ex-husband provided some support, she knew she would need extra income. She read an advertisement in her local newspaper that the local mailbox franchise needed a customer service representative. She answered the ad, and two weeks later she was working from 8:00 A.M. to 6:00 P.M. fixing office equipment, wrapping packages, advising people on the cheapest way to mail packages, renting mailboxes, copying bulk documents, and assembling mass mailings for the people who rented mailboxes or otherwise used the outlet as their office away from the office.

In the course of her duties she learned a lot about the businesses her customers were running, to say nothing of their personal lives (next to barbers and hairdressers, mailbox outlets are the best sources of local gossip), and in the course of time she became probably the best-informed person in the entire town. In time the franchise owner taught Rosa how to keep the books for the business and manage the other employees, all of whom were part-time college students or retired people who wanted to stay active.

Then disaster struck. The owner of the mailbox franchise outlet suffered a fatal aneurysm while on his summer vacation, leaving Rosa as the only person who understood every aspect of the business. The owner's wife liked Rosa, and with the cooperation of the franchise company (which did not want to see a profitable franchise go down the drain), the owner's wife sold her late husband's business to Rosa, agreeing to be paid over time out of the net proceeds of the business.

Rosa was terrified. Although she knew how to run the day-to-day operations of the business, keep the books, and pay the franchise company its monthly fees on time, she hadn't a single clue how to run and build a business. She took business courses in the adult-education program of the local community college, eventually earning a small-business certificate, which she had framed and proudly displayed over the cash register. She subscribed to every local and regional business newspaper, all the national business magazines, and every "home business" book and magazine she could find, and after the children were put to bed each night she would stay up past midnight reading about things that were happening in the community, things that might affect her business, trends in the business world generally, the new things people with home offices might need. If she read about something she didn't understand, she would ask one of her mailbox customers to explain it to her.

Still, she could never get over the nagging suspicion that she was missing something. She started asking her customers questions: What services would you like to see here that we don't already have here? Would you like to see more copiers? More fax machines? Would you like a private fax number for your business? How about office supplies? E-mail service? She placed monthly questionnaires in every mailbox at the outlet asking her customers their opinions on anything and everything that she felt would help her understand their needs.

Based on the feedback she received, she persuaded the franchise company to allow her to expand her services to include personal computers and printers and other back-office services—coffee machines and mailboxes on the Internet, among other things. The franchise company became so impressed with Rosa's research that she was invited to corporate headquarters on several occasions to advise senior management about possible new directions for the business. She received a national award from the franchise as their "franchisee of the year" and sat next to the franchise president at the Super Bowl. She paid her debt to the late owner's wife in half the time she had agreed, and within five years of the late owner's death she was grossing over $250,000 a year from the outlet, more than virtually any other franchisee.

Still, she worried. Would things change? Would the improving economy lead people back to big corporations and make them close down the home-based businesses she relied upon for her support? Would her success inspire someone else to set up shop in town and go *mano a mano* with her?

One night, while reading a local newspaper, her eyes glanced at the "new business listings" column, something she did not normally read. There was a listing that a company had leased store space directly across the street from Rosa's mailbox outlet. At first she didn't think much of it, but in the middle of the night she awoke from a nightmare that a competitor had opened up shop directly across the street. Although Rosa was not a superstitious person, she called her franchise headquarters the next morning and asked them for a list of competing franchise companies. When the list arrived by fax later that day, she scanned it, and sure enough, one of the names was suspiciously similar to that of the company opening up shop across the street.

Rosa could not sleep that night. Was it just a coincidence? Many companies have similar names, she tried to tell herself. She was tempted to forget about it, but something in the pit of her stomach told her she should at least check it out. The next morning she walked over to the beauty salon next to the mailbox outlet and asked the owner, a good friend, if she could use the telephone. This was a telephone call she knew she could not make from the mailbox outlet because she was afraid the call would be traced. Disguising her voice and using an assumed name, she called the competing franchise company and inquired about possibly opening one of their franchise outlets in her community. The reply sent chills down her spine: "We're sorry, but we've just signed up a franchisee in your town who's going to be opening a mailbox outlet at" . . . the address across the street!

Rosa panicked. She locked herself in her office and cried all morning. The part-time employees knocked on the door several times and asked if she was okay. She would only reply, "I'm working on something. Call me only if a customer needs something you don't understand."

She stayed in her office the entire day and late in the evening, paralyzed with fear. She literally did nothing all day, staring at her computer screen like a deer gazing at oncoming headlights.

At about midnight she decided to open some of her mail to try to take her mind off the problem. One of the first pieces Rosa opened was a reminder to pay for an advertisement she ran in a local "coupon shopper." No doubt many of you receive these in the mail on a weekly basis:

flyers that contain only advertisements and discount coupons from local businesses trying to generate traffic. In response to a question on one of Rosa's monthly questionnaires, her customers had told her (almost unanimously) that they first learned about the mailbox outlet from these coupon shoppers.

"Wait a minute," Rosa thought to herself. "This is where I get all of my new business from. So . . . this is where this new company across the street is going to have to go to get their business." Rosa rifled through her top desk drawer until she came upon a checkbook for a $50,000 line of credit she had signed up for at a local bank but never used.

The next morning Rosa went to work. She called every coupon shopper within a fifty-mile radius of her mailbox outlet (within the territory that had been assigned to her by the franchise company), and signed up for a full-page advertisement in every one, paying cash in advance for a full year of advertisements. She knew that coupon shoppers never run two or more ads by the same type of business, so once she had the space locked up for her business, the coupon shopper would refuse to let the new company across the street advertise. But that wasn't enough. Rosa worried that the new competitor across the street would find other ways to get business. So Rosa took out half-page advertisements in every local newspaper in town (one of her mailbox customers was a graphic designer), posted her business card on the bulletin boards in the lobbies of every Chinese restaurant and car wash in town, and signed up to teach an adult-education course at the local high school on "setting up your new home office." More than a hundred local residents signed up for the course.

Within a week she had used up over $25,000 of her line of credit, with no assurance whatsoever that she would be able to pay it back. Now she had something new to worry about. Like many new immigrants to the United States, Rosa had a morbid fear of debt, and she knew it would be difficult to pay back quickly the $25,000 with interest from the cash flow her business was then generating.

As it turned out, her new marketing efforts, motivated solely by her desire to lock her competitor out of the most desirable advertising sources, had an unexpected benefit. Within days after her "media blitz," the number of people renting new mailboxes doubled. The next week it tripled. The next week she was in danger of running out of mailboxes. Fortunately, she learned that an adjoining store had just been evicted by the landlord for failing to keep up with rent payments. Frantic, Rosa called her landlord and leased the adjoining space before the landlord even had time to list it with a broker. Rosa clinched the deal by offering to pay 150 percent of the previous tenant's rent as well as the three months' back rent that the previous tenant had been unable to pay! Within two weeks Rosa tore down the walls (one of her mailbox customers was a contractor) and doubled the size of her store. Rosa's mailbox outlet became the largest and most profitable outlet in the history of the franchise company, grossing over $1 million a year. The franchise company profiled Rosa in its annual report to franchisees and shareholders, calling her the "Mailbox Mogul."

A month or two later, Rosa was sitting in her kitchen after the children were put to bed, reading the local newspaper that had first alerted her to a potential competitor across the street. Under the "Bankruptcy Court Filings" column appeared a company name that looked suspiciously like the name of a competing mailbox franchise. . . .

Postscript: We talked to Rosa shortly after her profile in the franchise company annual report and congratulated her on her success. She thanked us for the compliment but seemed preoccupied by something. We asked what in the world could possibly be worrying her at this point? Her response was classic Rosa: "Yes, yes, you can help. Tell me, boys. You are the business experts, yes? I have an idea, but I'm not sure about it. I am thinking that maybe I should do a newsletter where my customers can buy and sell things to each other. . . ."

LESSONS FROM ROSA RODRIGUEZ

Rosa's fear and insecurity drove her to a level of success she never would have imagined possible. Her fear that she didn't know enough about business led her to become a voracious reader, a habit that eventually alerted her to a potential threat far enough in advance that she could deal with it before it became a major problem. Her sensitivity to all that was going on around her was so fine-tuned and honed by experience that her subconscious mind kept insisting "This is a hungry fox making that leaf move" when her conscious mind was trying to convince itself that "It's only raindrops causing that leaf to twitch." It would have been easy for Rosa to sit back and say "Okay, so there's a new kid on the block. I'm not worried. My customers have been with me for years and I've got strong name recognition in the community. It will take a lot for this new company to do damage to me. I'll let nature take its course, and this new company will fold when it realizes it can't beat my experience and knowledge of this business." That decision, however, would have been based not on an assessment of the facts but rather on self-confidence and arrogance. In business, you can never allow yourself to get comfortable with the status quo, because it's always changing. Fortunately for Rosa, she listened to her "inner rabbit," developed a winning strategy to overcome the threat, and in the process stumbled onto a marketing strategy that became a model for mailbox franchises around the country.

When you start your own business, the amount of information and raw data you will be exposed to every day can be simply mind-boggling. Many of you would not have thought twice about that notice in the "new business listings" column in a local newspaper. But sometimes the most valuable information about your marketplace, your competition, and your business risks comes from the least likely source. Sooner or later, your business will be threatened by something. Rosa was ready for the threat. Remember Rosa's decision to send monthly questionnaires to her mailbox customers, driven by the fear that she didn't understand enough what her customers wanted? Without the information those questionnaires provided her, she would not have realized the most effective way to prevent her new competitor from gaining exposure in the community. Staying in constant touch with your customers, asking them questions, getting feedback, is essential to developing the "sense of the environment" that will help you spot obstacles and threats before anyone else (especially your competition) does.

Rosa's decision to call the competing franchise company from the beauty salon next door to the mailbox outlet, for fear that the telephone call would be traced, contains the next lesson. Only a truly paranoid entrepreneur would think to do something like that. A less frightened entrepreneur would have called from the store, or their home, which may have tipped off the competing company that Rosa was "running scared." Having received this signal, they would have come out of the starting gate with a strong marketing campaign. In business, you always have to assume that your adversaries are smarter than you are. They usually are not, but then there's always the exception. The last thing you ever want to do in business is show your competition that they are getting to you and putting you in a weak position.

Based on years of feedback from her customers, Rosa realized that the best way to cut her competition off at the knees was to cut off its access to the most effective marketing media. Just as some say that "all politics is local," we would say that "all business is local," especially for a service business like Rosa's. Whatever you may read in business books (even this one), the best business information comes from your experience, your observations, and (most importantly) your customers. Rosa knew that she could count on only a trickle of new business from referrals and newspaper ads; the bulk of her business came from coupon shoppers. In other parts of the country, it might be quite different. What works for folks in Washington State may not work for folks in South Carolina. To beat your competition, especially new entries to the marketplace, you have to have better "local knowledge" than they do.

Now let's talk about Rosa's decision to draw down her bank line of credit to finance her advertising blitz. At first, you would say this was a courageous decision, as to do this she had to overcome her morbid fear of debt. What really happened, though, is that her fear of the new competitor was far greater than her fear of not being able to repay the bank. A friend of ours, a former Marine drill sergeant, told us once that he wanted his new recruits to be more afraid of him than of the enemy. When faced with competing fears, successful entrepreneurs place the fear of failure first and worry about the rest later.

After vanquishing her foe and gaining national recognition in the process, it would have been easy for Rosa to sit on her laurels and "cruise" for a while, resting secure that other mailbox franchise companies would think hard and long before expanding into her territory. But old habits, and old insecurities, die hard. No sooner had Rosa won the fight than she was already looking for something to worry about—how to expand her product line to make her outlet even more attractive to her existing and future customers. In the business world, insecurity never ends until the day you retire (if you're *really* good, it doesn't end even then). To be successful in business you must cultivate insecurity until it becomes a habit. The minute you let your guard down and put your business on "cruise control," sooner or later you expose yourself to the hungry fox who has been looking for an overly confident rabbit. Worse, once you start feeling complacent about your business and where it is going, that very complacency becomes a habit that will have to be overcome. The first step to success in any kind of business is to get out of your personal comfort zone and let your "inner rabbit" take over.

MONEYHUNT
RULE #2

"Heavy Hangs the Head That Wears the Crown"

<u>MoneyHunt</u> Hero: Herman Blazick

A veteran entrepreneur, one of our first advisory board members on *MoneyHunt*, once said to us, "Where the buck stops, loneliness begins." At first this seemed obvious—we all remember that Harry S. Truman had a sign on his Oval Office desk that said "The buck stops here." The full impact of this saying did not completely hit us until we started our own businesses (*MoneyHunt* for Miles, a niche publishing firm for Cliff). Starting and growing your own business is a very lonely game. Very often, the price you pay for your freedom is loneliness.

When you own your own business, you can work any time you want. When the business is just starting, however, if you don't work you don't do business, and if you don't do business you don't get paid. When you take a break to browse, you are not working. When you take a vacation, even one you and your spouse feel you desperately need, you are not working. Anything you do that does not involve working, you are not working.

While it's also true that entrepreneurs make their own hours, those hours become longer because it's your neck out there, not your company's or your division's. Of course, you can always hire employees to handle the grunt work, but that assumes you have the ready cash to make payroll, offer at least some rudimentary benefits, and pay federal and state employment taxes such as FICA and FUTA. (If these acronyms are new to you, do not even think of hiring employees!) Even if you do have the cash to hire employees, there is a quantum leap in psychology from being a "doer" to being a "manager," and many entrepreneurs fail to make the jump successfully.

It's Lonely at the Top, Especially When There's No One Beneath You

One of the hard realities of the entrepreneurial life is that business own-ers are lonely people. In a large corporation, that loneliness can be shared with a board of directors, with senior management, and with outside consultants who charge by the hour (if not by the heartbeat). In an entrepreneurial company, there is often no one to talk to. You cannot bounce ideas off of other people. You cannot hold a staff meeting and achieve a consensus decision. In the early years of a business's life, just about every important decision you make is a "bet the company" deci-sion. If a decision turns out badly, there are no scapegoats you can blame (or fire) but yourself.

In the words of Larry Fine of the Three Stooges, "What stupid imbe-cile . . . what moron . . . what idiot could have done such a stupid thing? . . . Oops, I did it!"

MoneyHunt Hero: Herman Blazick

Herman Blazick had a hell of a smile for a guy so deep in hot water, but then, anyone with a name like "Herman" is likely to be on the tough side. He had a little less hair than a twenty-nine-year-old male should hope for, but Herman seemed not the least bit apprehensive about his appearance during his initial MoneyHunt interview. A genuine and enthusiastic character with an ironic sense of humor and a low-key approach to life, Herman was the only entrepreneur in MoneyHunt history to bring his fiancée to the studio. They both seemed to be making a minivacation out of it—it was a welcome break from the trials and tribu-lations of a difficult business.

As we were to later learn, Herman's loyalty extended not only to his fiancée and his Main Line Philadelphia family but to his college alma mater and to his community in the Philadelphia suburbs. These three formed a Holy Trinity for Herman, to be cherished and protected at all costs.

Herman's business plan was one of the more interesting ones we had looked at that season. A molecular engineer by training, Herman had developed and patented a process that, through a chemical additive, made any fabric 99.9 percent waterproof. Cliff, ever the movie buff, compared Herman's business plan with that of the Alec Guinness character in that classic 1950s British film *The Man in the White Suit* (by the way, one of the top ten movies for entrepreneurs).

Herman's process involved impregnating the fabric particles such that, like a sponge that was full, nothing more could be absorbed. He developed this process while simultaneously completing his MBA degree at Harvard Business School. Two days after graduation, he was out in the field, selling the fabric to outerwear manufacturers like Nike and Adidas, who vied with each other to be the first to take advantage of Herman's innovation. Offers to purchase Herman's one-man start-up company came early and often, but Herman rebuffed them because he wanted to remain independent and grow his business as best he could.

Herman made a decision early on that would have a tremendous impact on his business later. Rather than license his process to the major outerwear manufacturers, sit back, and collect royalty checks every month as most professional inventors do, Herman decided to become a manufacturer of fabrics impregnated with his patented process, figuring he would make much more money that way. Initially, he was right—his patented waterproofing feature justified a higher price for his fabrics, which in turn enabled outerwear manufacturers to charge a higher price to consumers. In his first two years in business, Herman was showing a healthy margin on $5 million in sales.

Herman's growth came in the early 1990s, when the global activewear brands of Nike, Columbia, and Eddie Bauer (among others) were just taking off. These brands had tremendous influence in the marketplace; their ability to purchase and manufacture in any corner of the world gave them a price advantage. Because of the economies of scale that these new players in the outerwear business developed during this period, retail prices began to soften, and each brand started discounting against the others, which was all they could afford to do because of their already low costs. Discounting at retail put pressure on margins, and the lower margins in turn put pressure on raw-material costs.

Soon Herman found it was getting more and more difficult to generate repeat orders from his major customers—the premium outerwear manufacturers. The waterproof attributes of the fabrics were an easy sell, but complaints about Herman's premium prices continued to grow. Sales of premium outerwear were suffering, and some of his customers stopped returning his telephone calls. Herman came to refer to this as the "pruning process"—where those products that sold through were reordered and those that did not were allowed to die their slow but inevitable deaths.

Clearly, there was trouble down the road for Herman's company, and his life as a "professional student" prior to starting the company was not going to help him stop the slide. His wealthy Main Line Philadelphia family, who had invested heavily and indeed helped manage the company, could not save it. The closely knit Philadelphia business society, which was usually eager to protect its own, was unwilling to help with any follow-on investments, even though many of the most prominent angels in town had already sunk over a million dollars in Herman's company.

So Herman took the only course available to him. He had to lower the cost of manufacturing his waterproof fabrics, and that meant only one thing . . . going overseas. Herman bought a ticket for a plane trip to mainland China, Malaysia, Thailand, and Singapore, looking for the lowest-cost production he could find.

In China, Herman met with what he had heard was the lowest-cost producer of a fabric type to which Herman could apply his process. A few months previously, the Chinese manufacturer had been a branch of the provincial government and had just been privatized as part of China's efforts to modernize. During his first two days in China Herman was wined and dined by just about every manager in the manufacturing plant, as well as the local provincial government officials, members of their families, and even (Herman swore) the local tailors' association whose members would benefit from increased business at the manufacturing plant. Herman became comfortable that the Chinese plant could indeed manufacture a waterproof fabric using his patented process at a price almost 70 percent below his current cost, with a quality at or about his current level. Better still, the Chinese company was so excited by his new technology they were able to hammer out the framework of an investment by the Chinese in Herman's company.

The terms of this investment were very straightforward. The Chinese would invest enough money to capitalize Herman's growth plans and ensure that his family's capital, which represented a substantial chunk of their net worth, would be safe rather than at risk. However, there was a catch. Three of Herman's family members, employees of the company who had helped Herman grow the business to this point, would lose their jobs as those functions were transferred overseas to be performed by Chinese managers.

Herman had a hard choice. Not only was he choosing between independence and a partnership, he was choosing between a family business that gave him great emotional rewards and an international joint venture where he was but one cog (although an important one) in the wheel. The choice would mean the elimination of some family jobs, but with that came the opportunity to protect the family's net worth, which was significantly tied up in the company. It was a choice between retaining the "Made in the USA" label that Herman was so proud to display on his fabrics and the possibility that the Chinese plant was outsourcing some of its production to sweatshop facilities that would generate negative feedback in his marketplace.

The flight back from China is fifteen hours, but for Herman it was an eternity. Herman mulled his Hobson's choice over and over and over again in his mind. If he didn't do the deal with the Chinese company, his company would struggle on and might well go broke, leaving the family's small fortune in ruins and the family's jobs up in smoke. If he went forward with the Chinese deal, however, the tightly woven Philadelphia investment community would frown severely on the decision, and Herman's cherished reputation in that community would suffer, even though these same Philadelphia folks themselves had not been willing to provide second- or third-round financing.

Herman got no sleep and sat alone under the airplane reading light, reviewing the letter the Chinese company had given him indicating their willingness to go forward with a joint venture. Signing it would take him clearly in one direction that would force him to make great personal sacrifices but possibly save his company. Not signing it would salvage his reputation in the communities he cared about but might jeopardize his company's future.

He read the letter one more time, decided he would sign it after all, and deplaned, ready to face Philadelphia and all it had to throw at him.

LESSONS FROM HERMAN BLAZICK

Herman epitomizes the lonely entrepreneur. Over the objections of his family, alma mater, and early-stage investors, Herman boarded the plane for the Far East to pursue a course of action that even he himself wasn't completely sure about. Yet Herman was not yet faced with a decision. When you don't have any options, and only one course of action is open to you, decisions are easy to make. Once you have options, making the right decision gets tougher. Once the Chinese company offered him a relationship that would enable him to lower his costs dramatically and preserve his relationships with the outerwear manufacturers, Herman had a tough decision to make. The fact that no one from the company accompanied him on his trip to China made it all that much worse.

Herman needed to lower his manufacturing costs dramatically in order to preserve his relationship with the major outerwear manufacturers, and to do this he had no alternative but to seek an overseas source of supply. Sometimes in the business world decisions are actually easy, and this one was a "no-brainer." But sometimes not. We meet many entrepreneurs who are committed to putting a "Made in America" label on their products out of concern that too many key manufacturing industries are relocating their operations overseas. For some companies, a "Made in America" strategy works well, especially for products involving cutting-edge technology and a highly educated workforce. Sadly, for many basic industries, it is often dramatically cheaper to manufacture overseas than in the United States.

Herman had not expected and had not adequately prepared for the Chinese company's offer to invest in his U.S. operation. Decisions are a lot easier to make when you are not under time pressure to make them. Had Herman worked out all of the possible options in his head on the airplane flight to China, he might have been better prepared to respond to the Chinese company's offer on the spot, thereby saving himself the agony of a difficult decision. By defending his family and their management positions in the company, he could have worked out a face-saving solution for both companies that would have given his family members a continued role in the company while still permitting the Chinese investment.

Making the difficult decision isn't the end of the story. Often, it is only the beginning. Herman realized it was far more important that the company lower its costs and be properly capitalized than that the day-to-day operation of the company be controlled by members of Herman's family. Although he would not have admitted it to himself at the time, Herman had already made up his mind to accept the Chinese offer before he boarded the plane to Philadelphia. His agony on the plane trip home was not so much focused on which alternative he would accept; it was rather focused on trying to figure out how he would explain his decision to his family, angel investors, and other constituencies who had made the business possible in the first place. Herman could have signed the Chinese deal on the spot, which would have spared him the agony of decision on the plane trip back to Philadelphia, but he knew he would need this valuable "quiet time" to work through his options and figure out a way to sell the decision to his family and business colleagues before he could formally accept.

If you are considering going into business for yourself, picture yourself in Herman's shoes for a minute. The decisions you are called upon to make in the entrepreneurial world are often Hobson's choices such as the one Herman faced: a choice between bad and worse, not between bad and great. It's a haunting, lonely task that scares many first-time entrepreneurs right back into corporate life. Yet the decision must be made, the risk must be taken, and you must still be able to live with yourself and get a good night's sleep after the decision has been made. Don't say we didn't warn you.

MONEYHUNT
RULE #3

"If Life Hands You a Pickle, Relish It!"

<u>MoneyHunt</u> Hero: Jacob Rosenzweig

We have all heard since childhood that "when life hands you a lemon, make lemonade." Well, we're from New York originally, and we prefer pickles.

Most entrepreneurs, and virtually all of the great ones, are optimists. They take what they are given and, through a magical combination of creativity and terror, somehow make it work. If you choose the entrepreneurial path, you must become accustomed to problems and reversals because you will confront them virtually every day; the world of small business is not a user-friendly one. Not only do successful entrepreneurs accept problems, they cherish them, grabbing them by the throat and making them pour out their hidden secrets.

As one of our MoneyHunt advisers likes to say, "You're never broke until you say so." No matter what they throw at you, no matter how bleak the situation, by taking a different angle and a different approach, often seemingly horrible circumstances can be opportunities in disguise.

DON'T LOOK AT THE MOUNTAIN, START CLIMBING . . . AND DON'T FALL OFF

If you're thinking of starting a brand-new business, prepare yourself to face regular and recurring death blows to your company. No, this is not a conspiracy, although many would be tempted to think so for the regularity with which a business's viability is assaulted in its first few years. As David Chapman, one of our MoneyHunt advisory panelists from North Point Ventures in Boston, often reminds us, "Entrepreneurs make three or four 'bet the company' decisions each year in the first two years of their existence."

Still, many successful entrepreneurs we know got where they wanted to go precisely because they were confronted with a problem that forced them into a new, challenging, and ultimately profitable direction. Cliff likes to say (he's a lawyer, what can we tell you?) that "there are only two great motivators in business: fear and passion. Fear, by far, is the better motivator of the two."

One of Cliff's friends in college was an avid mountain climber. By the age of seventeen this fellow had climbed virtually every major peak in the Presidential Range of northern New England—an incredible feat that almost landed him in the *Guinness Book of World Records* back in the 1960s. The friend once told Cliff something about the adventurous life that he, and we, have never forgotten:

> The longer you spend looking at a tall mountain, the more good reasons you can think of not to climb the damned thing at all. There are always places where you can't see good handholds, and you can't quite figure out how you're going to get from point A to point B without a miracle. I've learned that the only way you are ever going to get to the top of that tall mountain is to put on your backpack, strap on your pitons and climbing tools, run up to the nearest face of the mountain, and keep putting one hand on top of the other until you are too far up the face to turn back safely. When you get to one of the points that you were so worried about, one of two things will happen. Most often, when you are right there you will see tiny little handholds and crevices that you could not have seen from the ground even with the most powerful pair of binoculars they make. And when you don't . . . well, let me tell you, hanging from a sheer cliff face two thousand feet above the ground is one hell of a motivator! You just find a way. . . .

This fellow, incidentally, has gone on to become a superstar entrepreneur in the telecommunications business—someone you've read about in business magazines. We hope to land him as a MoneyHunt Mentor someday.

IT'S A LOT OF FUN, BUT I'M SCARED TO DEATH!

Let's face it . . . most of us just don't have the spirit of adventure. We go to action-adventure movies like the *Indiana Jones* series precisely so we can see Harrison Ford (or more likely his stunt double) doing things we only dream of doing, from the safety of our air-conditioned movie seat. An adventure of any kind, but especially entrepreneurship, is one part fun and three parts terror. So it comes as no surprise that entrepreneurs often go to great lengths to avoid relishing the pickles life throws at them.

One of the most common ways is to just roll over, admitting that you can't turn it around to your advantage before you've even tried. Now, sometimes this is actually the case. Not everything can be turned around, especially not to a dramatic advantage. Sometimes it's just as important not to let it kill you and live to fight another battle on another day. To borrow from the German philosopher Friedrich Nietzsche, "That which does not kill me, makes me stronger." Well, most entrepreneurs can be happy with the first half of that. At least not getting killed is the first step.

The second way some entrepreneurs try to avoid dealing with their pickles is to treat problems when they arrive as nuisances to be solved and not opportunities to be cherished. Letting problems eat at your insides does not do anything but make your doctor and the pharmaceutical companies rich. Your attitude when a problem hits that really stymies you should be, but very often is not, "Thank God! Things were going a little smoothly there for a while. I was really getting worried there for a minute that I was out of touch with what's really going on. Reality is letting me know it likes me, and is favoring me with its challenges!"

This may sound utterly ridiculous when you first say it, but try it—you will feel much better, and when you are calm, cool, and collected on the inside, you are much more likely to see the opportunity hidden within even the most insurmountable problem.

It's Helpful to Remember This When:

- The big order has to go out tomorrow morning, and your packaging machine breaks down tonight when the parts stores are all closed.

- You are counting on one of your employees to make a key pitch to a new customer, and he comes down with a 102-degree fever the night before.

- You are counting on an infusion of equity from a venture-capital firm, the partner in charge (who loved your business) has left the firm for greener pastures, and his replacement looks upon your business as the flakiest thing he's ever seen.

- The main ingredient in your best-selling product has just been discovered to violate federal and state environmental standards for child
safety, and distributors around the country are demanding a recall.

MONEYHUNT HERO: JACOB ROSENZWEIG

Jacob Rosenzweig had the familiarity of a street kid from the old inner-
city neighborhood. No matter what the circumstances, Jacob seemed
like the type that would be organizing stickball games in the street and
"Johnny on the Pony" matches on the front stoop, his mother hollering
from an upstairs window about dinner being ready.

The son of a small-town dentist in northern California, Jacob was a solid
ball of pure energy and seemed to feed off the warmth of the crowds that
gathered around him; his favorite phrase was "G-o-o-o-o-o-O-O-D!",
echoing not a little a certain cereal-box feline. What you didn't catch on to
right away was that Jacob was a deeply religious man and Sabbath observer,
whose family and community commitments were just as strong as the passion that burned for his business.

Jacob was best at trade shows. He couldn't afford a big booth, and he
couldn't afford a fancy suit either. He wore clothes that came right off
the rack at Sy Syms and were too big in the shoulders, drove secondhand
American cars with six-figure mileage, and stayed in the sort of motels
where the neon signs out front were getting a little rusty. He relished
every minute on the trade-show floor, though, fairly jumping out into
the aisles to meet new people and draw them into his booth to show
them his new oral hygiene products.

Jacob's company, Carefree Industries, was a small player in the oral
hygiene marketplace. With the help of his father, who provided the only
market feedback Jacob had ever received, he had invented a few flossing
devices and two new toothpaste formulations. Jacob's great concept—a
combination toothbrush and dental floss dispenser—made his name in a
very stodgy business.

The irony was, however, that Jacob had never intended to go into the
oral hygiene business. He backed into the business, kicking and screaming all the way, before he knew what he had. Before Jacob became Mr.
Toothbrush, he was Mr. Odds-and-Ends Trader. A Russian major in college who graduated just as the Berlin Wall was coming down and the
former Soviet Union was breaking up, Jacob was always hustling. He
knew there would be opportunities in the former Soviet bloc, but where?
And for what? He bought his first airplane ticket to Moscow without
even knowing the answers to any of these questions.

On one of his early trips to the former Soviet bloc, Jacob learned a new word: "countertrade." None of the former Soviet bloc countries, nor, especially, the new ones formed by the breakup of the former USSR, had any real cash to pay for things. But they did have lots of cool stuff that Jacob knew he could sell back in America. So he became a raw-goods countertrader, living from deal to deal: buying vodka in Hungary, trading it in Russia for a caseload of those furry hats you used to see the soldiers wear for the May Day parade in Red Square, trading those for leather goods in England, trading those for Bulgarian plum brandy, and so forth. As long as there was cash somewhere at the end of this daisy chain of trades, Jacob made out all right. A lot of times, though, there was no cash at the end of the chain—just some really cool stuff—and Jacob had to figure out how to unload the mystery packages while at the same time keeping his creditors (mostly friends and family) at bay.

One day, he pulled off a cheese-for-vodka-for-sneakers-for-toothbrushes trade worthy of Rube Goldberg, one that snaked from the Soviet Union to eastern Europe to Turkmenistan and stuck him with two containers of soft-bristle brushes at his doorstep. No cash, just two boxes of bristle brushes made of the hair of God-only-knew what wild beast in the Caucasus Mountain hinterlands of Eurasia. Jacob had an idea, though. He caught the next flight down to Bentonville, Arkansas, and met with the oral-care products buyer at Wal-Mart. Not twenty minutes later, he walked out with an order for all the brushes and more.

On the plane back from Bentonville, Jacob had an epiphany: If he was nimble enough to put together complex trades in the former Soviet bloc that would end up giving him products that he could presell to the major discount chains like Wal-Mart, he knew that he had a career and a business and could pay off all his debts to friends and family.

Within a week of completing the bristle-brush trade, he started Carefree Industries, Inc. At the time, the major consumer-products players were playing a high-stakes game of hardball, introducing new products and new innovations in the market and engaging in costly price wars.

Most of them had advertising budgets of several hundreds of millions of dollars and would think nothing of dropping $20 million to introduce a new feature and advertise new products. In theory this would have the effect of crushing the smaller competitors, but it surprisingly had no effect on Jacob's business. Whenever he found out about a new bristle-brush launch from a major competitor, he would work feverishly with his overseas suppliers in the Caucasus Mountains (mostly farm families to whom he had provided cellular telephones) to introduce a similar knockoff brush at much lower cost.

There was nothing illegal about Jacob's business: Few new features in the bristle-brush market could be protected by patent, and he was free to do something similar to a competitor's product if he could do it quickly and compete at a lower price. Soon enough, almost by accident, Carefree Industries stumbled onto its own product, which was unique and patented. Called the "floss-brush," it was an innovative combination of the conventional toothbrush with a small round of dental floss in the handle, providing a tactile reminder to floss when you brush and vice versa. Of course, when the floss ran out, the consumer knew it was time to buy a new brush!

The one caveat that came with the deal was that the "floss-brush" had to be manufactured overseas. Jacob didn't see this as a major obstacle and decided to press on, thrilled at the prospect of having his own unique product in the marketplace. He arranged for a firm in Albania, probably the poorest of the former Soviet bloc nations (and therefore the cheapest place to manufacture anything), to manufacture the "floss-brush" to his specifications.

Unfortunately, the Albanian manufacturer of the product turned out to be incompetent, investing the seed money Jacob had lent to improve their assembly-line equipment in one of the government-sponsored "pyramid schemes" that bankrupted the Albanian government a couple of years ago. Jacob delayed his product launch several times, only to deliver substandard product that in the end had to be written off as totally worthless.

Soon Jacob was in the hole to the tune of over a million dollars on his new product, which could have easily bankrupted him and in fact nearly did.

Rather than shut down production, however, he began to think how he could exploit his existing contacts to get the "floss-brush" off the ground. Indeed, there was quite a market for his type of product in Europe; the only catch was that the manufacturer and distributors had to be based in one of the nations participating in the European Economic Community (EEC). As it happened, Spain and Greece—two low-cost countries—had just joined the EEC.

Jacob quickly redirected the flow of product to a manufacturer in Spain and began shipping his brushes through a distributor in the Netherlands throughout the European continent. He pushed through a backdoor distribution deal that kept the Albanian firm involved manufacturing some of the raw materials, which then would be shipped through Greece ultimately to Spain for assembly at the Spanish plant. European sales of the "floss-brush" took off, more than covering the losses caused by Jacob's faulty introduction of his new product in the United States the year before, and soon American companies were buying the "floss-brush" as a luxury import item!

Jacob had ridden this roller coaster for almost three years when he was approached by a major consumer-products firm that had an investment fund looking to finance growing companies just like Jacob's. Naturally, Jacob was interested. He met with the firm's representative several times, only gradually disclosing his strategy, tactics, and plans over the course of many meetings and many months.

Jacob developed quite a trust relationship with several of the principals of the firm, but at the same time, he was nervous that the confidential information he had always guarded so closely might leak out as a result of the informal familiarity that had developed between the parties. Sure enough his worst nightmare came to life, as he read in *The Wall Street Journal* and simultaneously heard from the president of the venture-capital firm that the "plug had been pulled" on Jacob's deal (and in fact all pending deals) due to a downturn in international markets.

Jacob was sick when he heard the news. He had given volumes of confidential information about his strategy and tactics to the very people who were now closing up shop on the investment side. After a day in bed spent staring at the ceiling, Jacob finally worked up the nerve to call one of the principals of the venture firm, with whom he had developed a working relationship. As Jacob calmly, deliberately asked question after question, it became clear to him that the firm's president had told only half the truth: The firm was indeed still making investments, but it was now focusing on outright purchases of companies rather than acquisitions of minority stakes.

Jacob hadn't planned on selling quite so soon, but he'd given the venture firm a major "peek under his kimono" without a written confidentiality agreement, and he was concerned that if the firm bought one of his competitors first, that information would be handed over to the competitor on a silver platter.

Thinking quickly on his feet, Jacob hatched a plan. "Bill," he said, "that's no problem. You go ahead and change your direction. As a matter of fact, we're sort of changing our direction at Carefree Industries as well. So many people have inquired about the availability of my company for sale during our negotiations that I feel obligated to pursue them now. Because of our relationship, however, I would be happy to give you an option at the same price per share as you would have invested, but this time for the whole company. Does thirty days sound right for the option, Bill? Let me know. Otherwise, I will have no choice but to go to the highest bidder, and of course you know what that means."

Bill responded to Jacob within twenty-four hours with an oral offer and followed it with a term sheet, offering Jacob $15 million in cash for the entire business and a $2 million advertising budget on a new product introduction.

Jacob responded, "Well, I'd hate to disappoint all these folks I'm talking to, but I really like the way you guys do things. Let's call it a deal. By the way, any of you guys need toothbrushes as a promotional handout for the trade shows you attend? I just got a box in from . . . "

LESSONS FROM JACOB ROSENZWEIG

Jacob Rosenzweig was the consummate survivor, living from deal to deal and from hand to mouth until it became a habit rather than a challenge. He actually reached the point, he told us once, where he would become suspicious if a deal came together too quickly and easily. If this ever happened he would know in his gut that something was wrong. When the problems inevitably surfaced, he would relax and go back to business as usual.

Sometimes in business you have to start down a road without knowing precisely where it will lead because there isn't time to analyze the situation. Business is, in many ways, a game, and who can predict the outcome of a chess match from the first couple of moves? Many of Jacob's deals were put together on the fly, with Jacob making up his plan as he went along. Of course, there was always the risk he would end up with more Bactrian camel bristle brushes than he could ever use in several lifetimes. But he learned early on that there's always a buyer for something if you look hard enough, and that keeps the trade going.

Jacob's decision to go head-to-head with the major international consumer-products companies, competing mostly on price, took nothing short of raw guts. Normally, small competitors like Jacob get chewed up by bigger companies that can achieve economies of scale in manufacturing and drive their per-unit costs far lower than any small company's. But Jacob had some advantages over the big folks: His command of the Russian language and extensive contacts in far-flung corners of the former Soviet empire enabled him to find sources of supply that could churn out brushes more quickly and cheaply than any larger competitor could hope for.

One of the great lessons in Jacob's story is the successful entrepreneur's response to disaster. When the Albanian manufacturer collapsed, leaving him with a big inventory of substandard products, Jacob did not panic or worry about it—he viewed it as a change in direction requiring a different view of his company's assets and strengths. Rather than continuing to sell in the United States, where he knew he would face product-quality concerns, he shifted his focus to the European market instead, where he knew any product sourced from the former Soviet Union would develop a luxury cachet—sure enough, even the "substandard" brushes were soon being imported to the United States from Europe at a premium price. The keys for success in any business are to always make sure (1) there is a market for your products and services, and (2) that you can sell them at a profit. Everything else is mere window dressing.

When venture capitalists started showing an interest in Jacob's business, he realized that any firm interested at a dime would be just as interested at a dollar, especially when they're part of a consumer-products group and were willing to drop $17 million into a new type of bristle brush. Too often entrepreneurs are so happy that professional investors are demonstrating interest in them that they end up leaving too much money on the table. If you don't ask for what you really need to grow your business, you won't get it, my friend.

Be assured . . . with $15 million in cash and a $2 million advertising budget, you can buy a lot of pickles.

MONEY HUNT
RULE #4

"When Push Comes to Shove, the Battle Goes to the Ruthless"

MoneyHunt Hero: Rocco D'Alessandro

et's face it—*ruthlessness* is not a nice word. When you refer to someone as a "ruthless _____ ," the word used to fill in the blank is usually not a nice word.

Yet ruthlessness is one of the critical traits of the successful entrepreneur. When we say someone is ruthless, what do we really mean? We mean that when that someone has set a certain goal, he or she does everything possible to reach that goal short of committing a felony and risking a jail sentence. Ruthless people do what the situation requires regardless of:

- What people may think of them (people who are too sensitive to what others think of them tend to be terrible entrepreneurs).

- Whether people will think they are crazy (sane, normal people do not normally become billionaires—they become middle managers at large, soulless corporations).

- The negative impact on other people that may result from their single-minded focus (after all, if you are so successful that you wipe out all your competitors, do you really care that the employees of those ex-competitors are now out of work?).

If the word *ruthless* bothers you, or cuts against your value system, you can substitute more politically friendly words like *dedicated, goal driven, determined,* or the ever popular *focused.* As for us, we like *ruthless.* It describes most of the successful entrepreneurs we know. It is the highest compliment we can pay a guest on MoneyHunt.

BEING ETHICAL VERSUS BEING SQUEAMISH

If we had to pick the toughest rule in this book to swallow, this one would win hands down. Most of us think of ourselves as nice, decent people; *ruthless* is not a word we would normally want applied to us.

Very often, however, growing businesses fail not because of legal, marketing, or financial problems but simply because the company founders didn't have the sheer guts to bull their way through a tough situation because they were squeamish about the consequences or too worried about what other people would think of them. Most entrepreneurs need to do a "ruthlessness check" on a daily basis to make sure they are not holding back when they should be going full throttle at all of their goals.

Because people don't like to think of themselves as ruthless, they go to great pains to avoid being ruthless, often to the detriment of their business. When entrepreneurs fail to capitalize on a business opportunity or they yield to an outside threat because of insufficient ruthlessness, they often rationalize it as follows: "I could have saved the situation by doing X, Y, or Z, but I couldn't bring myself to do that because, hey, I'm very concerned about my reputation in the marketplace (community, profession, whatever) and I wasn't about to let it get out that I'm somebody who would do X, Y, or Z."

Don't get us wrong. We do not support unethical behavior in business. If business becomes too competitive, ruthless, and cutthroat, everybody suffers. But in our experience, too many unsuccessful entrepreneurs have a difficult time distinguishing between a valid ethical position on the one hand, and squeamishness or cowardice on the other hand.

IT'S EASY TO BE RUTHLESS . . . SOMETIMES

The interesting part about ruthlessness is that it's surprisingly easy to rationalize away. If others complain or say something negative about something you did in business, you can simply say, "Well, I'm sorry

about that, but it was what I had to do to get where I wanted to go."
They probably will be jealous that they didn't think of it first.

As the old saying goes, "Necessity is the mother of invention." When
you only have one viable choice, it's easy to be ruthless. Let's say you
are in a supermarket with a small child. You turn your back on the
child momentarily, and when you turn back again, you see a total
stranger pick the child up and start running rapidly toward the store
exit with the child in his arms. Are you going to hesitate even a
moment before you start engaging in ruthless behavior to protect that
child, even at the risk of taking a bullet yourself? In business it's the
same way. If you have let someone else walk off with your "baby"—
your business—don't tell us you "didn't have the heart" to do what
was necessary to save the business, or that you "didn't think it was ethical" to do the brutal, cutthroat things that might—just might—have
worked. Tell us the truth: You didn't care enough about the business to
give 100 percent of yourself to solve the problem and move forward.
You cared more about your reputation, safety, or self-image than you
did about the business.

Remember to Be Ruthless When:

- You have to fire someone who's been with you for a long time
  but just isn't performing anymore.

- You learn your competition has a significant weakness that can
  easily be exploited without violating the law.

- Your current bills exceed your current income so that some folks
  (the nice ones) will have to wait awhile.

- Your customers make unreasonable demands that will require you
  to sell your goods or services at or below cost in order to satisfy
  them.

MoneyHunt Hero: Rocco D'Alessandro

Rocco was one of our first unofficial mentors at MoneyHunt. A millionaire several times over and an investor in start-up companies, Rocco
made his money in a most unusual way. While we love Rocco, it's fair to
say you will never see him, or his business plan, on MoneyHunt.

Born and raised on the South Side of Chicago, Illinois, Rocco didn't
make it much past high school. His dream was to drive trucks—the "big

rigs"—and for twenty years he worked as a trucker hauling hazardous chemicals, industrial waste, liquid nitrogen, explosives, and other toxic goo. These truckers, who are called "suicide jockeys" in the industry for obvious reasons, command incredible salaries for blue-collar workers. There is a downside, though. Driving trucks that carry hazardous materials, which could explode and cause untold damage if spilled, takes nerves of steel and reflexes like a cat. One small error of judgment could cause an accident, which in turn would cause a spill of toxic materials, which in turn would cause an explosion and (in many cases) a release of toxic gases, which in turn would be a disaster of epic proportions (think Bhopal or Chernobyl). To put it bluntly, suicide jockeying is a young person's game; once you reach a certain age, your reflexes and physical stamina just aren't what they once were, and the risk of a major accident increases geometrically each year after you turn thirty-five.

By the early 1980s, Rocco had reached the ripe old age of forty and realized he couldn't continue as a suicide jockey much longer. His trucking company was pressuring him to quit. He wanted a desk job at his trucking company, but there was no room for him. Besides, the company required a college degree for clerical jobs, and he didn't have one. After some negotiation, the company offered him a generous severance package he couldn't refuse. He left the trucking business and decided to try something new.

After years of living on the road away from his wife and children, who had grown up without him, Rocco decided he would start his own business with his wife as partner so they could have more time together. He had read about franchises, where you buy a proven business plan and get training and support for starting a new retail business. After looking at several franchises, Rocco and his wife decided to buy into a home video rental franchise. This was in 1982.

Do you remember what the video rental business was like in the early 1980s? Unlike today, it was largely a mom-and-pop industry. A number of video rental chains opened branches across the country, and they all worked the same way. You paid an up-front fee for the privilege of becoming a "member" of the video rental store, and the membership had to be renewed on a monthly or annual basis; these membership fees usually ran between $50 and $100 per year. On top of that, rentals were $7 to $10 a night. Because the stores were small, you rarely found the video you wanted to rent. Instead, the helpful store owner would order the video from the store's voluminous catalog. You waited anywhere from two days to two weeks to get your video, and once you got it you had to return it to the store in twenty-four hours because someone in another state wanted to rent it.

Rocco purchased a video rental franchise and opened a store in an upper-middle-class suburb of Chicago. For several years, Rocco and his wife ran a highly successful business. Having always been a deeply religious person, Rocco was a deacon of the largest church in town, with over two thousand parishioners, and headed up just about every church committee there. By publicizing his business in the weekly church bulletin, Rocco had more business than he could handle. Within six months of opening his video rental store, Rocco and his wife were grossing over $20,000 per month on average, which netted him $15,000 a month after paying the franchise fee, utility bills, and other out-of-pocket expenses. Not bad for an ex-trucker with a high school diploma!

This, of course, did not last. In 1988, five years after he opened the business, Rocco read some disturbing news in his local newspaper. A company called Blockbuster Video was going to open a giant video rental store right down the street from Rocco's store. At first, Rocco wasn't worried. When the Blockbuster Video opened, however, he worried plenty. Unlike Rocco's store, Blockbuster Video did not charge an annual membership fee. Rentals were only $2 to $3 a night. Because the store had a warehouse-size floor space, it could stock thousands of video titles to Rocco's two hundred or so. And if you didn't find the video you wanted, Blockbuster would guarantee delivery within twenty-four hours.

Rocco knew he couldn't compete with Blockbuster Video, but he pressed on, hoping his customers would remain loyal. Sadly, that didn't happen. Within two months of the Blockbuster Video grand opening, Rocco's gross had declined from $20,000 to less than $1,000 a month, which was not even enough to pay the franchise fee. Rocco called the franchise company and asked for help. He was told, in effect, "We're sorry, Rocco, but Blockbuster's killing us all over the country. We're getting ready to file for bankruptcy. If you pay us $5,000, we'll be happy to release you from your franchise contract and you can do whatever you want with the store." Rocco may not have been an educated man, but he was not stupid. He was not about to pay $5,000 to get out of a contract when he didn't even know he could keep the business running. Where would he get his videos from? How could he compete with Blockbuster's massive advertising and promotional budget?

Rocco was scared out of his wits. He had two kids in college, a heavy mortgage, and the only two businesses he knew were trucking and video rental. His back was literally against the wall; he was behind in his rent, his mortgage, his credit cards, and just about every other debt he owed. A lesser person would have given up and filed for bankruptcy—thrown in the towel and gotten a job flipping hamburgers at a fast-food joint or working as a clerk in a grocery store.

But not Rocco. Rocco was made of sterner stuff.

One night on his way home from work, an idea occurred to Rocco, seemingly out of nowhere. A strange idea . . . a crazy idea . . . an idea that would make him the most hated man in town and cost him every friend he ever had, but maybe . . . just maybe . . . might save him. He talked it over with his wife that night. At first she thought it was crazy, but after a while she realized they didn't really have any other choice. She hated the idea, but she went along.

Rocco paid the $5,000 to the failing franchise, got a release from the franchise agreement, and went into . . . the adult video business.

Adult videos. Triple-X stuff. Naked people on the covers. Black tape over the store windows so teenage kids can't peer through and see anything. People protesting with picket signs outside your doors. Local zoning officials trying to shut you down on legal technicalities. Nasty editorials in the local newspapers with your picture on the front page. But . . . perfectly legal, and . . . highly profitable.

Rocco did some research and discovered his store was properly zoned for an adult video business. He scoured downtown Chicago looking for XXX-rated videos and bought as many as he could afford, usually by paying cash. Rocco instinctively knew that the people who rented adult videos on a regular basis weren't the local citizenry, who were horrified at the idea of an adult video store in their neighborhood. Instead, Rocco knew, his key customers were transients, people who were just passing through town, such as traveling salespeople, corporate executives on business trips, college fraternity boys, and . . . truckers. Rocco knew how to sell to truckers. He advertised in truck stops, got a mailing list from the local Teamsters union, and started mailing flyers to truckers around the country. Pretty soon, word got around in the trucking community that a "brother trucker" was running one of the hottest adult video stores in the midwestern United States. Truckers went out of their way to visit Rocco's store and paid premium prices to buy or rent Rocco's videos. While most adult video stores have theft and nonreturn rates of 50 percent or more, Rocco's was less than 2 percent. If you didn't return a video on time, he knew who you were, and knew where he could find you. Within three months of opening his adult video store, Rocco was grossing $10,000 a month; within six months, he was grossing $25,000 a month, more than he had ever made in his "legitimate" video business.

His success, however, came at a huge price. Within a week of opening his store, nobody would sit near him and his wife at church on Sunday. He was removed from all of his church committees and was eventually asked to leave the church, as the pastor found it embarrassing that the largest single contributor to the church was running a business in viola-tion of the church's highest principles. Weeks after he opened his busi-ness, picketers (some from his old church) set up in front of Rocco's store claiming he was the "agent of the Devil" who was "polluting the minds of our young people." These pickets were front-page news, and every edition of the local newspaper carried editorials and letters to the editor condemning Rocco, his wife, and his business. His children were afraid to tell their friends what Daddy did for a living. Rocco's landlord tried to evict him three times without success, as Rocco always paid his rent on time and complied strictly with the terms of his lease. The local zoning board hauled him in for hearings several times and tried to declare his business illegal because of highly technical zoning violations. Lawyers and accountants wouldn't return his phone calls asking for help because they were afraid for their reputations in the community. Rocco and his wife were eventually forced to sell their home and move to a neighboring suburb where they were not as well known.

Rocco soldiered on. He ran a tight ship, as clean an operation as you can in the video rental business. If you even looked like you were under twenty-one years of age, you were carded at the door. Rocco painted his windows black so nothing could be seen from the outside. He offered a delivery service for those customers who were afraid to visit his store in person. Still, the efforts to shut him down continued.

All the adverse publicity, the pickets, the sermons from the pulpit con-demning Rocco, and the general opprobrium directed at Rocco, his fam-ily, his business, his dog, and everything connected with Rocco, had one peculiar impact on his business: Sales kept on increasing. Rocco had to hire people to handle the volume, something he never had done before.

Pretty soon Rocco was receiving inquiries from people who wanted to franchise his concept and open stores in other areas. Rocco agreed, pro-vided the new store owners adhered to his "keep a low profile/keep your nose clean" policies. Not knowing how to put together a franchise agreement (no decent lawyer in town would even talk to him), Rocco just took the old contract and disclosure documents from his "legiti-mate" video rental franchise, changed the company name to his own, and offered exactly the same terms. Within two years of opening his XXX-rated adult video store, Rocco was running a chain of five franchise stores throughout the greater Chicago area. Within five years Rocco had thirty adult video stores throughout the Midwest, some of which were franchised, and some of which were company owned, all generating incredible revenues from franchise fees and "percentage of sale" over-rides, with hardly any cost. By the end of 1994, Rocco was a "porn-lord" millionaire, the sole owner of a franchise business with over $5,000,000 in revenue and $3,500,000 in earnings.

In early 1995, Rocco was approached by a major chain of adult video stores based in California. He sold his stores to the chain for $10,000,000 in cash. He has since contributed a significant portion of the proceeds of this sale to church-related charities in the Chicago area.

LESSONS FROM ROCCO D'ALESSANDRO

How many of you would have made the decision Rocco made when his initial franchise venture was going down the tubes? How many of you would have risked your entire reputation, your standing in the community, your friends, your respectability, to stay alive and prosper? Many of you, I'm sure, would not have. You would have taken your lumps, filed for bankruptcy, and started from scratch. But Rocco was willing to become a pariah in his community to avoid losing his home, pulling his kids out of college, and going on welfare. Frankly, I'm not sure we would have made the decision Rocco made, yet Rocco remains one of our all-time entrepreneurial heroes, the poster child for what it means to be ruthless in business.

Obviously, deciding to open an adult video store violated just about every major ethical principle Rocco and his wife held dear. We are sure Rocco lay awake at nights wondering how he could continue in a business that was so contrary to his upbringing and values. But did Rocco really have a choice? In Rocco's value system, going broke and filing for welfare was one of the most shameful things that could happen to a person. Any legitimate business was preferable to being a "bum" living off the generosity of others. Rocco chose to survive, despite the fact that his whole world (except, of course, the adult video marketplace) would be against him.

In the beginning, Rocco knew nothing about the XXX-rated movie business except . . . the most important things. He knew his customers and how to reach them, and he knew that to avoid the inevitable legal hassles of running an unpopular business he had to run a tight ship with zero tolerance for mistakes that would give his enemies ammunition to use against him. Similarly, Rocco didn't know the first thing about franchising, but having been a franchisee once, he figured that what was good enough for him to sign would probably be good enough for others to sign. Why reinvent the wheel, and spend thousands of dollars in legal fees, when you have ready at hand something that's been proven to work?

Rocco also learned that, in the words of a famous movie actress, "All publicity is good publicity." Much of the negative press he generated in his community served ironically to get his message out and increase his sales, without costing him a penny. His enemies would have done more harm to Rocco's business by just ignoring him.

When Rocco sold his adult video franchise for $10,000,000, he donated a large portion of that sum to charity. While we're sure Rocco did this partly to reduce his tax exposure, we know Rocco well enough to know that something else was going on there. It is amazing how often successful entrepreneurs, once they have reached the point where they are no longer concerned about sheer survival, become philanthropists and benefactors of their communities. Think of all the good that has been done in the world because of the bequests of the nineteenth century "robber barons" like Andrew Carnegie and John D. Rockefeller. If these were such sweet, lovable people, why are they known as "robber barons"? Were their contributions to society just part of a Machiavellian marketing or public-relations plan? Or did they feel a certain need to compensate for all the dirty, nasty, ruthless things they had to do to people to get where they wanted to go? Only they can tell us for sure.

PART TWO

The Right Idea, at the Right Time

"Look Between Your Toes, and Stoop to Conquer"

<u>MoneyHunt</u> Heroine: *Alice Gobineaux*

Why are you thinking of starting your own business and becoming an entrepreneur? Why did you buy this book instead of the latest Stephen King or Barbara Bradford novel? We hope it was because you want to make some serious money and achieve a return on your time and talent far greater than you could possibly hope to achieve by working for someone else.

Yet there is no guarantee that the type of business that will most likely bring you the riches and material rewards you want will be challenging, fulfilling, or intellectually stimulating. Some of the most exciting (from a financial point of view) business opportunities we can think of can be executed by people with high school educations.

Just about every day, we meet a would-be entrepreneur who is spending serious time and money developing a next-generation computer software product for the year 3000 when his community is screaming for a dry-cleaning business or ethnic grocery store that could easily be launched with the entrepreneur's current abilities and resources. In the words of the eighteenth-century playwright Oliver Goldsmith, to succeed in business sometimes you must "stoop to conquer."

I'VE GOT THREE PH.D.'S, SO HOW COME I'M NOT RICH?

The current generation of Americans is probably the most educated generation in human history. We say "most" educated, not necessarily the "best" educated. Most of the people we met in our live *MoneyHunt* presentations have at least four years of college, and in many cases two years or more of graduate school.

Education can be a two-edged sword, however, especially in the entrepreneurial world. Read biographies of famous entrepreneurs and rarely if ever will you see advanced degrees in their backgrounds; probably the best-known entrepreneur of our times, Bill Gates of Microsoft Corp., dropped out of college to go into the computer software business.

When you are a highly educated person, it usually means you did well in school. You were a good student. How did you get to be a good student? By following rules. By learning what the teachers wanted and then giving it to them. By demonstrating an enthusiasm for the subject matter (whatever the subject matter was) that equaled or surpassed that of the teacher.

In other words, you learned to live inside your head—building theories and constructs and rationales and proofs that, while beautiful and logical and coherent, had little if anything to do with the real world. You also learned that things must happen in a certain order—"I can't take American History II until I've taken and passed American History I."

Yet, as we all know (but sometimes won't admit), the real world is anything but beautiful, logical, and coherent, and often you have to skip the "introductory courses" in life because you aren't given the time to take them. As we point out throughout this book, opportunities do not wait for you to take time preparing for them.

EDUCATION IS GREAT, BUT DON'T LET IT GET IN THE WAY

Again, don't get us wrong. We have nothing against education or advanced degrees. In certain highly technical fields you cannot succeed without an extensive background in engineering, mathematics, or the physical sciences. Some of the most successful entrepreneurs we've known have been highly educated people. We merely submit, based on our experience and observation of successful entrepreneurs, that many highly educated people fail to succeed in business because they let their education get in their way, while less educated people often succeed precisely because they do not look beyond the obvious (indeed because they are incapable of doing so). In the words of a famous, and very successful, entrepreneur: "If I had known it was going to be this difficult making my first $100 million, I would have finished high school." Business success depends more on street smarts, acute perception and awareness of your external environment, and sheer dogged determination than it does on "what you know."

You must learn to beware your education when evaluating ideas for a new business. Too many first-time entrepreneurs look for something interesting, exciting, or "sexy" that will make use of their education, intellect, and creative imagination. Yet often successful business ideas are literally right in front of you, staring you in the face and screaming "Do me! Do me and get rich!" But because they are simple, obvious ideas that do not require imagination, creativity, or intellect, educated people tend to ignore them, either out of fear that they will be bored silly or because they feel the business is "beneath their dignity."

If we were to tell you there was a wonderful business opportunity in your town, one that could easily bring you income of more than $100,000 a year within the first twelve months of operations, with a start-up investment of only a few hundred dollars, would you be interested? Would you want to know more? We suspect that you would.

Now, let's say we told you that the "opportunity" was a janitorial service—cleaning offices, kitchens, and toilets for small- to medium-sized businesses. How do you feel about the opportunity now? You are probably not as wild about it as you were a minute ago. Why not? With your college degree, you have more than enough skills and expertise to do the job, and the start-up costs are well within your means. We have just guaranteed you a six-figure income within one year. Yet you are hesitant. Why? Could it be that your education, and the image of yourself that it has engendered, is getting in the way of your success?

People with less education, who spend more time looking at the world around them than focusing on the space between their ears, and whose expectations haven't been artificially built up by diplomas hanging on the wall, are often better suited to the world of entrepreneurship, because they have no choice but to see, and reach out for, the obvious. No one likes to feel that they are overqualified for a particular job or career. Yet passing up solid business opportunities while you wait for something that will make use of your master's degree in existential philosophy is not going to make you rich, famous, or in control of your destiny.

"TODAY I WILL MAKE MONEY; TOMORROW I WILL DO SOMETHING INTERESTING"

One way entrepreneurs try to ignore what is between their toes is to pretend that they would not be happy in a situation that, they are convinced, is beneath their dignity. "I realize I could make a lot of money, but I wouldn't be happy, and ultimately I'd end up making a big mistake or losing interest in the business, so I'd rather not go down that road." Perhaps this is true, but most of us can find it within ourselves to take on something we find unpleasant, uninteresting, or unsavory for a short period of time, if we decide up front that it will be only for a short period of time and then we will be able to resume our upward path. If someone offers you the chance to make $1 million in five years doing something distasteful or unchallenging, the correct response might be "Okay, I'll take it, I'll make my million, and then I'll go back to school for my Ph.D. and become the Egyptian archaeologist I've always wanted to be."

Another common way entrepreneurs turn their backs on the obvious is to pretend that uninteresting but highly lucrative business opportunities do not have long-term potential. "I realize that what my community needs more than anything else is a good ethnic grocery store, but hey, it's only a matter of time before someone franchises the concept, develops a 'big box' retailer in this area, or starts selling ethnic food on the Internet, which will wipe out all of the 'mom and pop' stores." That may be true, but did you stop to think that you might be just the person (with your superior education and all that) to carry it to the next level?

MoneyHunt Heroine: Alice Gobineux

Alice Gobineux, *née* Schoenblum, began life as a professional student. A star athlete and valedictorian of her high school class in the rural New Hampshire community in which she was raised, she attended an elite college in the greater Philadelphia area, carrying two majors, in philosophy and French. Upon graduation from college she won a postgraduate fellowship to attend an elite university in France, where she was to pick up an advanced degree in her major field of study (twentieth-century continental philosophy) and return to her alma mater with a guaranteed teaching position.

On her sojourn in France she met Charles Gobineux, the son of a prominent Paris attorney who, having been trained as a sous chef at one of the elite French cooking schools, was working in one of Paris's most exclusive restaurants as an apprentice, making the stock for soups and occasionally getting a shot at an hors d'oeuvre or two. The two fell in love, and later married.

On returning to the United States, Alice took up a teaching position in the philosophy department of her alma mater, while Charles worked as assistant chef in a French restaurant in Philadelphia. Alice went on to obtain a Ph.D. in philosophy, writing several articles (some in the French language) for leading academic journals in her field as well as one book (on the Spanish philosophers of the "Generation of 1898" and their impact on the development of French existentialism). She became a top scholar in a very narrow field. Nonetheless, when the time came, she was passed over for tenure, as there was no room for her in the small (and getting smaller) philosophy department at the college. Despite valiant efforts and glowing recommendations from some of the leading experts in existential philosophy in the world, she was unable to secure a position at another college. At one point a local prep school asked her to consider joining their faculty, as they desperately needed someone to teach French, but she turned it down in the hopes that a position in philosophy would open up somewhere.

Meanwhile, her husband, Charles, had advanced to the position of head chef at the French restaurant, winning acclaim for some of his new recipes and reviews as one of the up-and-coming French chefs in the Philadelphia area. After considerable discussion, Alice and Charles decided to open up a catering service specializing in state-of-the-art French cuisine, so the two could spend more time together. Charles planned the meals and did the cooking, while Alice learned to keep the books, interface with the customers, and handle the back-office functions so Charles could be free to indulge his creativity in the kitchen.

Their catering business was moderately successful; in fact, we met Alice and Charles when they were recommended to cater lunches and dinners during one of our marathon *MoneyHunt* shoots at WHYY Channel 12 in Philadelphia. During a break in the shooting, over one of Charles's fabulous lunches, Alice shared with us an idea she had (and was in the process of selling to Charles) for opening a gourmet French restaurant. The couple had recently moved to a town in southern New Jersey, ten miles outside of Philadelphia, and soon realized that there wasn't a French restaurant anywhere in the vicinity. "With Charles's reputation," Alice said, "there's no way we can lose!"

Whenever we hear an entrepreneur tell us "it's never been done before," we worry that there might very well be a very good reason why it has never been done before. We asked Alice to tell us something about the community. "It's a pretty big place—about thirty thousand people— with two colleges." We then asked about demographics and learned that Alice had clearly done her homework. "It's mostly a young person's town—lots of college kids of course, and young families with small children. Not many older folks."

With this disclosure, alarm bells started going off in our heads. Alice's market was heavily composed of:

- Parents of young children (with no time or patience for formal dining and three-hour sittings).

- College students (who either don't appreciate, or can't afford, gourmet French cuisine).

We expressed our concern that a gourmet French restaurant might not be a good "fit" for the community. Alice sighed and said, "Yes, that's what the banks have been telling us. We have a great location in mind, right in the center of everything, but with an astronomical rental. I don't see how we can do the kind of restaurant we want without charging $20 to $30 per entrée."

We like nothing so much as a good business challenge, so we asked Alice to tell us something about the competition. "Well, there's more Chinese restaurants than you can shake a stick at, several pizzerias and trattoria-style Italian restaurants, and an Indian place."

At this, Cliff's eyes widened and he smiled, a sure sign that he was onto something. "Alice, you're going to think I've lost my marbles, but have you thought about opening a Mexican restaurant?" Alice indeed looked at Cliff as if he had just arrived from another planet and said, grimacing with each word, "Mexican? As in tacos, enchiladas, and refried beans?"

"Precisely," Cliff said, warming to the subject despite Miles's gently kicking him under the table. "Think about it, Alice. You've got a lot of parents of young children, who want good, cheap food that everybody can enjoy in a family setting. That's why you've got all the pizzerias and Chinese restaurants in town, all apparently doing quite well from what you've told me so far. And the college kids . . . I don't know about you, Alice, but when I was in college Mexican takeout was one of the major food groups! Those kids must be going crazy without it."

"Well," Alice stammered, "there is a Mexican place two towns over from us. . . ."

"And," Cliff interrupted, "most of the college kids don't have cars to get there! They need a local place they can walk to, and your location is within easy walking distance of both campuses. Sounds like a perfect idea to me! And from what you've told me, there's no competition."

By this time Charles, who had been listening to the conversation with one ear while standing behind the serving table, chimed in. "Mexican food? But . . . but . . . any fool can cook Mexican food. There is . . . how do you say? . . . there is . . . no challenge, no sophistication, at all to it!"

Alice agreed. "I hear what you're saying, Cliff, but Charles has spent his entire career at the cutting edge of gourmet French cuisine. He's won awards for his creations. It would be like asking Julia Child to work at McDonald's. It does sound like a good idea, but . . ."

Miles jumped into the fray. "Alice, do you want a four-star rating in the Michelin guide, or do you want to make a ton of money?"

Charles cut off Alice's reply. "Thank you for the advice. We will think about it. We appreciate your good intentions." We decided to change the subject before we ended up being doused with vichyssoise.

Six months later, we were back in the studios shooting another season of *MoneyHunt*. One of the first decisions we made was to ask Alice and Charles to do the catering for us again.

We asked Alice how her plans for the gourmet French restaurant were going. After a long hesitation, she said, "Dead in the water. We lost the location."

"I'm sorry to hear that," Cliff replied.

"We are even more sorry than that," said Alice. "You know, you guys really ARE good. Want to take a wild guess what opened up in that location?"

Miles smiled. "A Mexican restaurant?"

Alice nodded. "Not only that . . . a franchise . . . a 'chain' Mexican restaurant where everything looks and tastes the same no matter where you go. The people who opened it—they never even ran a restaurant before! They didn't know a taco from a tostada. They just took a three-week course on Mexican cooking from the franchise company and opened their doors."

Cliff, trying hard not to look too smug, asked, "And how are they doing?"

The answer came back slowly and quietly. "It's the hottest place in town. You can't get near it on the weekends."

LESSONS FROM ALICE GOBINEUX

Given her academic background, it would have been asking a great deal of Alice to take Cliff's suggestion of a Mexican restaurant seriously. People with Ph.D.'s in existential philosophy usually don't open Mexican restaurants. It's just not done. Besides, she probably would never have persuaded Charles to go along with the idea.

Yet by ignoring the obvious, she and Charles passed up an opportunity that might have made them rich enough to eventually get back to France and that little bistro on the Côte d'Azur with the four-star Michelin rating.

Alice's first clue that it was time for a change in her outlook on life came when she was denied tenure at the college where she had spent most of her working life. Admittedly, this was not her fault; her academic credentials were excellent. Unfortunately, she was in the "wrong place at the wrong time," and there was no demand in her chosen field of specialization (a common problem in academia, especially in the humanities). Because of her past successes in the academic world, however, she continued to think of herself as a scholar and college professor. Even when a prestigious prep school offered her the chance to salvage her academic career by teaching French, a language she obviously loved, she turned it down because it meant ultimately turning her back on a college teaching career and accepting what she perceived as a second-class academic career track.

We all have in our heads images of who we are that have been shaped by our upbringing, our education, our tastes, our prior experiences, and our goals in life. To succeed in business, we have to get over these self-images. There is no such thing as a "proper" business for an Ivy League graduate, just as there is no such thing as a "proper" business for someone with only a grade school education. What is "proper," frankly, is whatever works. It is better to be "nouveau riche" than not "riche" at all.

Joining her husband Charles in the catering business must have required quite an adjustment on Alice's part. Having no prior business experience, only a talented husband who did not speak English as a first language, Alice had a very steep learning curve. What enabled her to make the adjustment, psychologically speaking, was that in her mind she was still dealing with the crème de la crème of society—the Main Line Philadelphia carriage trade. Cliff's suggestion that she lower her sights and focus on a middle-class market (including college students, who once had to satisfy her demands rather than the other way around) was bound to fall on deaf ears.

Alice's focus on a four-star French restaurant was consistent with her background and her (and her husband's) ambitions. Unfortunately, it did not fit the market demographics of the community in which she chose to open the restaurant. A gourmet French restaurant in downtown Philadelphia might have survived, depending upon the location, Charles's reputation as a top-notch chef, and Alice's marketing talent, which was not insignificant. A gourmet French restaurant in sport-utility-van suburbia was not such a promising proposition.

In refusing to even consider opening a Mexican restaurant, Alice did not consider the possibility that she and her husband could still establish the gourmet restaurant they dreamed of. Mexican cuisine, like French cuisine, lends itself to wide variation in quality and execution. There are four-star restaurants in Mexico City, just as there are four-star restaurants in Paris. There is low-quality fast food in Paris, just as there is low-quality fast food in Mexico City. Alice's prejudice against Mexican cuisine as "tacos and enchiladas" prevented her from seeing the possibility of an upscale Mexican restaurant that would challenge Charles's culinary talents and satisfy Alice's concern that they not compromise their exacting standards. With Charles's amazing talent in the kitchen, they might have set a new paradigm for Mexican cuisine, much as the great New Orleans chef Paul Prudhomme set a new paradigm for Cajun/Louisiana cooking a few years ago. Sometimes, when you have superior skills, it's better (and more profitable) to go where the talent is lacking so you stand out in the crowd that much more quickly and easily.

MONEYHUNT
RULE #6

"Don't Waste Time Making Someone Else Rich"

MoneyHunt Hero: Roberto Saville

Most of us want to become entrepreneurs precisely because we are tired of working long hours to make someone else rich. We want to work long hours making ourselves rich.

Yet it is surprising just how often we see entrepreneurs spend years of their lives developing business ideas that they themselves cannot exploit for their own benefit.

Hardly a week passes that we don't see a business plan for an interesting and potentially great idea. The only problem is that the entrepreneur, a first-timer with few resources, is looking to raise $5 million in venture capital just to get the idea past the prototype/development stage. To put it simply, venture money (in that amount, at least) is not going to be wasted on an unproven idea developed by unproven talent. Professional investors (like all investors) want to back proven technology and proven entrepreneurs. They want to know "where you have been," not "where you think you can go." This is sad, perhaps, but it is true.

Sometimes an idea, however great, is too big for you to handle. In that case it is better to pass on it and focus on something that you can do with the resources you have available.

BEING TOO FAR AHEAD OF YOUR TIME IS JUST AS BAD AS NOT BEING FAR ENOUGH AHEAD OF YOUR TIME

We all have ideas, and some ideas are bigger than others. For example, we are certain that science will prove the existence of significant quantities of strategic metals on Mars and other planets in the solar system—minerals such as titanium and cesium that are extremely costly to extract on Earth but may be as common on other planets as water is here. Surely the first entrepreneur to develop a means of finding and extracting these minerals on other planets will be richer and more famous than anyone in human history.

Well, it isn't too hard to see the problem here. What do you think the start-up capital for such a venture would be? How much money would have to be spent before the first spadeful of strategic minerals left for planet Earth? Our best guess (we are not rocket scientists) is that it would cost more than the entire combined net worth of the "*Forbes* 400" list of the richest individuals on Earth.

Such an example may sound silly, but you would be surprised how many earnest entrepreneurs are wasting years of their lives and thousands of dollars of their hard-earned money to develop ideas that are just as far-fetched and that no investor in his or her right mind would even consider financing.

A GREAT IDEA, BUT ARE YOU THE PERSON TO DO IT?

The idea that we may not be the people to bring to fruition a truly great idea is one we cannot readily accept. We are all the heroes of our own lives, and in our minds there is nothing we cannot do with the right amount of spunk, intellect, and hard work. Sadly, that is not always true. Very frequently, even solid ideas that are carefully researched and extremely persuasive on paper will fall short of the mark if they are too far ahead of their time. Even venture capitalists, who are accustomed to taking risks on new technologies and companies, are hesitant to "take a flier" on something they are hearing about for the first time.

We have been taught, thanks to P. T. Barnum, that there is a "sucker born every minute" and that there are people in the world crazy enough to put money behind something we wouldn't (or couldn't) finance ourselves. Sadly, this is another bubble that must be burst. The kind of money that it will take to realize a truly great idea will not come from unsophisticated mom-and-pop investors (even if you fully comply with the securities laws). It takes great capital to realize great ideas, and only the largest and most powerful investors have the leverage to make it happen. Trouble is, these titans of industry will probably want to exploit the idea themselves, leaving you (at best) with a small finder's fee and a footnote in the history books.

It's not just a question of money (although in our experience money is the most formidable barrier to realizing a breakthrough idea). If your great idea requires skills and talents you don't have, a large number of employees who will demand to be paid for their time, a large quantity of expensive real estate, access to supplies that have to be imported from hard-to-reach locations, or indeed any other resource that you do not possess and cannot obtain with the resources reasonably available to you in the next year or two, the idea is probably too great for you to exploit. Rather than waste years of your life trying to realize an impossible (for you, at least) dream, find something you can do with the resources you have available or can easily obtain with a minimum of time and money.

We are not suggesting that you cannot "stretch" your resources a little to realize an excellent business idea. We merely suggest that you do a "reality check" before committing your precious resources.

A Reality Check Is Called for When:

- You come up with a great idea for a new product, but it will require at least $1 million in start-up costs before the product can even be test-marketed.

- You come up with a great idea for a business book, but it will require two years of full-time research and development without pay, and your spouse is home raising three children.

- You read in a "futurist" magazine about a product or service people are likely to be using a hundred years from now, and you think it would be great to get into the market now when there's no competition;

- Noting two current trends in the Broadway theater—"dumbed down" musical versions of classic books, and plays featuring nude scenes by Hollywood celebrities—you decide to write an all-nude musical comedy based on Gustave Flaubert's Madame Bovary and pitch the title role to Gwyneth Paltrow.

- You come up with a great new invention, but you think you should put off doing any marketing research until you have built a detailed prototype you are satisfied will work.

MONEYHUNT HERO: ROBERTO SAVILLE

Roberto Saville was one of our early mentors on MoneyHunt and a truly American success story. An energetic, intense, bespectacled African American who vaguely resembles Woodrow Wilson, Roberto was the fifth of seven children of a forklift driver for a St. Louis, Missouri, warehouse. As a teenager Roberto was plucked from the ghetto of East St. Louis, Illinois, by the ABC program *A Better Chance*, and placed in one of America's most exclusive, prestigious, and demanding prep schools. Rising to the challenge, and working twice as hard as his more privileged white competition, Roberto graduated at the top of his class, distinguished himself as both a scholar and an athlete at an Ivy League college, and rose through the ranks of a leading management consulting firm to become, by his early thirties, a partner in the firm's St. Louis office and one of its top technology consultants. When it came to designing and implementing complex information systems (IS) for large corporations, there wasn't anything Roberto didn't know. He was considered a rocket scientist within the firm—the guy you went to when a client wanted something no one else had ever seen before.

One night Miles was working late at the office when he received a telephone call from Roberto. Roberto started talking before Miles could even say hello: "Miles, I'm in New York City meeting a new client. Listen, I need to see you. Tonight, if possible. I've been working on something for a while, and it's becoming an obsession. I'm onto something, man, something big. I need to talk to you. Can you see me tonight?" Before Miles could say yes, Roberto continued: "It really can't wait past tonight. I'm going out to San Francisco tomorrow to see another client, and it will take about three weeks. I won't be able to sleep out there until I know I've shared this with you and gotten your feedback." What could Miles say but yes? "Great. I'll meet you in two hours at ———— [a local sports bar within walking distance of the Bridgeport, Connecticut, train station]." Click.

Miles thought for a moment and figured Cliff should sit in on this meeting, since it was Cliff who had introduced Roberto to MoneyHunt in the first place. Miles called Cliff at his home, and within two hours Miles and Cliff were sitting in the smoke-filled back room of the sports bar watching a jai alai match on closed-circuit television. Precisely two minutes before he was scheduled to appear, Roberto burst into the sports bar, wearing his trademark horn-rimmed spectacles, a trench coat, and a $2,000 suit and carrying two large scrolls of drawing paper (the kind used by architects when designing skyscrapers and sports stadiums) under his arm.

After exchanging greetings, they moved to a private booth where they wouldn't be overheard. Roberto looked as if he hadn't slept in a week, but that wasn't surprising, as long hours and frequent travel are part of the life of a young management consultant. What was surprising were the two scrolls that Roberto coddled and fussed over as if they were a newly found book of the New Testament claiming that Jesus and Mary Magdalene had six kids and a condo on the Sea of Galilee.

"I'll get right to the point," Roberto promised. "About six months ago I was on the floor of the Chicago Options Exchange visiting a friend of mine and looking at all the pieces of paper being thrown around by the floor brokers as they were yelling and screaming at the specialists trying to execute trades. I said to myself, hey, why can't computers do all this? Why do you even need a trading floor? Try as I might, I couldn't get this idea out of my head. This is the kind of systems-integration stuff I do for a living. I began to sketch out a plan, and once I got started I just couldn't stop. Every spare moment, whenever I get a chance, I work this thing out, and guys, I think I have it. I have found a new way to organize a stock exchange, commodities exchange, options exchange, you name it, around personal-computer technology. This thing has the potential to make billions, man. Billions!"

Miles and Cliff looked at each other. Had Roberto, one of the most analytical and even-tempered people either of them knew, lost it? Before they could suggest to Roberto that maybe it was time for a weekend at the beach, Roberto rolled out the scrolls on the table. What the scrolls contained was a schematic, or "flow chart," of a personal-computer-based stock-trading system (this was in 1991). Roberto walked through the system step by step, showing how the interfaces between different parts of the system would be constructed, describing the type of computer equipment that would be required, and working through the costs of putting the system together.

Having both cut their teeth on Wall Street, Miles and Cliff both knew something about stock exchanges and started asking questions. Roberto had answers to every question—good ones. He had clearly thought through every aspect of the business plan and had worked out feasible solutions to all the potential problems Miles and Cliff could think of. No question about it—Roberto was onto something, something big. He had in six months figured out something it would take large corporations years of time, hundreds of man-hours, and millions of dollars to develop. And it all fit on two scrolls.

After winding up his presentation and taking the first few swigs of the Guinness Stout that had been sitting in front of him while Miles and Cliff grilled him as if he were a contestant on *MoneyHunt*, Roberto sat back.

"You see what I mean, guys. This isn't 'pie in the sky.' This is real, man. This can be done!"

After a long silence, it was Miles who spoke. "You got us, Roberto. This is absolutely fantastic—the most amazing thing I've ever seen. Cliff, what about you?"

"No doubt about it, Roberto. This is a work of true genius—Leonardo da Vinci with a degree in computer science couldn't have done this." Clearing his throat, Cliff added, "Tell me, have you figured out how much capital you would need to get this past the design stage and into implementation—I mean buying the hardware, developing the software, building a prototype system, and getting it into the brokerage houses?"

"That's what's been keeping me up nights," Roberto admitted. "The best I can figure is that I can do it for about $5 million."

Everybody took a swig on their beers. Miles said, "Well, Roberto, as best I can figure you're a little short. You'll need a bit more than that."

Roberto looked at Miles suspiciously: "How much more?"

Miles answered: "About $45 million more."

Roberto stared straight at Miles. "Fifty million dollars?"

Cliff chimed in. "I agree with Miles. Don't get me wrong, Roberto. You've really done your homework here, and we're not about to second-guess you. I think you could do the hardware and software development and the initial marketing for under five million as you predicted, but that's only the first step in the process."

Roberto looked stunned. "What do you mean, the first step?"

Miles started to speak, but Cliff interrupted: "You know I'm a lawyer, Roberto. Tell me, is it possible to start up a national securities exchange without government approval?"

Roberto stiffened slightly in his seat: "I know where you're going, Cliff. Of course I know. The Securities and Exchange Commission (SEC) has to bless this thing before we proceed. I understand that."

"Correct," Cliff replied. "And tell me, when do you think the SEC last approved a new national securities exchange?"

Roberto suddenly looked puzzled and settled back into his seat: "That's a good one. I really don't know."

"Try . . . 1939," Cliff said.

Roberto's eyes widened in amazement: "1939 . . . fifty-two years ago?"

"Right as rain," Miles confirmed. "When you go to the SEC with this thing, it isn't like there's a whole bunch of analysts waiting for something like this to come in the door. It will take months, maybe years, to get the approval you need. The SEC isn't going to just roll over and give you a rubber stamp on this. Somebody is going to have to tell the SEC that this is a priority and that they'd better make it happen. They will need to be pushed, most likely by the congressional committees that oversee the SEC's activities. Which means that somebody is going to have to push some buttons with the right people in Congress. You're a great guy, Roberto, but you will need to hook up with someone who has a lot more political clout in Washington and can get to the right people."

Roberto instinctively went on the offensive: "But lots of people will want this. They'll help get the political clout we need to push this through the SEC."

"Sorry," Cliff answered. "Think again. Think hard and long, Roberto. Can you think of a few people who might actually oppose this thing?"

Roberto's face went blank: "Oppose . . . ?"

"Not everybody is in love with new technology," Miles agreed. "Technology changes the status quo in dramatic ways, and there are a lot of entrenched interests who would not want this thing to happen. Try the stock exchanges. The options exchanges. The commodities exchanges. The major brokerage houses that have invested millions in the existing system. Your new system is going to hit the marketplace like a bowling ball crashing through tenpins. People in the industry will see this as taking their jobs away, and they'll fight it to the death."

"But it makes so much sense. . . ."

"Perfect sense," Cliff confirmed. "An idea that is way ahead of its time and well executed. Something that the brokerage houses, computer, and telecommunications companies will want someday. But not today. And when they do, they will want to develop it internally, because they're not about to buy something this big from an outside vendor, no matter how solid his credentials."

"Of course, you could try to sell this to one of the big computer and telecommunications companies," Miles added. "But they probably will want to steal your idea, which they probably will be able to do, as you can't patent or copyright something like this. A few changes in the system and they will be able to pass it off as their own creation. Besides, do you really want your consulting firm to hear through the grapevine that you're peddling something to their Fortune 500 corporations on the side? I don't think you're ready to give up the consulting game quite yet."

Roberto sat back, clearly disgusted, and let one of the scrolls fall to the floor. "I guess I didn't think through all the angles," he muttered, almost to himself.

"Don't be hard on yourself," Cliff said. "From a technological and feasibility point of view, you've done a hell of a job here. I've always thought you were something of a genius, Roberto, and this only confirms it. When your head is so into the details of a complex system like this, it's only too easy to lose sight of the political and 'people' problems you will face getting your idea across. All true visionaries have that problem. We see inventors and other technology entrepreneurs make that mistake all the time."

"I'm not big on making mistakes," Roberto said, "of any kind."

They were silent for a few minutes. The waitress came by with the tab. We paid for Roberto's beer. It was the least we could do.

Postscript: Two years later Miles read an article in a national business magazine about a new joint venture between a Fortune 100 computer company, a Fortune 200 telecommunications company, and a major brokerage house. According to the article, the three companies were planning to pool resources with the goal of creating a personal-computer-based system for trading stock, bonds, options, and commodities within two years. He called Roberto, who had left the consulting business to become chief operating officer of a fast-growing technology company in California. When asked if he had seen the article, Roberto laughed. "Yeah," he said, "you're about the third person who's pointed it out to me. Looks like they're heading in exactly the same direction I was going two years ago." With a chuckle, Roberto added, "After our meeting in the sports bar, I admit I was pretty down. You guys did exactly what I hoped you would do, and when I got over my initial frustration I realized just how right you were—it was a great idea, but I wasn't the guy to make it happen. I left the two scrolls on the train when I headed back to New York that night, because I just didn't want to waste any more of my life on them. Too bad. Some homeless person in Grand Central Station is probably sitting on a fortune right now and doesn't even know it."

LESSONS FROM ROBERTO SAVILLE

If we had to pick the five most brilliant people we've ever known in our careers, we would both put Roberto Saville on the list without a moment's argument. Roberto has the combination of visionary mind, restless energy, and intellectual candlepower that can lead to major breakthroughs in any field of human endeavor. A similar plan for a PC-based stock-trading system was eventually adopted by a consortium of three Fortune 100 companies after years of effort by dozens of technicians and systems designers. Yet Roberto learned that even great ideas aren't so great if you are just going to hand them over to someone else and watch them get rich off of them while you stand by with your hands in your pockets.

A lot of entrepreneurs we know would not have gotten as far even as Roberto did with his plan for a PC-based stock-trading system. For too many entrepreneurs, a great idea remains just that—a great idea that doesn't ever see the light of day. Roberto's vision that someday stock exchanges would be computerized, and his decision to devote virtually all of his nonworking time to the development and articulation of a working computer-based stock exchange, is a credit to his energy, stamina, and sheer force of will.

Like many people working in technical fields, Roberto decided he shouldn't even discuss the idea with other people until he had worked all the "bugs" out in his own mind, and this was his biggest mistake. While he accurately assessed the cost of developing his system, and sincerely believed (perhaps correctly—we would never bet against Roberto) that he could raise $5 million with only two scrolls of drawing paper and a business plan, he did not think about the political and regulatory obstacles he would have had to overcome to make his vision a reality. Had he done so, he would have realized sooner than he did that only someone much bigger and much more powerful than he could capitalize on the idea and make money at it.

The history of American business is full of brilliant inventors and visionaries who died in poverty after seeing their ideas make other, less deserving but better-capitalized people wealthy. When you are developing a new product or service, you can't operate in a vacuum. You need feedback at every stage of the development process, to serve as a reality check on your plans and a guarantee that you won't devote years of your life to a truly brilliant idea that will improve the lives of everyone . . . except you.

MONEYHUNT
RULE #7

"Sometimes Overnight Success Takes Twenty Years"

MoneyHunt Hero: Douglas MacAllaster

P ersistence is the hallmark of the successful entrepreneur. The entertainment business offers thousands of examples where, after laboring in obscurity for years upon years, an actor finally hits the big time and becomes an overnight success, when in fact he spent a lifetime working for that moment.

Well, we believe the entrepreneur market probably has more of those stories than even the entertainment business. Entrepreneurs sometimes spend decades learning an industry and working for others before one day they get their big breakthrough and start off on their own. Others get their industry experience by failing, sometimes two or three times, before finally the stars align and everything clicks and success comes easily, after decades of hard work.

SOONER OR LATER, IT COMES DOWN TO EXPERIENCE

"Staying in the game" is a crucial element of eventual success. The knowledge base and contacts that take years to build are very comforting to investors who are counting on your knowledge of the marketplace to pull "their" company through.

For example, we once knew an entrepreneur who labored in the bicycle business for twenty years, during which the most exciting new things to come along were the banana seat and butterfly handlebars. Then, in the early 1990s, the "mountain bike" craze hit and high-tech applications flourished for frames and shocks and wheel hubs. The big wheels (sorry) in the business were those who knew how to apply this new technology, and they inevitably were the ones who had labored in the fields of obscurity during the years when nothing much was happening in the bicycle business.

NEW INDUSTRIES SOMETIMES CREATE NEW TRICKS FOR OLD DOGS

Every once in a blue moon, a new industry appears out of nowhere. The rise in popularity of the Internet, for example, created many companies that are truly "overnight" successes because no one had had any prior experience in on-line communications. But where did the people come from to run these companies, since by definition only a handful of people had any prior experience in on-line communications and marketing? Many came from the publishing industry, which has been around since Gutenberg first put a piece of parchment between two hot plates. Most new industries are really incremental developments or extensions of existing industries—in such situations the marketplace puts a premium on experience.

Even in the Internet industry, as the market is maturing (slightly), the opportunities in Internet technology are going to people with experience in related fields. For example, Candice Carpenter, the founder of the iVillage on-line network and one of our *MoneyHunt* Mentors, was an accomplished media maven for decades in New York City, having built businesses for the likes of Time Warner and American Express.

Candice was an acknowledged expert at building a following when she hit upon a perfect way to deliver her contacts to women throughout the world and create an on-line forum for women to exchange information. Her comprehensive media background generated tremendous confidence among investors, who to date have pumped more money into iVillage than any private company in the Internet space. Although her success can be termed "overnight," Candice spent lots of time building her network and her knowledge until finally the right moment came about.

Remember That "Persistence Pays" When:
- You are slugging it out building a reputation in an industry that doesn't show much sign of long-term growth.

- You have started a number of companies that have crashed and burned with all passengers on board and are thinking of giving it up to run a bed-and-breakfast in rural Wyoming.

- You are an archaeologist with a passion for dead languages and ancient Greek and Roman coins, and you overhear at a party one of your lawyer friends tell someone that one of the lawyer's clients is looking for someone to help start an archaeology-related site on the Internet.

- You find yourself inundated with telephone calls from entrepreneurs who want your help to launch their new start-ups because over the years you have established yourself as the world's leading authority on _____ [fill this blank in yourself, if you dare!].

MoneyHunt Hero: Douglas MacAllaster

Doug was probably the perfect *MoneyHunt* guest. Energetic far beyond his fifty-odd years, passionate about his product and his company, with a flair for drama, and emotionally demonstrative, Doug was probably the star attraction at every one of the family gatherings he experienced growing up in Dubuque, Iowa. No doubt he tap-danced on the coffee table more than once for his proud parents. Doug thrived on attention.

Doug was great when he was on a roll. He would start most of his pitches slowly, as he did when he was in our studio for his initial *MoneyHunt* interview. Once this average-looking, midwestern, balding, fifty-something guy started rolling, and the arms and legs on his body began to flail like one of those plastic air-filled dolls that keep coming back up at you when you knock them over, Doug was hilarious and believable all at once. Even when you disagreed with Doug or challenged him on a point in his business plan, you couldn't help but laugh along with him.

Doug was founder of the Precocious Pen Corporation, an Iowa-based maker of pens, pencils, markers, and just about anything else you would use to color a piece of paper. Precocious Pen and Doug both had their roots thirty years in the past. Fresh out of college, and with nary a penny to his name, Doug was an inventor. Marking instruments were his medium. Back in the early 1960s, he was one of the successful early creators of new products like ball points for pens, markers that erase themselves, and special inks that dried before they could smudge.

Doug seemed to have been involved in every conceivable way to make a mark on a piece of paper, including space pens, ball points, cartridges, and felt and razor tips. Owner of over a hundred patents, all in the writing-instrument field, Doug absolutely loved coming up with new writing products. Sometimes he didn't even feel badly when no one bought them, because the kick he got out of creating something totally new was almost reason enough to pursue his trade. Unfortunately, in the 1970s Doug and a couple of business associates formed a company around a few of his patents and got off to an impressive start before getting sidetracked by a real estate venture that went bust in 1975 and landed them promptly in bankruptcy court.

Doug pressed on and almost busted a second company in the 1980s because of the same speculation habit, but he was able to sell his real estate interests off in early 1989 just as the spike in interest rates later that year would have buried him. So by 1991 Doug was making his third go of it after twenty-five years in the writing-instruments business, with the Precocious Pen Corporation. The name was a little crazy, but Doug seemed to be doing everything right this time. He surrounded himself with people who were able to hold him in check and to quell his temptation to speculate in real estate and thereby overleverage the company. This time he made sure that he raised enough capital up front to start the business, so he wouldn't have to go begging as he had to with his previous companies.

Doug started Precocious Pen Corporation with a few core product lines based on some old patents that he had held back from other partners or never got around to introducing because his other companies were in such trouble. The company got off to a solid, if undistinguished, start, chugging along at a few million dollars in sales and 20 percent year-to-year growth, enough to pay the bills but certainly nothing over the top. Moreover, being an inventor at heart, Doug's creative juices were sated by the development and introduction of about three new products twice a year, which he directed from start to finish.

Meanwhile the retail environment was changing dramatically. Large market discounters such as Wal-Mart, Kmart, and Target Stores—the so-called big box retailers—were controlling more and more of the retail space nationwide. The mom-and-pop stationery stores that had bought from Doug's former businesses were gone, replaced by Staples, Office Depot, and Office Max. Fewer and fewer big box chains were controlling a higher and higher volume of business in the stationery products industry. Margins were tightening, and seasonal promotions were becoming bigger and bigger business.

Besides Christmas, Halloween, and Easter, new seasonal promotions emerged on the horizon that would change Doug's fortunes forever. The back-to-school concept blossomed as a promotion angle from the big box retailers. They were looking for an excuse for parents and kids to go to the stores and had a captive market for repeat sales in that kids needed to return to school each year. So along with the new clothes and new lunch boxes, the mass marketers wanted to add some more school products to the list.

Precocious Pen was ideally positioned. Doug's line of "hot" pencils, pens, organizers, stickers, and project kits was exactly what the mass merchants were looking for. The margins in his products were excellent, the terms above average, the sell-through tremendous. Suddenly, instead of introducing three new products a season, Precocious Pens was being asked to introduce twenty-five or more.

Doug's salesmanship and the consolidated buying power of the big box retailers made for huge orders. Sure enough, Precocious Pen became the little company everybody had to have a piece of. Precocious Pen went on a tear of 100 percent growth in each of the following three years, topping out at $40 million in sales and delivering a hefty bottom line.

Investors piled in, first in a private round of venture capital, then in a public offering, and then in a series of secondary public offerings. The stock eventually hit a market capitalization of $50 million as the investors were convinced that Doug and his thirty years' expertise in the market would develop more products, more orders, and more profits. Doug and Precocious Pens were finally having their day in the sun.

LESSONS FROM DOUGLAS MACALLASTER

Precocious Pen achieved its $50 million market capitalization because Doug managed always to keep himself in the game. His in-depth knowledge of the industry and his gift for new product development were enough to convince investors that there would be a constant flow of new opportunities at Precocious Pen despite the occasional loser.

Although he had run through a few companies in his long history in the industry and had made some disastrous investment decisions, he had in fact invented and patented more products in the writing-implement industry than just about anyone else. Success had come fast for Doug, but only after thirty years of hard work, preparation, and patience.

Doug's penchant for speculative real estate deals had been his undoing on not just one but two occasions. When you have expertise in a given field, it is often wise to follow the advice of Mark Twain's Pudd'nhead Wilson and "put all your eggs in one basket . . . but watch that basket!" Rarely do we see entrepreneurs succeed in two such wholly different businesses as writing implements and real estate. What usually happens is that the gains in one field of endeavor end up financing the losses in the other. It took Doug two decades to recognize this. When he finally got wise with the start-up of Precocious Pen, Doug made sure there were people around him who would say "no" to his wilder impulses and keep the company—and him—on track.

In every business there are certain fundamental keys to success; while they are usually simple and straightforward once you recognize them, it often takes years before they make themselves apparent. With over twenty years in the writing-implement business, Doug realized that no company would survive for long with a product base consisting of only one or two items. Doug knew that the ability to come up with "cool" new products in rapid succession was the key to success in the pen business and that he needed to build a product catalog that was both wide and deep. As a result, Doug worked like a dog to make sure Precocious Pen had a product in every major market category.

Luck is a factor in business success—we don't deny that—but things change so fast in the business world that sooner or later things will break your way if you hang around long enough. The trick is to be ready for it, as Doug was. In the early 1990s a combination of two trends—an increase in back-to-school promotions outside the clothing industries and the rise to dominance of big box retailers who bought in bulk—enabled Precocious Pen to grow in a way Doug could not have imagined when he was at the helm of his former companies. If he had become disgruntled and changed industries while waiting for the big break, say by putting more of his time into his real estate activities, he would have missed out on the opportunities these trends created in the market for pens and writing utensils.

Sometimes an "overnight success" can take decades. Stick it out until it's your turn to shine.

PART THREE

Markets

and

Competition

MONEYHUNT
RULE #8

"When People Call You a Donkey, Buy a Saddle"

<u>MoneyHunt</u> Hero: Vinod S.V. Jhairaputra

One of the best quotations we have come across for new entrepreneurs was coined by no less a personage than Cliff's late grandmother, Almerinda Ruggiero ("Irene" to her friends and family). An immigrant from a village near Salerno, Italy, in the early 1900s with a third-grade education, Irene married a barber in Brooklyn and raised four children. She learned English when, finding a "Complete Works of Shakespeare" in the trash one day, she read it cover to cover by lamplight, looking up the words in an English-Italian dictionary and asking her children for clarification if she still couldn't grasp the meaning of the old-fashioned Elizabethan words. She never started a business herself, but she had the entrepreneurial spirit. And she spoke the most beautiful English, full of philosophy and two thousand years of Mediterranean stoicism in the face of adversity.

Cliff remembers that when he was a small boy, he once complained to Irene that the boys and girls at school were making fun of him because he liked books more than sports. He never forgot his beloved "Nonny's" response: "Cliffie, we used to have a saying when I was a girl in Italy. 'If someone calls you a donkey, laugh at him. If ten people call you a donkey, buy a saddle and charge for donkey rides.'"

Cliff also remembers his response to this wisdom: "Nonny, that's beautiful . . . but what does it mean?"

We at *MoneyHunt* know what Cliff's "Nonny" was talking about. It is one of the most profound quotes any entrepreneur can live by. When you are thinking up a business, you do not decide what the business will be and how well it will do. Your marketplace decides that for you.

Your customers and clients tell you who you are, what you can and cannot do, what business you are in, and how you conduct it. Listening to your marketplace, learning what it wants, and giving it to them even though it doesn't exactly fit what your business plan calls for can often be the key to greatness in an entrepreneurial company.

YOU DON'T DECIDE WHAT BUSINESS YOU ARE IN; THE MARKETPLACE DECIDES THAT FOR YOU

On *MoneyHunt* we see too many entrepreneurs, especially (although not exclusively) first-timers, who know too well what they want to do with their business. Their business plans are highly detailed, with comprehensive descriptions of the products and services they intend to provide, how they intend to deliver the goods, and how much money they will make based on "best case," "worst case," and "likely" scenarios.

There is only one problem with their plans. They do not anticipate the curveballs that the marketplace will throw at them and that will cause them to change direction against their will. Like it or not, the marketplace gets what it wants. You do not always get what you want from the marketplace (although, to paraphrase Mick Jagger of the Rolling Stones, if you try, sometimes you get what you need). Tailoring your business plan to what the market will buy is always a better, more successful strategy than thinking up something in your head and hoping the market will buy it.

In our small-business seminars and live presentations, we emphasize that often it is the person who doesn't know what type of business he or she wants to be in who has an easier time building a successful business. Having no prejudices or preconceptions, such a person is highly receptive to what the marketplace wants and will buy and is less likely to make value judgments about those desires, fears, and needs of the marketplace that drive their purchasing decisions.

When ten people call you a donkey, buy a saddle . . . and charge handsomely for the donkey rides. Accept that you are who you are, and use it to make money.

WHY PEOPLE DON'T BUY WHAT THEY "SHOULD" BUY

"When people call you a donkey, buy a saddle" is an unpleasant truth for those who think they will be masters of their own destinies once they set out on the entrepreneurial path. It often comes as a bitter surprise that what the marketplace will buy and pay for is something quite different from what you had in mind. We all fall in love with our ideas, and it's hard to let go of them even when reality steps in and gives us a body check.

Many entrepreneurs say that people "ought" to buy their products and services because they "need" them. Let us tell you a dirty little secret: Nobody buys what they need. Before people will buy something they "need," two things have to happen:

They have to recognize and accept that they need it.

They must act upon that recognition and acceptance.

Let's take the first part. Do we really know all the things we need in life? Of course not. If we did there would be no need for entrepreneurs, business plans, or MoneyHunt. There would be no wars or lawsuits. We would not need radio psychiatrists, "lonely hearts" columnists, churches, synagogues, mosques, ashrams, and self-help gurus. We would not need adult-education courses and group therapy to better ourselves and improve the quality of our lives. What a wonderful world this would be if everyone knew instinctively and instantaneously what they needed out of life. Before people know they need something, you often have to spend lots of money educating them about why they need it.

But if you are one of that rare and disciplined breed who truly know what they need out of life, do you always act on that recognition and buy the things you really need? Before you say yes and turn to the next chapter, consider this: Let's say you are hungry, and I tell you I've got someone in the back room steaming up a huge heaping bowlful of cauliflower, Brussels sprouts, carrots, cabbage, and broccoli, and I offer you some. How much are you really looking forward to this tasty treat? We suspect that if you are like the vast majority of Americans, not a whole lot. But why not? Surely you read magazines and health articles in newspapers. Surely you know that these great vegetables contain all the major vitamins, minerals, antioxidants, and beta-carotene. Hell's bells, the stuff can probably cure cancer for all we know. Yet you are not exactly smacking your lips at the thought of this life-giving concoction, are you?

Now . . . what if, instead of the vegetable medley described above, I

were to say, "You know, I'm hungry too. Let's go out and grab a pizza."
Sounds a lot more appetizing, doesn't it? Yet you know pizza is not exactly
a health food that will improve your energy level or increase your life
expectancy.

We repeat the question: Even if you know you need something,
do you always buy what you need? In our humble opinion, we think
not.

"Fears" and "Passions" Rule the Marketplace

One of the toughest lessons in entrepreneurship is that people will only
buy what they want to buy, or are afraid not to buy, at a given moment
in time. You cannot change these "fears and passions" of the marketplace;
you can only respond to them. Keep this in mind when:

- You think people "should" buy a particular good or service.

- You think you have a new idea for a new business but the only
  people confirming your opinion are those you talk to about it at
  cocktail parties (sad truth: People will tell you only what they
  think you want to hear).

- Your marketing research is showing less than dynamic enthusiasm
  for your product or service, but you dismiss it as a statistical aber-
  ration that does not reflect mass-market views.

- You are tempted to invent or develop a new product without
  knowing precisely the customers for it, and how and why they
  will buy it.

- You think a product or service will sell because "I would buy such
  a product or service if I saw it in a local store."

MoneyHunt Hero: Vinod S. V. Jhairaputra

When we first started *MoneyHunt*, Cliff had a small law practice in
southern Connecticut. As a result of a favor Cliff did for a well-
connected Indian venture capitalist in our area, quite a few of Cliff's early
clients were Indian entrepreneurs in technology-related businesses,
whom the venture capitalist referred to Cliff. So it came as no surprise
when the Internet server that ran our *MoneyHunt* Web site crashed for the

first time, Cliff recommended Vinod S. V. Jhairaputra, one of his clients, to help fix it.

Miles's first encounter with Vinod was one he will never forget: Vinod was a strikingly handsome man who vaguely resembled Omar Sharif, in a double-breasted three-piece suit and Florsheim broughams (the ones with the little airholes in them), wearing a turban and a chest-length beard. "My name is Vinod," Vinod said in a crisp English accent. "Please take one of my pens." He handed Miles a pen that was nine inches long and thicker than your thumb—something that would actually hurt somebody if you threw it at them. Along the side of the pen was a metal strip that seemed to be connected to something inside the pen. Miles pulled on the metal strip, and out scrolled a six-inch white-and-gold banner on pure silk, bearing a silk-screened, four-color photo of a smiling Vinod and the slogan "Vinod S. V. Jhairaputra—Your Database Doctor" in both English and Hindi.

Well, it was different.

Miles stumbled on Vinod's name, accidentally calling him "vineyard," as in Martha's, where Miles and his wife had just vacationed. "That is all right," Vinod assured him with a smile. "You may call me V. J., or you may call me Vinnie as some of my friends here in Connecticut do. You must be the My-less that Cliff has told me so much about."

Miles, or My-less, stuck with V. J. This was clearly no Vinnie.

V. J. may have had some thinking to do on the marketing side of his business plan, but he was a wizard at fixing computers. Within three hours he had rewritten several faulty software interfaces, salvaged and replaced virtually all of the Web site data that Miles had feared was lost forever, and fine-tuned the server so that it ran even faster than before.

Miles, extremely impressed, wanted to know more about the colorful V. J., who could make hard drives sing like a caged nightingale. It was quite a story V. J. told.

Born and raised in Uttar Pradesh, a poor province in southern India, V. J. was a mathematical prodigy, winning several state and national math competitions by the time he was eight years of age. After graduating from a local seminary school (the equivalent of our high school) at the tender age of twelve, V. J. won a scholarship to India's elite Bombay School of Science and Technology—perhaps the toughest and most prestigious training ground for software engineers in the world.

In a school that routinely gave out Cs and Ds to its students—to keep them humble—V. J. never came back to Uttar Pradesh with less than an A average. Finishing his degree in computer science in the late 1980s, V. J. caught the attention of a visiting scientist from Bell Laboratories in New Jersey who was teaching as a visiting fellow at the Bombay School. V. J.

became seduced by America, joined Bell Laboratories, and quickly rose to the top of Bell Labs' elite corps of software engineers. After several years at Bell Labs, he married a girl from his native province in India, bought a house in the New Jersey suburbs, earned a Ph.D. in mathematics from a prestigious university, and arranged to obtain permanent resident visas in the United States for several of his relatives who were engaged in technical careers.

V. J. worked on many state-of-the-art technology projects at Bell Labs, but his passion was the type of software known as the "relational database," then in its infancy. A relational database is software that enables a large company to archive and keep track of large volumes of data, allowing access from multiple personal-computer servers at multiple locations to the central database. The mathematics involved in creating and upgrading a relational database had at that time been mastered by only a handful of software engineers in the world. One of them was V. J.

In the early 1990s, the old Bell Labs was broken up into several pieces, which all merged into large companies. As part of the breakup, V. J.'s development team was dismissed, and V. J. was given three months' severance. V. J. had never been out of work before, and the idea of preparing a résumé and networking at business luncheons was foreign to him. But after a few sessions with an outplacement counselor, he found he enjoyed selling and marketing himself very much indeed. He had started to read some of the magazines for entrepreneurs that he found at his local Barnes & Noble bookstore, and liked very much the idea of starting his own computer-software consulting business.

Having been introduced to Cliff by the Connecticut-based Indian venture capitalist V. J. met at a meeting of the MIT Enterprise Forum in New Jersey, V. J. was now "Vinod S. V. Jhairaputra, Inc.," doing business as "The Database Doctor."

"So what is the primary focus of your business, V. J.?" Miles asked over a cup of herbal tea.

"Well, what I really want to do is work on relational databases," V. J. replied. "There are a lot of large corporations here in southern Connecticut, which is why my wife and I just moved here. These big corporations all use many relational database programs. I know they are having problems with them, and with this software there are no off-the-shelf solutions. Everything is custom tailored. It is a fascinating challenge, these database programs, and I love working on them."

"Interesting," Miles rejoined. "And how has it been going for you? How many of the local Fortune 500 have signed up for the Database Doctor?"

After a moment's pause, V. J. sighed, "Unfortunately, no one. Not a single corporation has expressed an interest in me. I was glad when Cliff referred me to you; I needed this business."

Miles decided that V. J. could use some help; clearly it was more than just his pens and cute slogan that were costing him business. Miles began to ask marketing questions just as he would a guest on *MoneyHunt:*

"Tell me, who are you pitching to within the corporate hierarchy of these corporations? Are you getting through to the right people?" V. J. replied that he always spoke to the head of information services within each company, and that with his credentials he had had no difficulty obtaining interviews with these highly placed executives.

"Well, that's certainly the right person, so no problem there. Okay, now walk me through a typical sales pitch." V. J. complied, pretending to sell Miles on a database-upgrading and bug-correction project. V. J. was an excellent presenter and made a compelling case for his services.

"Well, that sounds pretty good, V. J. Anyone who listens to you will know you're the right person for the job. What do they say when they turn you down?"

"They say they already have a project team working on their relational databases. They feel that because the data in the databases is so highly confidential, they are nervous about entrusting this task to an outsider. Believe me, I have had offers to become an employee of several very good companies, but they do not pay enough. Sooner or later, though, I will have to take one of these jobs or my goose will be cooked. I cannot live on my family's charity much longer."

"Well, they certainly have a good reason not to hire outside consultants—corporations are paranoid about their internal data," Miles mused out loud. After a long moment of silence, Miles asked, "V. J., after they turn you down and you are chatting informally with these IS people, do they say anything else? Anything else at all that might give me a clue to what's really happening in this market?"

V. J. thought for a moment and said slowly, "Well, yes, now that you have mentioned it, I do hear something from quite a few of these people."

"What is it?" Miles asked.

"Well, you probably won't believe it. They ask me if I know anyone who can work on word-processing programs."

"Word-processing programs? You mean the software people use to write letters and memos and such?"

"Precisely. They tell me they are large corporations with offices and plants scattered around the country. Many of these offices and plants were acquired from other companies, or they were established at different times. They all are using different word-processing programs that do not talk to one another. The IS people say the problem is driving them crazy."

Stunned by this revelation, Miles leaned forward in his chair. "V. J., I've seen what you've done with our server. Can you work on the software interfaces that will help these word-processing programs talk to each other? Can you solve this problem?"

"Of course!" V. J. replied, raising his voice as if he had received a mild insult. "Word-processing programs are based on the simplest algorithms and mathematical models in existence. They are . . . child's . . . play. . . ." The look on V. J.'s face changed to one of almost pure wonder—the sort of look you would expect from a novice Hindu monk who has just achieved spiritual enlightenment for the first time after long months of bodily deprivation.

"V. J., why don't you go back to these companies and tell them you will work on their word-processing solution? It sounds to me like these companies were giving you a hint of what they really needed, and you weren't listening to them. I know working on word-processing programs is 'child's play' for you, but you have to get your foot in the door somewhere with these big companies. They don't farm out their top projects to people they don't know. Once they see what you can do on some lower priority projects, I think you will be pleasantly surprised by what happens next."

V. J. thanked Miles. When he left the office V. J. was so engrossed in his thoughts he neglected to give Miles his invoice for fixing the Web site server.

V. J. did go back to the large corporations. Within a month he was performing consulting work on word-processing programs for several of the large corporations in our area. Working eighteen hours a day, seven days a week, V. J. turned around project solutions so quickly and creatively that he amazed senior management virtually everywhere he went. Pretty soon, the corporations were giving him the relational database work he had originally wanted, because unlike then, he was now "one of the family" to the IS department's technical employees. V. J.'s workload became so great he had to hire employees, some of them former friends and colleagues from his days at Bell Labs and student interns from the Bombay School of Science and Technology, some of whom V. J. has sponsored for U.S. citizenship.

In 1997, when many large corporations learned to their horror about the "Year 2000 Problem," a software bug that causes software programs to recognize dates that begin only with the numbers "19" and will cause computer systems of all kinds to shut down on the first day of the year 2000, they realized that only a mathematical genius could solve the problem. V. J.'s telephone rang off the hook, and his consulting business tripled in size in a single three-month period. Today V. J. runs one of the fastest-growing technology consulting firms in New England, and has even begun to dabble in venture capital.

During the Christmas and Hanukkah season we receive a lot of gifts from clients and friends. Two days before Christmas in 1998 Miles received a small oblong cardboard box from "Vineyard Technology Consultants, Inc." that looked as if it contained a cigar. Not recognizing the company name, Miles opened the package. When a large pen fell into his hands, Miles laughed, knowing it was from V. J.

Miles grasped the metal piece on the side of the pen and pulled. Sure enough, out came a six-inch piece of silk bearing a color photo of V. J. and his company name, along with his new slogan:

"FOR YOUR COMPANY, LET JANUARY 1, 2000 BE V. J. DAY!"

LESSONS FROM VINOD S. V. JHAIRAPUTRA

Many times, it is difficult to figure out what people in your marketplace really want. People don't always tell you the truth, either because they haven't admitted to themselves the real reasons they buy certain products and services or because they like you and will tell you only what they think you want to hear. The marketplace can be coy and must sometimes be coaxed into giving away its secrets.

This was not, however, the case with V. J. His market was screaming at him that it wanted something right now and was willing to pay tons of money to have a particular problem solved. Being focused on what he wanted to do, V. J. was not listening to these pleas for help. In the process he almost walked away from a business that has put him in the big leagues of technology consulting.

V. J. was lucky that he was able to go back to the Fortune 500 corporations after initially rejecting their offers of consulting work. As a result of his irrepressible personality and good-natured charm, he did not burn any bridges with the IS directors who had interviewed him. Another entrepreneur would have said or done something negative when his services were rejected or would have been embarrassed to go back and volunteer for a job he had previously turned down. V. J.'s character and skill, however, made it possible for him to go back and get the work from the large corporations, which opened the door to other, more exciting opportunities.

Ultimately, V. J.'s success depended upon his finding a way to distinguish his business from the host of competing, and highly qualified,

computer consultants who were pitching their services to the same customers V. J. hoped to reach. In a highly competitive field with many players, you need to be able to articulate your competitive advantage in a
matter of minutes, if not seconds. If you cannot, you will lose your
prospective customer's attention, and the business. There were many
computer consultants in the market with skills that match and even excel
V. J.'s, but nobody else had those pens! You may laugh at V. J.'s corny slo-
gans and his self-promoting pens, but they acted as excellent door openers that attracted people's attention and kept V. J.'s name in people's
minds.

MONEYHUNT
RULE #9

"During a Gold Rush, Sell Shovels"

<u>MoneyHunt</u> Hero: Adrian Hewitt

There is a famous old joke about a kindergarten teacher who asks three of her students what they want to be when they grow up. The first child says, "I want to be a surgeon and do heart transplants." The second child says, "I want to be a lawyer and help people get out of jail." The third child says, "I want to open a clothing store." When the teacher expresses surprise at the third child's seeming lack of ambition, the third child responds, "Hey, some people need heart transplants, and some people need help getting out of jail. But everyone needs clothes!"

If you find yourself in the middle of a great Gold Rush, you have a number of choices open to you. You can become a gold miner, buy some picks, shovels, pans, and other mining utensils, stake out a claim in the wilderness, and rough it for a while until you either strike it rich or starve to death. Or . . . you can be the one selling the picks, shovels, and pans to the would-be miners.

BECOME AN "ENABLER" RATHER THAN A "DOER"

In times of "national obsessions," sell a tool that enables participation. For example, the Alaskan gold rush of the 1890s had many more miners than there was gold in them thar hills. But everybody needed a shovel.

More recently, in the Internet gold rush of the mid- to late 1990s, thousands of entrepreneurs are designing Web sites and providing cool things to do on-line. The trouble is, the average person needs a way to access all these goodies. Enter companies like Yahoo! and America Online (AOL), which provide the directories and other software (known as portals) that enable people to find the things they like on the Internet.

Keep in mind, though, that fads, crazes, "gold rushes," and other hot markets seldom last forever. If the gold veins dry up, so does the need for shovels. So be prepared to adapt quickly to the market—use the gold rush to build your brand name, and then when the gold rush ends find some other uses for those shovels.

When a hot new industry, fad, or craze takes off, everybody wants to be on the bandwagon. Many entrepreneurs want to be in the epicenter of the new market, where all of the glamour, visibility, and fame is concentrated. When the disco-dancing craze of the mid-1970s was at its height, everybody wanted to own the hottest dance club in town. The only trouble is . . . so did everyone else. Soon even small suburban towns had two or more competing discos, creating a saturated market. Meanwhile, the manufacturers of strobe lights, polyester fabric, and state-of-the-art sound systems were having a field day, and nobody was looking their way.

In a hot market, the most profitable place to be isn't often the most exciting or glamorous place to be, and you will have to choose between making money and making a magazine cover.

MoneyHunt Hero: Adrian Hewitt

Adrian Hewitt loved science and he loved his laboratory. A perfect day for him would be to drive his beat-up 1968 Chevy pickup truck out of his small farmhouse in the Rocky Mountains of western Wyoming, grab two coffees on the way to work, and spend the entire day with his lab coat on, tinkering with beakers and burners and grinders, all in an effort to improve the property of the single element that had become his life: urethane. He was as passionate about urethane as anything else in his life.

In fact, it was one of three things that mattered most to him in life. The other two (in no particular order) were his marriage of thirty years to a lab assistant he had met while obtaining his Ph.D. in chemistry at Columbia University, and his volunteer work as a paratrooper for the local ski patrol, performing high-altitude search-and-rescue missions for lost or injured skiers.

Adrian was a scientist through and through. When he came to our studio for his initial MoneyHunt interview, we were impressed by how thoroughly Adrian knew his specialty. He told us things about urethane we never knew (and probably would never have thought to ask) and pulled out published papers in scientific journals and certificates of meritorious advancement from the Urethane Manufacturers of America Association.

In fact, our biggest worry about Adrian was that we would have to "humanize" him on camera, as we sometimes have to do with some of our technology-driven guests. We need not have worried; on camera Adrian was ebullient and articulate, explaining in plain and simple language what urethanes were, how they worked, and why anyone in the world should care about them. His performance was a magical combination of Albert Einstein and Mister Rogers.

Adrian's company had literally "reinvented the wheel." Realizing that urethanes could be used to make low-cost, strong wheels and cylinders, Adrian started a company that developed and manufactured urethane rollers, the cylindrical wheels that feed $20 bills out of automated teller machines (ATMs), among other uses. Soon his company branched out into such mundane, low-margin but essential products as luggage castors and skateboard wheels. The business had bumped along for years, as Adrian improved his existing products to make them cheaper and more durable, but he was not about to attract venture financing anytime soon, because high performance wasn't a major concern in the ATM, luggage, and skateboard industries.

Then, in the late 1980s, a former professional ice hockey player in Minnesota named Scott Hallstrom was looking for a way to continue his ice skating training throughout the summer months. Tinkering in his garage, he invented what has become the in-line skate, otherwise known as "Rollerblades."

The first Rollerblades were very crude. Laced up like hockey skates, the boots were made of hard plastic, and the wheels were made either of plastic or hardened rubber. The product got off to a very slow start mainly because the wheels were so bad—either they weren't fast enough or they wore out quickly, or both.

Then one fateful day Scott read about a speech Adrian had given to an industry group on the qualities of urethane wheels, whose speed, grip, and durability made them ideal for high-performance applications. Scott knew that if anyone in the world could develop a high performance wheel for his in-line skates, it was Adrian. The first time Adrian and Scott spoke, Adrian sensed that with the right wheel, in-line skating had the potential of becoming a national, if not an international, craze. Now was the time when twenty years of urethane research was going to pay off. Working nights and weekends, Adrian developed the best high-performance urethane wheel that his lab could produce. Within two minutes after demonstrating them to Scott, Adrian had an order for 500,000 wheels.

It might have ended there, but Scott and Adrian were on the cusp of a wave. The timing could not have been better. Americans were beginning to recognize the benefits of regular exercise. In-line skating was an excellent cross-training activity for lifestyles on the go, and it was easy . . . anyone with two feet could do it. It was a new sport, it was a year-round sport, and (for some) it was a fast sport. The early 1990s saw growth in the Rollerblade industry that topped 100 percent a year for five years straight, until in-line skating became the second most popular sport in America after bicycling.

When a new wave hits the sporting-goods industry, there is no shortage of entrepreneurs to surf it. Everyone and his brother got into the in-line skate business. Dozens of new manufacturers arrived on the scene within the first two years of the in-line skating craze. For Scott's company, it was not such great news, as he now had plenty of competition for his innovation. But for Adrian's company it was fabulous news. All those different brands of skates . . . and they all needed wheels. Every pair of skates needed eight wheels, and on average the wheels wore out in six months. Skate manufacturers would sell their boots once, but Adrian would sell his wheels over and over and over again.

The market for in-line skates evolved quickly during the 1990s and segmented into recreational, aggressive, racing, and hockey categories. Adrian followed suit and developed a number of different wheel designs that had specific performance attributes. Each new design sent Adrian back to the lab, where he was truly happiest. Before long, Adrian's company was the leading worldwide manufacturer of in-line skate wheels.

Two years into his growth spurt, the nimbleness of Adrian's company was put to the test, as he received a letter from an in-line skate manufacturer that accounted for more than 50 percent of his business. The letter stated that despite their prior exclusive supply arrangement, the manufacturer would be buying wheels on the open market from other competitors. Shortly thereafter the manufacturer canceled an order of 1.2 million wheels right at the beginning of the in-line skating season, leaving Adrian with $600,000 worth of inventory sitting on his shelf. If he couldn't sell those wheels quickly, the cash crunch would be enormous, potentially throwing his business into bankruptcy.

Fortunately for Adrian, another force was at work in the marketplace. As the wheels on the first wave of in-line skating boots had begun wearing out, a demand was being created for replacement wheels at the retail level. Every store in North America that sold sporting goods was under pressure to stock replacement wheels. Adrian saw a way to access this market without going to the boot manufacturers. With 1.2 million wheels gathering dust in his inventory, Adrian put his own brand name on the wheels and started selling them directly to sporting-goods stores and other retailers. His packaging allowed him to fully describe the unique performance characteristics of each set of wheels, and he used different colored packages to identify the different performance attributes of each wheel type. His reputation for quality grew to the point where in-line skaters actually began asking boot manufacturers if Adrian's wheels were on the boots before they bought them.

So when Adrian decided he wanted to raise money to fuel additional growth, investors lined up at the door. When he sought $3 million of financing to buy out some existing shareholders and add an international operation, he had three bidders fighting for the deal. He closed his financing within twenty-six days of signing the letter of intent.

Adrian's ability to adapt quickly to changes in the marketplace, coupled with a knowledge of urethane chemistry that enabled him to innovate faster and better than any of his competitors, made his personal fortune. Nothing succeeds like success. As the market for in-line skates topped out and both boot and wheel manufacturers were squeezed when the growth spurt ended around 1995, Adrian's prominence in the market for in-line skating wheels made it easy for him to win big contracts for casters, rollers, and other urethane wheels for industrial applications.

LESSONS FROM ADRIAN HEWITT

It is difficult, if not impossible, to predict the next major trend in any industry. But if you are in the right place at the right time, life can be beautiful. Ironically, when a new trend sweeps an industry, as in-line skating swept the sporting-goods field in the early 1990s, the most exciting, glamorous, and visible part of an industry (making the in-line skating boots) often isn't where the money is to be made. Adrian had the wisdom to realize that the rush was going nowhere fast without wheels.

Adrian was perfectly positioned to take advantage of the boom in in-line skating. He had spent a lifetime becoming one of the world's leading authorities on urethane chemistry, and his experience in manufacturing urethane wheels for more mundane applications made him the obvious choice for developing a high-performance urethane wheel once the infant Rollerblade industry realized it was needed.

Adrian took on Scott Hallstrom's challenge to develop a Rollerblade wheel, even though Adrian hadn't a clue what Rollerblades were. If

Adrian had delayed, or had not anticipated the potential of Hallstrom's invention, or waited until the Rollerblade industry became more established, other urethane companies might have edged into the market earlier and forged relationships with the key in-line skate manufacturers.

When Adrian's customer canceled the order for 1.2 million Rollerblade wheels, Adrian could have written off the inventory at a huge loss but instead capitalized on the growing demand for replacement wheels at the retail level. This thought probably would never have occurred to him at the beginning of the in-line skating boom, when every new pair of boots sold came with a new set of wheels and nobody was thinking about "spare parts." Once the boom was a few years old and the original sets of wheels started wearing out, the market for replacement wheels was born. And there was Adrian sitting on 1.2 million wheels wondering what to do with them.

Key to Adrian's success, and what made his business unique, was his ability to capitalize on his comprehensive knowledge of urethane chemistry even as the in-line skating boom wound down. Having built a nationally recognized brand in the in-line skating industry, he was uniquely positioned to transform his company into one that could provide a wide variety of urethane wheel products. After all, nothing succeeds like success, and everyone who has met Adrian for even a few minutes knows you can't tell him anything about urethanes that he doesn't already know.

MONEYHUNT
RULE #10

"Seemed Like Such a
Good Idea at the Time"

<u>MoneyHunt</u> Hero: Kirk Samuels

Every good business begins with a great idea, but not every great idea makes a good business. The trouble with ideas . . . any ideas . . . is that they tend to take on lives of their own after a while. Many of the entrepreneurs we meet on MoneyHunt and in our live presentations are so enamored with their ideas that they forget to research the market, competition, legal environment, and other major factors thoroughly enough to determine whether or not their business idea is feasible. Occasionally, even entrepreneurs with great ideas are run over by freight trains over which they have no control. You are much more likely to be run over by freight trains, however, if you develop the habit of not looking for them.

When entrepreneurs get run over by freight trains that gave plenty of warning of their impending approach, we frequently hear, "It seemed like such a good idea at the time."

THERE IS NO SUBSTITUTE FOR MARKET RESEARCH

We all have ideas. Some of us have an idea every ten minutes. That does not mean we should spend years of our lives and thousands of dollars building businesses out of our ideas.

One of the questions you are almost certain to be asked if you appear on MoneyHunt is: Why will people buy your products or services? Now, this is a straightforward question. There is nothing devious or tricky about it. Yet you would be amazed how few entrepreneurs have a really satisfying answer. The answer we get is frequently phrased, "Well, people ought to buy my stuff because . . ." or "People need my products because . . ."

Yet look closely—this is not the answer we are looking for. We did not ask you "Why should people buy your stuff?" Instead, we are asking, "Why will they?" In other words, "What has your marketing research revealed about your customers' buying preferences, and why do you have an advantage there?" People ought to buy lots of things, but they don't. They don't buy things if they don't know they need them. Even if they know they need things, they still often don't buy because there are things they would rather buy.

Funny thing about suppliers and customers: They just never do what they ought to do. Before you can succeed in business, you have to find out how the world really works and tailor your business plan to the real people who inhabit the real world. Don't expect them to adjust their behavior so that your brilliant idea will become reality.

TALKING TO YOUR FRIENDS IS NOT MARKET RESEARCH

Entrepreneurs are usually terrific salespeople—so good they sometimes even sell themselves. They often convince themselves that people will recognize the brilliance of their idea and conform their behavior to it, even though this means changing their established practices and acting contrary to their vested interests. This rarely happens in practice. If you truly believe you can change the way the world works with your little idea, you will be in for a sad comeuppance.

A more common way to run into trouble here is to base your business plan upon informal, perfunctory, and half-assed marketing research. You get a bunch of your friends in a room, walk through your business plan, and ask them what they think about it. They all say "great idea!" so you start spending money and building the prototype. Trouble is, your friends are not telling you the truth. They are telling you what you want to hear, as any good friend would. This is one of the many reasons you should be very careful when doing business with friends. Be assured that as your friends are leaving the room, they are all saying to themselves, "Boy, old ————'s really gone off the deep end this time! I wouldn't pay a dime for that crap he was talking about!"

MONEYHUNT HERO: KIRK SAMUELS

Kirk Samuels could easily have played one of the investment bankers in the 1987 movie *Wall Street*, with his slicked-back hair, tailored suit, suspenders, and Gucci loafers. A management consultant to *Fortune* 500 corporations, Kirk had seen many senior executives at large companies leave to start their own entrepreneurial businesses. Like many professionals who advise and consult to businesses, Kirk indulged in the belief that he knew more about business than his clients did, and that he could do a better job of running a company than they could. Little did he know . . .

Kirk was at his beach house one summer in the Hamptons, knocking back a few brews with a bunch of his thirty-something Wall Street friends after a bruising beach volleyball game, when he started kicking around a new business idea that they eventually, but unanimously, decided was too cool not to pursue.

His company, "Gimme CD," was a concept born out of his love of music. When he was in college, Kirk hated the idea of buying record albums because, as he observed, "There were only one or two songs on each album that were really good." As he worked for the college radio station, though, Kirk saw an opportunity to get all the music he liked without having to pay for all the albums. Kirk bought blank cassette tapes in bulk and then went to the radio station late at night after the station had shut down for the day. He made up his own selection of the music he liked from the LPs at the radio station, recorded the selections on the cassettes using the radio station's equipment, and then made copies for his friends . . . for a small fee. Kirk's custom-made cassettes were the hit of every fraternity party on campus. Even though Kirk knew that he was technically violating the copyright laws with his "bootleg" cassettes, he also knew that his operation was so small that the record labels were not likely to do anything about it. In fact, it's fair to say that every college campus in the 1980s had at least one Kirk Samuels doing pretty much the same thing.

Kirk's idea was to take this practice to the Internet, although legally this time. "Gimme CD" would provide an on-line database of music that, Kirk hoped, would eventually include thousands of songs. With just a few clicks of the mouse, customers could listen to various selections, choose up to fifteen songs from different artists and different record labels, and make up their own customized compact disc (CD) of the music they liked. If someone wanted to put Richard Wagner and the Beastie Boys on the same CD, he or she could do so for the first time. Once the customer had created a customized CD and paid by credit card, the customized CD would be assembled electronically and shipped by overnight courier service within twenty-four hours. Everyone at the beach party agreed it was an idea whose time had come. It wasn't long after his return from that weekend in the Hamptons that he plunged into researching the technology that would enable him to create the "Gimme CD" Web site.

Surprisingly, Kirk found it was not all that difficult to construct a music database that would enable customers to select and assemble songs in random sequence. He hooked up with a software design firm that had spun off from one of Kirk's corporate clients, and in a matter of weeks Kirk was looking at a demonstration Web site. The designers had included a feature even Kirk hadn't thought of. On the "Gimme CD" site you could be listening to a song on your personal computer and if you liked it, you could add it to your customized CD *while the selection was still playing*. Try doing that with a radio. Sooner than he thought possible, Kirk had a dynamite Web site that in his mind could not fail.

Kirk felt that his timing was right. It was the beginning of the Internet boom, and everybody was looking for ways to sell more books, tapes, and information products on the Web. Amazon.com had already gone public selling books on the Internet, and CDNow was selling music CDs on America Online (but without Kirk's customization feature). Selling CDs over the Internet was a natural—you could list thousands of titles and not stock a single CD in inventory. When somebody ordered, you merely passed the order on to the record company and took your cut. The record labels and publishers would love "Gimme CD," Kirk reasoned, because it would increase their overall sales. The college kids who were bootlegging cassettes could now do so legally, with CD-quality sound and without the time and trouble of recording cassettes one cut at a time, and the record companies and artists would now be getting a piece of that action.

Moreover, Kirk thought, the "Gimme CD" site was a major step up from the current way of doing things. He knew he could easily position it as the next wave in music merchandising on the Internet, and since he was the first to develop the technology that made CD customization possible, investors would perceive him as a market leader. Sure enough, within a month Kirk had raised almost $250,000 in seed capital to develop and launch the "Gimme CD" Web site. Kirk needed the money because there was still one piece missing from the puzzle. He had the technology, the market was ripe, and he had investors lined up. All he had to do was to license records from the major record labels, so that he could build his database and make them available on his Web site for custom mixing. Business plan in hand (and a song in his heart?), Kirk went out to make presentations to the five major record labels that control more than 90 percent of the international record business. He was asking them to hand over an exclusive "Internet custom mix" license of their entire catalogs.

Within a week, Kirk had fallen into the abyss. Not one of the five major labels would even talk to him, let alone meet with him. Kirk was stunned. At first he thought it was because he didn't have the right connections, so he hired a high-powered entertainment attorney and the Big Six accounting firm that worked with most of the major record companies. They made introductions, and Kirk had one or two meetings with record company executives who, he suspected, were meeting with him out of deference to the attorneys and accountants rather than genuine interest in Kirk's concept. Kirk had a great Web site and a great concept . . . but no records, except for a couple of minor-league classical music labels that said they would "try it for six months and see how it worked."

After six months of banging on doors, Kirk awoke to the hard realities of the record business. The record companies were not willing to part with their libraries bit by bit. They were not willing to share their properties with those of their competitors. They would not give Kirk an exclusive license of their properties on an exclusive basis without proven results. Even if they liked Kirk's concept, there was nothing to prevent them from creating their own custom mix Internet sites, where the selections would be limited exclusively to their titles and artists.

Kirk knew he had been beaten. He had spent a small fortune building a Web site with all the benefits of selecting the music you want, except that four out of the five titles most customers would be looking for would not be available. Kirk realized that although he might have some success with smaller labels, this would not give him the critical mass necessary to build a multimillion-dollar business. If the big five record companies wouldn't play, Kirk had no business.

When he thought about it, Kirk remembered something from his college disc-jockey days. He had always wondered, when looking at "golden oldies" music collections, why all of the selections were limited to artists from the same label. "Why is it," he had wondered back then, "that you can't get a collection of all the greatest hits of, say, 1975, featuring artists from all the different labels?" Now he knew.

LESSONS FROM KIRK SAMUELS

The concept that Kirk and his friends had developed on a hot August night in the Hamptons was a nice idea at the time but impossible to pull off given the realities of the record business, which none of them really knew. The record companies "should have" been interested, because the

"Gimme CD" Web site could make them additional money with no additional cost, but the idea of combining their catalogs with those of their competitors was simply not something they were willing to risk for an upstart kid in a fancy suit.

While a good idea, youth, and energy can help build a dynamic business, there is no substitute for knowing the industry and how it works. Polls taken at the beach after a few pitchers of beer are not adequate market research. Kirk should have worked in the record industry, or scheduled a few information interviews with record company executives, before spending time and other people's money developing the "Gimme CD" concept. If he had, he would have quickly learned that his idea could not be executed in a recording business in which most of the music content is controlled by a handful of large, powerful companies.

When you are in a distribution business such as "Gimme CD," you must take into account not only the demand side of your business but the supply side as well in building your business plan. It is not always true that supply will automatically follow demand, especially when it is in the supplier's best interest to limit distribution to a few controllable channels.

Finally, a word to you management consultants, financial advisers, and business experts out there who are thinking about starting your own companies. Just because you have made a career out of advising entrepreneurs and businesspeople doesn't mean you will necessarily be better at the game than they are. We've been on both sides of the fence, and let us assure you—it's a lot different when you're on the inside. Many were the times that, in order to survive and grow, we had to break the rules we used to teach in our small-business seminars and programs. In the process, we learned new rules we never would have learned from the outside looking in. So will you.

PART FOUR

People

MONEY HUNT
RULE #11

"Delegate the Small Stuff . . . and It's Mostly Small Stuff"

<u>MoneyHunt</u> Heroine: Dagmar Svenson

I t is hard for entrepreneurs to delegate. When you are first starting out in business, there is no one to delegate to, so you get into the habit of doing everything yourself. Successful entrepreneurs, at least in the early years, are "utility infielders"—capable of playing a variety of positions and executing them all at least somewhat well.

Yet there comes a point in every business where it becomes impossible to do everything yourself. At such a point the successful entrepreneur learns to perform "triage"—separating those things that must be done by the entrepreneur himself in order to ensure the company's survival, and delegating everything else to employees and outside help (such as lawyers, accountants, and advisers).

Learning to distinguish between the essential activities—those tasks that cannot be delegated—from the nonessential activities—those tasks that must be delegated—is what often separates successful entrepreneurs from business failures.

DON'T DELEGATE THE ESSENTIAL STUFF . . .

In looking at a wide variety of businesses, as we do on MoneyHunt, it is amazing how few activities are really essential to success. Rarely are there more than four or five tasks an entrepreneur must perform himself or herself to ensure that the business will survive and grow. These tasks will vary, of course, from business to business and from industry to industry. We can offer a hint, though: The "essential activities" that must be performed by the entrepreneur—because no one else can be counted on to perform them as well as the company founder—are those that give the company its competitive advantage over other companies in the industry. In other words, the tasks that an entrepreneur cannot afford to delegate are those that cannot be trusted in the hands of others.

Yet many entrepreneurs we see on *MoneyHunt* fail to distinguish between these "essential activities" and other—less essential, more marginal—activities that can often easily be delegated to other people. In order for a company to advance beyond the primitive start-up stage, when virtually every task must be performed by the company founders, the company founders simply must learn to delegate those tasks that are not essential to the company's success. Another way of saying this is that the company founders must learn to "do" less and "manage" more—making sure the nonessential activities get done while at the same time making sure they are doing the essential activities.

. . . But Delegate Everything Else

Let's face it—most of us are terrible delegators. We all think we can do things better than other people or that we care more about our business than any other person could possibly care. Sometimes we are right about that, but we overlook an important question: Does it matter that this particular activity be done perfectly? Even in a highly competitive environment, there are many activities that need only be performed 75 percent or 90 percent well in order for the company's operations to run smoothly. Attempting to reach 100 percent performance in these areas may distract an entrepreneur's attention from those areas of the company's business where 100 percent performance is essential. Given the choice, you want to be 100 percent on essential activities, and 80 to 90 percent on everything else—not 80 to 90 percent on everything.

Many entrepreneurs pretend that all activities—however insignificant and trifling—are key to the company's success, as if the failure to put stamps on an envelope right side up will lead to the company's ruin. While sweating the details is a key attribute of successful entrepreneurs and is often a product of the insecurity that can lead to success, it can be overdone. If you have to stay up late at night, which would you rather be doing—licking stamps for a mass mailing to your customers, or planning a strategy to outwit your key competitors?

Don't Expect Others to Assume Responsibility You Never Intended to Give Them

Sometimes, entrepreneurs pretend to delegate without ever really giving up control of the details. This often happens in small manufacturing companies, where the entrepreneur will tell an employee, "This must be done by thus and such a date" and then five minutes later ask "How is it coming?" When the employee responds "fine," the entrepreneur counters by asking, "Well, have you thought of this? And this? And this? When will this be done? And that? And that?" Sooner or later clever employees give up trying to think for themselves, refusing to accept responsibility, and simply let the boss take over, as this is clearly what the boss wants.

Remember to Distinguish Between "Essentials" and "Nonessentials" When:

- You set yourself three tasks in the morning and none of them are done by the evening.

- Clerical tasks are consuming an increasing amount of your evenings and weekends.

- You have not spoken to your advisers, lawyers, accountants, and other support professionals in at least two months.

- You are reacting to customer-service problems instead of adopting proactive solutions.

- Your business plan is completely free of typographical errors but is six months out of date.

- Someone asks you, "What is your twelve-month plan for raising revenue?" and you admit you haven't given it much thought.

MoneyHunt Heroine: Dagmar Svenson

In the fashion industry, it helps to have a distinctive name, but it is also essential to have carved out a niche where that name can be established as a "brand." Dagmar Svenson had both.

One of our first guests on MoneyHunt, back in the days when the show was running only on public-access cable television in southern Connecticut, was a leading entrepreneur in the bridal-wear business. Through his influence and contacts, we were introduced to several interesting entrepreneurs in the bridal business, including Dagmar.

Born and raised in northern Minnesota of solid Norwegian Lutheran stock, Dagmar was not exactly the stereotypically glamorous fashion-industry entrepreneur. In fact, she never really intended to be an entrepreneur. Dagmar married young and was raising four children in the suburbs of Minneapolis–St. Paul when her husband was downsized from a lucrative corporate job and had to scrape by as a consultant to his former employer. Realizing the need to supplement her husband's income, Dagmar looked for something she could do in her spare time that would leave her enough time for her children and household responsibilities.

An accomplished seamstress, Dagmar had won acclaim at her wedding by designing her own bridal headpiece. A number of friends asked her to create unique bridal headpiece designs for their own weddings. When a leading bridal magazine took note of her creations and profiled her in one of its spring bridal issues, Dagmar's bridal headpiece business was off and running. Soon most of the leading bridal-wear designers in New York, California, and eventually Europe were making the pilgrimage to suburban Minneapolis–St. Paul to view Dagmar's latest designs and listen to her views on headpiece trends. Within a year Dagmar was earning more than her husband, and within two years Dagmar's husband quit the consulting business and starting working full-time as Dagmar's chief operating officer.

The bridal-wear manufacturers loved Dagmar, because she turned around orders for custom headpieces in ten days or less. Her competitors would only guarantee turnaround in thirty days, and sometimes longer. Her advantage over her competition was nothing more complicated than her flexibility. Working alone and out of her home, she could control her schedule and meet deadlines that other, more established headpiece manufacturers could not meet. Why was this such an advantage? Because like most other players in the high fashion industry, bridal-wear designers like to wait until the last minute before launching their creations. Even as the models are being fitted for their walks down the runway at the annual spring and fall bridal shows, the designers are tinkering with the details of their designs, adjusting a pin here, moving a flounce there. Dagmar's quick turnaround on the headpiece designs gave the designers more time to finely tune their creations to a fickle and fast-moving marketplace.

One day Cliff, who occasionally did legal work for Dagmar, received a telephone call. "Cliff," Dagmar began, "I've decided that I really don't want to fly around the country attending trade shows anymore. It takes too much time away from the business, and I'm not really a salesperson. I've found this absolutely wonderful woman who understands everything about the bridal business, and she has agreed to drop her other clients and work for me full-time as my vice president of sales."

"Fine," Cliff replied. "You'll need an employment agreement, of course. I'll get started . . ."

"Uh, that won't be necessary, Cliff. I was in the library the other day and I found this absolutely wonderful book on how to draft your own employment agreements. There was a form in the back of the book that looked absolutely wonderful, so I just typed it onto my personal computer and made a few changes. Do you think you can give it a quick look, Cliff, just to make sure I haven't overlooked anything? Please don't be upset with me, Cliff, but I needed this done quickly and I can't afford a big legal bill right now."

"Okay, Dagmar. Send it over. I know this is your busy season and you can't afford a big legal bill, so I'll only give it an hour." Cliff hung up the telephone and shook his head. He had seen many legal forms in "self-help legal books" before, and he was not impressed. Contrary to popular opinion, you really can't just take a boilerplate legal form, fill in the blanks, and use it. Forms need to be tailored to the particular business and situation. Sometimes forms prepared in one state would not work in another state. Sometimes forms contained irrelevant provisions that needed to be deleted, or omitted important provisions that were specific to a particular industry. Cliff knew instinctively he would spend at least three to four hours cleaning up the agreement for Dagmar, and he had reluctantly agreed to limit his fee to one hour.

A few minutes later Dagmar's employment agreement for the vice president of sales came over the fax machine. Cliff read it and it was . . . perfect. In Dagmar's favorite phrase, it was "absolutely wonderful!" Every word was in place, all the irrelevant language had been deleted, and Dagmar had even added two or three provisions to account for some of the unique aspects of her business.

Cliff called Dagmar upon reading the agreement. "Dagmar, I've got a pleasant surprise for you. This one's on me. I'm not even going to bill you an hour. This form is terrific, and you've done a great job with it! Frankly, I can't add any value, and I don't charge clients if I can't add any value." He added with a chuckle, "By the way, you will tell me the name of that book, won't you? I may want to look at some of the other forms in the back if they're anything like this. By the way, how's your business going? I know you're starting to get into your busy season."

"Oh, Cliff, not so good," Dagmar wailed in response. "I'm backlogged thirty days on my orders right now, and they're coming in the door faster than I can turn them around."

Cliff sat back in his chair, stunned. "Forgive me, Dagmar, but you're one of the better time managers I've ever worked with. You guarantee turnaround in ten days or less; that's what gets you the business. I have to believe some of your customers are a little ticked off at you right now. How could you let something like that happen?"

After a long pause, Dagmar answered. "I didn't want to say anything before, Cliff, but I've been so focused on getting every word of that goldarned employment agreement right that I haven't had time to do anything else for the past couple of weeks!"

Lessons from Dagmar Svenson

Okay, here's a pop quiz.

Question Number One: Did Dagmar save money in legal fees? The answer is yes—Cliff didn't even charge Dagmar for reviewing the employment agreement because he couldn't improve upon what Dagmar had done.

Question Number Two: Did Dagmar do just as good a job drafting the employment agreement as Cliff would have done for her? Again, the answer is yes—she picked a good form and obviously spent way too much time getting every word right. Cliff admitted he couldn't improve upon it, and even asked Dagmar for the name of the book from which the form was taken.

Question Number Three: Did Dagmar do the right thing for her business? Clearly, the answer is no. While Dagmar saved money in legal fees and did an excellent job on the agreement, she became so absorbed in the details of the agreement that she took her attention away from an essential activity in her business—namely, ensuring that orders were processed within ten days or less.

Although Dagmar ultimately was able to get back on schedule and calm down some unhappy customers, she had to offer discounts for late delivery that cut deeply into her operating profit, and the survival of her business was put in jeopardy for several months thereafter.

Clearly, one of Dagmar's essential activities—an activity that she couldn't afford to delegate to anyone else—was ensuring that orders for bridal headpieces were filled within ten days as she promised. This in fact was the key to her business success and her principal advantage over her slower-footed competition. By allowing herself to become distracted by a nonessential activity, Dagmar put her entire business in jeopardy even though she successfully executed the nonessential activity of drafting the employment agreement.

Dagmar later admitted to Cliff that she had worked a solid two weeks on the employment agreement, with little time for anything else. Cliff, who had been drafting employment agreements for over fifteen years when he started working with Dagmar, would probably have needed no more than two to three hours to generate a draft employment agreement for Dagmar. It might not have been as "perfect" as Dagmar's draft, but it likely would have served her purposes and protected her interests well enough. Having Cliff draft the agreement would have cost Dagmar some money, of course, but in terms of lost time and opportunity, which was the cheaper alternative?

Nobody enjoys paying fees to lawyers, accountants, and other professionals. Like taxes, though, they are a cost of doing business. People ask Cliff what he does for his clients—expecting a traditional answer such as "I perform legal services" or "I draft and negotiate contracts." Cliff's answer usually surprises them: "I help my clients manage their time." Given the right amount of time and training, you can learn to do just about anything yourself—draft your own contracts, prepare your own tax returns, handle your own payroll. There's no rocket science involved in any of these tasks. But why should you, when others can do these jobs in a fraction of the time it would take you to do them?

By focusing your energy and time on those activities that will ensure your success in business, and delegating all other tasks to those who can perform them efficiently and quickly, you will soon reach a stage where you can easily afford the fees and salaries these people will charge to manage the nonessential activities of your business.

MONEYHUNT
RULE #12

"Don't Confuse Partnership with Friendship"

MoneyHunt Heroes: "Phineas" and "Phil"

When you are first starting out in a new business venture, it is tempting—in fact, it is almost irresistible—to bring on board friends, family members, college roommates, and other significant others. First of all, these are people with whom you know you can communicate. Especially among downsized corporate executives accustomed to working long hours away from home, we frequently hear "I am starting a new business with my spouse (or a child, lover, favorite cousin, whatever) because I want to spend more time with him or her."

Secondly, friends and family are usually willing to work cheaply, out of respect for you and the friendship. At least in the beginning, they don't expect much and don't ask for anything.

Most importantly, for many start-up entrepreneurs, friends and family are the only people they know whom they can call upon for help on short notice. "I need some help, and Mom does know how to type."

THEY'RE CHEAP, AND THEY CAN'T SAY "NO"

Even at *MoneyHunt* it has been difficult to resist this temptation to use family and friends as temporary help. Miles had to draft his mother as a cameraperson when we first launched the show on public-access cable television, while personal friends of both Miles and Cliff have been called upon on short notice to take the late-night Amtrak to Philadelphia to fill in for a MoneyHunt Mentor who has called in sick at the last minute.

Yet doing business with friends, family, and significant others with whom you have a relationship outside the business is a very tricky affair. More often than not, it does not work.

WHY PARTNERS ARE NOT NECESSARILY "FRIENDS"

When you are doing business with "friends and family," there are two relationships going on at the same time—a business relationship and a friendship—and frequently the two come into conflict. Someone who's a friend, for example, may resent the fact that he has been given only a small percentage of your company's stock; he may see himself as equal partners with you, when you know his contribution to the business does not entitle him to more than a piece of the action.

Sometimes friends and family cease to become friends and family when there's real money on the table worth fighting for. The legal books are filled with cases involving the breakups of family businesses, and they are among the most heartbreaking stories we can tell.

Succeeding in business requires a cold, detached, analytical look at the world around you; it is at the heart of what we mean when we say on MoneyHunt that entrepreneurs must be cynical—taking the world at face value and doing what the situation requires, not what they themselves would do in a perfect world. It is difficult to maintain that sense of detachment when the person you have to fire (because she can't do the job) is your mother.

Beyond that, however, business communication often requires a directness and forthrightness (and sometimes crude bluntness) that is difficult to pull off in a relationship. Let's face it—most of us find it very difficult to be confrontational with a spouse or someone else we love or like. While we may disagree with our friends and loved ones, and occasionally argue with them, deep down inside we are thinking, "Gee, I better hold off telling him or her what I really think, because if I do he or she may cease to like me and it will affect our relationship." If you disagree, think about it: When was the last time you looked your spouse straight in the eyes and called him or her a shit-head?

Holding back information and pulling punches in business discussions is precisely what business partners cannot afford to do. As we will see elsewhere in this book, discussions among successful partners often become knock-down-drag-out arguments which, while painful in the short run, nonetheless help to strengthen the business by weeding out bad ideas, opinions that are unsupported by facts, and so forth. Making the right business decisions requires that everything be put out on the table and that no topic is ever too sacred to be thrashed out. Worrying too much about what the other person thinks of you, and whether "winning a point" will hurt a longer term relationship, can be an unnecessary obstacle to the brutally candid communication that makes successful businesses work. Given the choice, many successful entrepreneurs have chosen to work with people who are relative strangers to them because their discussions will not be impeded by concerns about preserving a relationship. At the end of the day, each of them goes home and forgets about what happened until the next heated discussion.

SOMETIMES CONFRONTATION IS THE ONLY WAY TO COMMUNICATE

For most of us, confrontation is painful, and we try to dodge it in any way we can, especially with friends and loved ones. Entrepreneurs frequently try to avoid the need to be confrontational by:

- Looking for complementary business skills in a friend or loved one that are not really there.

- Prohibiting business discussions away from the office (which is precisely the time when the most productive business discussions can take place), and imposing artificial deadlines on when they and their significant others will talk about the business.

- Pretending that the nonbusiness relationship does not really exist.

- Limiting the scope of business discussions to matters on which the significant other is in general agreement.

You should remember that family and friends do not always make the best business partners when:

- You are building your first management team in a start-up company.

- The pressure is on for you to deliver on a promise and you are short of staff.

- You are tempted to borrow money from a wealthy relative to start a business (the distinction between investors and business partners is often a hairline one, as you will see elsewhere in this book).

- You are tempted to turn a business relationship into something a bit more personal and intimate.

MONEYHUNT HEROES: PHINEAS AND PHIL

Even their wives agreed: "You couldn't imagine two more different people than Phineas and Phil, but when you really get to know them and see them together, you realize they are one and the same person."

By his own admission, Phineas had a golden life. The youngest son of a powerful Wall Street investment banker, he belonged to a prominent WASP family in New England with roots that went back to the *Mayflower* and sixteenth-century England. Boyish, fun-loving, articulate, handsome, and stylish, he was the sort of man who made women go weak at the knees and who could talk you into just about anything. You were his friend for life the moment he smiled at you. A star football player at one of New England's most exclusive private schools, he was the darling of the suburban New York City country clubs, debutante balls, and cotillions.

But *pampered aristocrat* is not a phrase you would use to describe Phineas. A year after he entered an exclusive private college, some bad business deals forced his father into bankruptcy. Phineas was forced to quit college, and he never went back. He started out as an options trader at a Wall Street brokerage firm during the go-go 1980s; within a year he was the firm's star trader, and by age twenty-seven he had earned his first million dollars. By his early thirties he was financially secure enough to strike out on his own, forming his own investment banking firm in rural New England. Within two years his multimillion-dollar investment portfolio included several fast-growing technology companies, oil and gas drilling rigs, and real estate development projects. Everyone agreed Phineas was a "young man in a hurry." During most of his adult life he slept only three or four hours a night.

Phil's background was altogether different. Born in Brooklyn, New York, Phil was the son of working-class immigrants and was as "ethnic" as they come. He learned early on the streets of New York that nothing ever comes easy to those without money, and nothing ever came to Phil without a hard uphill fight. But whenever Phil was in the fight, you didn't want to be on the other side. Tough, focused, plain speaking, gregarious, but as stubborn as concrete when he felt he was in the right, he was a top student in high school, captain of the debating team, and offensive line-backer for his school's all-state champion football team, while also hold-ing down two daily newspaper routes with over a hundred private homes. He won two scholarships to an Ivy League college and graduated at the top of his class.

He went to a top law school in a faraway city and was soon at the head of the class. At the beginning of his last year of law school, his student loan money ran out. At the same time, his father became ill and was hos-pitalized for several months. With no other way to pay his tuition bills, room, and board, Phil took on two outside jobs—as a law librarian for the local courthouse and typing term papers for undergraduates at the university he attended. He graduated from law school with top honors and $10 in his pocket.

When Phineas and Phil first met, they were both at the top of their forms. Phineas was branching out into new types of investment for his firm, and Phil was climbing the ladder as a young corporate lawyer in a prominent Wall Street law firm. Despite the 180-degree difference in their upbringing and personal style, they became fast friends. Both had experienced firsthand the school of hard knocks and knew what it meant not to know where your next meal was coming from. Neither of them wanted to repeat the experience.

One day Phineas came up with a brilliant idea for a new business— one that would involve manufacturing a specialized line of consumer products. He immediately discussed the idea with Phil, who agreed to help out in any way he could. The two started spending weekends and "all-nighters" together in Phil's garage, working on the prototype prod-uct and a detailed business plan. Phineas had an intuitive feel for the market and the product design; Phil researched the competition and legal risks and put together the projections of start-up costs and anticipated revenue.

Phil was happy to help out his friend Phineas but had an ulterior motive for spending so much of his precious free time on something that had a very uncertain reward. Secretly, and unbeknownst to anyone (including his own wife and children), Phil had come to the conclusion that he did not want to practice law the rest of his life and was looking for an opportunity to join a fast-growing entrepreneurial company, per-haps as general counsel or chief operating officer. Phil would have killed for the opportunity to work with his close friend Phineas on such a ven-ture and was only too happy to go through walls for his friend if it meant being offered a senior management post at the new company. Phil assumed that as soon as the business was put together he would be offered a position in the new business and didn't bring up the subject with Phineas because he was concerned about appearing greedy.

Realizing that the venture would require more start-up capital than he could afford to spare at that time, Phineas started casting about for start-up capital from the network of professional investors who participated in his firm's merger-and-acquisition deals. Despite competing offers, he settled on Joe, the owner of a small venture firm that had taken minority positions in some of Phineas's deals. Not even thinking to involve Phil in the discussions, since "this doesn't really concern the legal aspects of the business," Phineas and Joe each decided to put $100,000 of their own money into the business.

When Phineas asked Phil to prepare the legal documents for his and Joe's investment, Phil was delighted to help, as this type of transaction would make him look like a "rainmaker" to his superiors at the law firm. He agreed to attend a meeting with Phineas and Joe to discuss the terms of the investment.

When the topic of management came up, though, Phil received the surprise of his life. He was told that the new company would be owned fifty-fifty by Phineas and Joe; there would be no room in the organization for Phil.

Like any lawyer, Phil did not like unpleasant surprises, especially when they shattered his expectation of being a part of the entrepreneurial team. "Wait a minute, Phineas; I've been a part of this thing from the very beginning. I was kind of hoping you would offer to bring me on board."

Phineas, understanding for the first time why Phil had put in all those free hours developing the product, avoided Phil's stare and stammered, "Well, to be frank, I never thought about it, Phil. We want you to do the legal work for this thing, and of course we will pay your firm's fees. We need a good lawyer to help us out, and we've budgeted for that. But I admit I never thought about bringing you on as a partner. I mean, I would love to bring you on board . . . you'd be great. If you are willing to put in $100,000 as Joe and I have . . ."

At this Phil went into battle mode. "Oh, cut the crap, Phineas. We've known each other for years. You know how badly I want to get in on the ground floor of something; God only knows I've sent you enough signals. And you also know damn well that I can't afford a $100,000 investment. For you that's pocket change, but I have a wife, two kids, and a mortgage. Look, I know you've got what it takes to make this thing happen, and I have some clients on the side who could provide me with extra income if I left the firm. I would be willing to work for half my current base salary if you would let me have some stock now and maybe some options going forward if we hit our revenue targets. But I need at least $50,000 a year to live on for the first couple of years. You're asking me to take a big risk and I want to make sure I can meet my obligations. Can't you guys help me out there?"

Bristling slightly at the reference to "pocket change," Phineas cleared his throat. "You know there's nothing I'd like more than to work with you, Phil. But this is just a start-up now, and we really don't need a full-time lawyer in house. What we need now is money, and lots of it. And believe me, it's more than the $100,000 investment. I'm going to be sweating blood for the next couple of years to get this going. And nobody's going to be paying me a red cent for that."

"So you're giving up the investment firm?" Phil retorted.

"Of course not, Phil. The investment firm is my current income, my bread and butter. This is more like an aggressive growth fund."

"So who's going to run this business?"

"Me, myself, and I."

"Forgive me, Phineas, I love you like a brother. You're a great salesperson—one of the best I've ever known. And as a dealmaker you've got few equals. You're a smart guy, and you learn quickly. But I've worked with a lot of companies, Phineas, and believe me there's a lot more to running a business day to day than you realize. It takes a different kind of guy, a different kind of mentality. You're going to need help there, and you know I can do that. I've been sweating the details on business transactions my entire career."

"I hear you, Phil, but to be fair, you haven't run a business yourself either," Phineas snapped, and realized for the first time just how hurt Phil was. Not wishing to offend his friend, and wanting to deflect the conversation to friendlier turf, Phineas smiled and said, "Don't worry, Phil. I know what I'm getting into. I've been reading business plans and studying entrepreneurs close-up my entire life. I know how hard it is. If things get too tough, I'll take out an ad in the *New York Times* for a 'guy or gal Friday, part-time, ten to twenty hours a week.' That's all we will probably need, and I can't ask you to be our errand boy. That would be an insult to you and to our friendship. I promise you that when the money is there, I will do something for you—something that will work for both of us. But it's going to have to come out of the company, not my own pocket."

The next few months were difficult ones for Phineas and Phil. Phil did the legal work for the new company and billed his time at a discounted hourly rate. Phineas did everything he could to steer legal work to Phil on his investment firm's transactions. Phineas and Phil remained friends, thanks largely to their wives, who kept the lines of communication open between them. Soon the scars had healed and they were joking around like before, but both were embarrassed by their mutual misunderstanding, and they avoided discussing any aspect of the business except for legal issues.

In the beginning Phineas and Joe ran the company together, but soon Joe's other activities required a lot more of his time and Phineas found himself running the company without help. As he promised, he hired a succession of "guy and gal Fridays," each of whom lasted about a month, and Phineas couldn't figure out why they didn't stay longer. Wasn't this, after all, the best possible opportunity for a twenty-something college graduate—getting in on the ground floor of a dynamic start-up company? The new venture took more and more of Phineas's time away from his investment firm, and he had to work harder than ever to keep on top of everything. At one point he told his wife, "I feel like that circus act where the guy is spinning a hundred porcelain plates on top of bamboo poles. He can't relax for a second because there's always one plate that's starting to wobble and he's got to get it spinning fast again so it doesn't crash."

After his initial investment, Joe refused to put up any additional capital, so when cash was tight (as it usually is for any start-up company), Phineas either had to dig deeper into his own pockets or tap one of his other investor friends, calling in favors from prior deals. Soon the start-up company had over twenty investors around the country, but only a few thousand dollars of revenue.

One day Phil received a panicked telephone call from Phineas. "Phil, it's really hit the fan at the start-up. Some of the investors are threatening to sue."

"Okay, Phineas, calm down. Tell me what happened. Why are they angry?"

"They're saying we've missed our revenue projections two quarters in a row. They're saying it's my fault. God damn it, Phil, I've been working my ass off. . . ."

"Calm down, Phineas. Now I know you've got good accounting support. Why did you miss your revenue projections two quarters in a row?"

"Well, the product's great, and getting orders is no problem. The independent sales representatives we hired have done a world-class job. But we keep losing the orders."

"Why is that happening, Phineas?"

"Well, part of the problem is we're not getting orders out on time, but . . . hey, I know what you're thinking! It's not because of me! It's

that these people just don't communicate! The design person doesn't
call the manufacturer to discuss the specs for the packaging, so the
mechanicals come in the wrong size, and then the manufacturer gets
bent out of shape because he has to call the designer and meantime
he's set aside plant time for us and . . . "

"Wait a minute, Phineas. You've outsourced your design, your packaging, your manufacturing, and your marketing?"

"Yeah, of course, Phil. We're a virtual company. We don't have employees, except of course for me. But I can't do everything here—I rely on
these people to communicate with each other."

"But of course they don't. Is that the only problem—fulfilling
orders?"

"Well, no. Not really."

"Uh huh. Drop the other shoe, Phineas."

"Well, I'll admit I've also been blindsided a couple of times by our
customers. I work hard to get a big order, and the guy . . . the purchasing guy . . . he tells me . . . he looks me straight in the face and tells me
I've got the order, so many units, etc., etc. And I go back and start the
wheels going so we have the products ready on time. And then the next
thing I know I'm ready to deliver and they've had a 'corporate restructuring' and the new guy says he doesn't know a thing about the order and
doesn't want the stuff!"

"Well, Phineas, that's clearly a breach of their contract with you. I can
go after them for that. You want me to write the usual nasty letter?"

After a moment of silence, Phil heard Phineas say quietly, "Well . . .
there's not really a contract as such . . . not in writing, anyway. . . ."

Phil heard the music. Realizing that his friend was in way over his
head, Phil took time off from the law firm and spent the next several
weeks piecing together the day-to-day operations of Phineas's start-up
company. The two friends agreed that Phineas's time would best be spent
dealing with the company's battered relationships with its investors.
Thanks to Phineas's charm, integrity, and commitment to turning things
around, the dissenting investors were dissuaded from suing, which
bought the company some time. Phineas also successfully persuaded a
local bank to grant the company a working-capital line of credit.

Phil, for his part, took over the day-to-day operations of the company.
He hired two full-time employees to manage the production and marketing efforts, under his own direction, and paid them out of the proceeds
of the line of credit. When Phineas's salespeople generated new orders,
Phil drafted a short purchase contract and made sure the customer
signed it before the manufacturer was told to begin production. Phil also
worked closely with the company's accountants to tone down the finan-

cial projections so that investors were always promised less than Phil knew the company could deliver. The two friends also set up a reserve fund, earmarking a portion of the company's revenues to buy back the stock of the dissenting investor group. Within a year the company, having tripled its operating revenue, was making regular distributions to all of its investors and had cut the number of investors in half by buying out their positions.

After returning to his law practice, Phil made it a point to stay in daily touch with Phineas and his two employees to make sure things were running smoothly. Saturday mornings were spent over coffee and bagels discussing precisely who was going to do what in the coming week, and updating monthly, quarterly, and yearly operating budgets and marketing plans.

Two years after the company's dramatic turnaround, Phil received a call from Phineas: "Phil, I've got terrific news. One of the top venture-capital firms in the country wants to come on board, and they're talking seven figures. They say we can definitely go public in three to five years. The only thing they said that concerned them was that we had out-sourced our chief operating officer, and they want to see more of a com-mitment there. My friend, I think it's time I fulfill my promise of a couple of years ago and bring you on board full-time so we can get rich together. Believe me, there's plenty of money to take care of you now. What do you say?"

Phil was so happy he nearly jumped out of his chair. "Phineas, I've been waiting for this for years. You bet!" adding slyly, "Now . . . about the terms of my employment contract . . ."

LESSONS FROM PHINEAS AND PHIL

Phineas and Phil were the ideal business partners, but they didn't realize it until it was almost too late. Long before bringing in Joe as the compa-ny's first investor, Phineas and Phil should have had a heart-to-heart dis-cussion of the role each would play in the company before they committed time, effort, and money to build the business. Ideally, this should have been committed to writing and the details ironed out so there would be no surprises once the company was formed.

Phineas and Phil had a serious misunderstanding because neither one could tell where the friendship ended and the business relationship began. Phineas blithely assumed that Phil was supporting his business start-up out of pure friendship, and so never thought to bring up the subject of what Phil expected to get out of the business once it started. Phil, for his part, blithely assumed that Phineas was looking out for him and was planning to make him an offer he couldn't refuse, even though Phineas hadn't said a word to Phil about a future with the company. Because Phineas was focused on keeping Phil as the company's outside legal counsel, and Phil had his heart set on a full-time job offer, neither Phineas nor Phil thought to discuss compromise solutions—such as an evenings/weekends commitment by Phil with payment as a percentage of the company's revenue—that would have gotten Phineas the "detail person" he so desperately needed without forcing Phil into a full-time entrepreneur position he could ill afford.

Both Phineas and Phil were afraid to speak plainly about their goals and objectives for the business because they were afraid their friend-ship—which both of them valued highly—would be threatened by any strong disagreement. Friendships and business partnerships require dif-ferent styles of communication and interaction. Some of the best busi-ness partnerships we've seen on MoneyHunt involve partners who never socialize or even see each other outside the office. By contrast, some of the worst business partnerships we've seen involve partners who are afraid to speak their minds because they are too concerned about what the other person will think of them. In doing business with anyone, be partners first, and then maybe friends.

When doing business with friends and loved ones, it is a good idea to have everything documented in legal agreements, just the same as if you were doing business with a total stranger. Just as Robert Frost once wrote that "good fences make good neighbors," most lawyers will tell you that well-crafted legal agreements make for good business relationships, and may even save a few friendships as well.

MONEYHUNT
RULE #13

"Who Do You Want to Get into Trouble With?"

<u>MoneyHunt</u> Heroes: Steve Caldwell and Jimmy Salvato

This chapter is about people—specifically, the people you choose to be partners with when growing your business. Entrepreneurship is about sacrifice, and sacrifice often causes strain on relationships and living habits. Making these sacrifices with people who aren't worth the time and bother is one of the worst things that can happen to your start-up or early-stage company.

John Doerr, a partner in the legendary Silicon Valley venture capital firm Kleiner Perkins Caufield & Byers, introduced us to this rule of entrepreneurship by telling a story. Imagine sitting around a table at a diner or a pancake place with several other people, discussing with great enthusiasm an idea for a wonderful business that you all have just created and are about to grow. Set aside all the product questions and marketing ideas, and ask yourself: Are these the people you are willing to get into trouble with? Are these people for whom you're willing to be more than five hours late for dinner, three nights in a row, every week?

So the big pitch wasn't quite right? Are these the guys you'd be willing to sacrifice your summer vacation for because the factory broke down, the big shipment is due, and you have to go in and help do it yourself? Imagine yourself asking your wife or significant other, twenty times in a row, to please understand that these are the folks you have chosen to throw in with, and these are the folks that you're willing to sacrifice for.

Very often you can't please both your business partners and your family. If these conflicting sacrifices aren't balanced in some way, or your significant other just doesn't buy off on the credibility or integrity of the group you've chosen to associate with, watch out. The emotional bank accounts of each respective party will become overdrawn.

If you don't have support from both sides you will end up either crapping out on the business (and hearing a chorus of I-told-you-sos from your family) or crapping out on your family, marriage, and other emotional commitments (and hearing a chorus of I-told-you-sos from your business partners).

DON'T BE AFRAID TO RESEARCH YOUR PROSPECTIVE BUSINESS PARTNERS

Many entrepreneurs turn a blind eye to their business partners, especially if they started out as personal friends, college roommates, or family members. "Well, let's try it and see how it works out," becomes the mantra of the entrepreneur who doesn't ask the tough questions of his business partners up front.

Sometimes an entrepreneur willingly goes into business with someone he doesn't like or trust all that much, in the belief that "he really can't be all that bad, and anyway, working in the business will change him!" Those of you who have married someone who wasn't 100 percent right for you in the mistaken belief that you will change the person can spot this train wreck coming ten miles away.

As for trust . . . if you ask yourself, "Do I really trust this person?" and it takes more than a second for you to answer yes, the correct answer is no.

MONEYHUNT HEROES:
STEVE CALDWELL AND JIMMY SALVATO

We had never seen the likes of Jimmy Salvato on MoneyHunt before, and we really doubt we'll see another one like him for some time. Wearing long, flowing, curly black hair halfway down his back, dressed in sterling-silver earrings, blue jeans, and a leather jacket, Jimmy looked more like a roadie for the rock band ZZ Top than the accomplished restaurateur that he was. Jimmy's tan was so even, he was able to appear on MoneyHunt wearing absolutely no makeup. Needless to say, he didn't fit the classic entrepreneur mold in terms of appearances, but he was dynamic, well spoken, and a great showman.

Jimmy delivered an absolutely flawless presentation in his ten minutes on the show, and despite his unconventional trappings, if you closed your eyes and listened, he sounded like one hell of an entrepreneur. From all the evidence it would appear that that's just what Jimmy was— the founder of a chain of Italian trattoria-style restaurants called Jimmy Pimento's that were sweeping the New England shopping malls.

The reason he was on *MoneyHunt* had nothing to do with his restaurant chain, however. Jimmy wanted to pitch a new company he had developed around a new prepackaged garlic bread. To make the business happen, Jimmy knew he desperately needed the support and commitment of a young executive chef named Steve Caldwell. Jimmy had formed a limited liability company (LLC) to run the business and had drafted an operating agreement (like a partnership agreement) showing him and Steve as fifty-fifty partners. Steve was dragging his feet on signing the operating agreement for the new company, and it was making Jimmy increasingly nervous.

Steve was the operations chief for Jimmy's chain of Jimmy Pimento's restaurants. Just out of high school, Steve had started as a restaurant chef and evolved into an excellent food-service operations chief, despite his lack of formal education. Steve excelled at making each plate make money and was a fine buyer and skilled menu planner who knew by heart the portions, ingredients, and costs of each dish. If market fluctuations forced ingredient costs above a certain level, Steve's computer database would set an alarm and pull the item off the menu until costs were in line and his margin goals could be met.

What made him truly exceptional was that he didn't leave the kitchen completely, as many executive chefs do. Steve organized a chain of command, from chef to wait staff to table, that assured efficient delivery and excellent customer service.

When Steve weighed the opportunity to go in with Jimmy on the garlic bread deal, many of the things Jimmy had done for him weighed heavily in his decision making. Jimmy had sent Steve to classes at the Culinary Institute of America from which Steve graduated with the only diploma he ever had. Jimmy's publicity machine facilitated Steve's appearing on various talk shows as a cooking expert, and he was getting a share of high-society catering as well. But Jimmy's munificence did not stop there. He took Steve with him on tours of Europe to research recipes, and he always seemed to be there with a little extra cash bonus whenever Steve needed some, which was fairly frequently. In Steve's eyes, Jimmy could do no wrong.

When Steve reviewed the opportunity with Anna, his live-in girl-friend, it got a little rockier. Anna, coincidentally, was the bookkeeper for many of Jimmy's restaurant operations. When they first talked about it, Anna was skeptical, so Steve laid out his case. Jimmy was asking Steve to put up his share of the capital at risk. Risk capital was more dear to him obviously than it was to Jimmy, but Steve thought that Jimmy had been grooming him for this opportunity, and the other partners couldn't argue against Steve's involvement.

So Anna fought the battle a little closer to home. "Whatever you work for would mean much less time together for us," she pointed out, "and with a kid on the way there might be better places for a little nest egg." Steve took Anna's arguments to heart but was still determined to consider every facet of the opportunity before jumping in with both feet.

The business itself was beautifully simple, as are most great ideas. After being responsible for making millions of loaves of garlic bread for restaurant customers, Steve, in an effort to save time, had developed a superior loaf of bread perfectly sliced, seasoned with garlic and cheese, and ready to be toasted at a moment's notice. It was a necessity brought on by the tremendous demand from the patrons of the restaurants.

Jimmy thought, why limit this product just to the Jimmy Pimento's restaurants? When people started asking to go home with his frozen loaves, Jimmy developed the idea of a prepackaged garlic bread product for sale to grocery stores and Italian delicatessens. Steve and Jimmy did a bit of research and realized that the product category simply did not exist in any of the local grocery chains they checked out. Presto! Jimmy Pimento's garlic bread was born.

The branding was a snap because they could build off of their success-ful restaurant's brand, at least in New England. The initial production runs were done after-hours in the restaurant ovens, so no additional expense was incurred in putting together an independent baking facility. To encourage regional distribution of the garlic bread products, Jimmy developed the practice of providing complimentary meals for all of the grocery buyers and their families at the nearest Jimmy Pimento's restau-rant. It wasn't too much of a push either, because they were going into a the frozen-foods section of the supermarket, where the competition for shelf space wasn't quite as intense as in the bread section. So the bread got tested, sold through, and the business began to grow. Further, growth was augmented by decent sales through mail order, the Internet, and dis-count coupons that were given out with the checks in each one of the Jimmy Pimento's restaurants.

Soon, however, the growth spurt was over, and the big push to go national loomed large. It would require separate production facilities, marketing strategies, and of course loads of new capital. Hence Jimmy's appearance on MoneyHunt.

Steve desperately wanted to believe Jimmy would be able to make the garlic bread business happen. He had watched Jimmy's empire grow from one diner on the wrong side of New Haven, Connecticut, to ten Jimmy Pimento's restaurants, located in each of the major New England cities. All of them were big, often full, and pushed out $20 plates of pasta like a sausage machine. The masses flocked to the place, because it was flashy, fun, and a little bit cosmopolitan. Which means a lot when you're looking for a special night out in New Haven or Hartford, Connecticut.

Going by appearances alone, Jimmy was the epitome of the successful restaurateur. He drove two Porsches, though only one at a time. He had a beautiful ex-model girlfriend who made it a point when she was any-where near a Jimmy Pimento's to show up with some of her equally attractive friends to throw smiles and laughter around in the busy cock-tail lounge. The places were packed six nights a week, so much so that they didn't even bother opening for lunch, which is rare for this type of restaurant. And . . . there was always Jimmy, flitting from one spot to another to accept congratulations on this new menu item or that new grand opening. He accepted all with big smiles and seemed to be always working the room, maybe looking for partners for his next conquest.

Jimmy's magnanimous style may indeed have been his undoing, for Jimmy lavished benefits on key personnel, including Steve and potential investors. It was common for five limos to be lined up outside a Jimmy Pimento's to take key personnel on "research trips" to other cities where they partied all night, checked out the best restaurants, and came back with a few new recipes. Even that was nothing compared to regular all-expense junkets with twenty restaurant personnel, customers, and investors to southern Italy, and particularly Sicily, that Jimmy would pay for. They'd go for four, five, or six days, check out the palaces, ruins, churches, and art museums, ride in helicopters, and come back with a few items of unique research. During these trips Jimmy would disappear for hours at a time to "scout out some new restaurants" in one of the mountain towns.

No doubt the menu benefited from these extravagant fact-finding mis-sions, but Steve's girlfriend Anna was the first to suggest that maybe it didn't all add up. Despite the fact that the restaurants were often packed, no one supports a pasha lifestyle on 350 tables and $20 pasta plates. The margins in the restaurant business just are not that good.

The only evidence that Steve ever saw any chink in Jimmy's armor was how edgy he would be whenever "business associates" would show up. He entertained them in a different way, often shuffling them off to a cor ner of the restaurant, loading them up with rounds of drinks or food or both, and then escaping himself out the back door for walks in the night air in the parking lot. Sometimes this would happen two or three times a week. He always returned in a better frame of mind and seemed to be able to calm down whoever was asking him questions and giving him pressure at the moment.

Steve actually liked these "business associate" functions because with Jimmy gone he became the focus of attention, and with carte blanche he would go over the top preparing special plates from his kitchen and picking great wines for each course. Still, the risk came up time and again in conversations with Anna. Anna seemed to suggest that Jimmy had a whole posse of old investors chasing him for returns they never got. As the Jimmy Pimento's bookkeeper, she was privy to increasingly frequent intercompany transfers (each restaurant was owned by a separate corporation, as is typical in the industry) to cover Jimmy's wheeling and dealing.

Steve agonized over the investment and partnership in Jimmy's garlic bread company. He spent many sleepless nights with an uncomfortable mix of excitement and fear. For the first time Steve would be an equal with Jimmy in the business venture, and this had even greater meaning, since he had risen from nowhere because of Jimmy's mentorship. But it seemed to him that Anna may have been right after all. Jimmy's base was starting to fold, and Steve realized that the demands of starting a food business from scratch would strain Steve's relationship with Anna and his new child.

One of the other drawbacks was that he never had too clear an idea why Jimmy needed so much more money, $2 million, on the bread deal. Steve had never seen a business plan, but he was half afraid to ask for one for fear that he couldn't understand it even if he did get it. This was an important nonaction on Steve's part. Not only is a business plan necessary as a road map for investing and building a business but it would have provided a forum for Steve to ask several additional questions of Jimmy, based on the document. A business plan really is a statement of fact or intent that is one of the most crucial elements of any new partnership.

With all of these thoughts running around in Steve's head, Steve finally did something that he'd learned years ago from his grandfather. He simply took a blank page of paper and drew a line down the middle of it, listing and writing each of the benefits and drawbacks of the new deal. When he had it all down on paper, he resolved in his mind to proceed over Anna's protests, risk their nest egg, and become a full partner with Jimmy in the bread company. After four consecutive sleepless nights, he put down his pen and resolved to announce his decision to Jimmy in the morning, knowing this was the critical last piece of the puzzle that would allow Jimmy to put the whole deal together.

When he finally rolled out of bed at 11:00 (a typical hour for a restaurateur), he was greeted with his customary cup of cappuccino on the kitchen table and the newspaper. Except today's newspaper had a headline that made Steve drop his cappuccino.

LOCAL RESTAURATEUR NABBED IN NEW HAVEN'S LARGEST COCAINE BUST

Jimmy Salvato, the top owner and founder of the Jimmy Pimento's Italian trattoria-style restaurants in New Haven and other major New England cities, was apprehended in the parking lot of his New Haven restaurant at the wheel of a delivery truck allegedly carrying cocaine with a street value of $2.2 million. Bricks of the drug were concealed in drums of olive oil with false bottoms. Agents who knew of the case said they had been observing Jimmy for many months after being tipped off by an FBI undercover agent during his regular meetings with known crime families in southern Europe.

Officials are moving to seize companies and assets under control by Jimmy Salvato (story continued, page B3).

LESSONS FROM STEVE CALDWELL AND JIMMY SALVATO

Steve Caldwell almost got into big trouble because, despite a long-standing business and personal relationship with Jimmy, he didn't really know his partner-to-be. Because of the many good things Jimmy had done for Steve over the years, it was difficult for Steve to face up to the possibility that his benefactor might—just possibly—be a crook. Steve never checked into the backgrounds of Jimmy's "business associates," never asked questions of other investors in other deals, and accepted everything Jimmy told him as the gospel truth.

Needless to say, the results of the garlic bread partnership would have been disastrous. Had Steve committed to Jimmy earlier, the long hours, travel, and the strain on his new family would have surely changed his life for the worse. More importantly, he surely would have lost his entire investment and would have been back where he started, cooking pasta in a kitchen somewhere, once the Jimmy Pimento's restaurant chain folded. Contrary to the old saying "He who hesitates is lost," it was precisely Steve's hesitation to join Jimmy that saved him in the end—the police got to Jimmy first.

There were plenty of clues that Jimmy Salvato was not exactly an Eagle

Scout. The late-night meetings with "business associates," the transactions in the company van in the parking lot, the extravagant trips to southern Italy and Sicily were blatant tip-offs that Jimmy might have a few business "connections" Steve wouldn't be happy meeting in a dark alley. Add to that Steve's girlfriend's report about the transfers of cash from one Jimmy Pimento's company to another, and it doesn't paint a pretty picture.

Still, Steve was loyal to Jimmy, who after all had made Steve's entire career possible. Saying no to Jimmy probably would not have been possible for Steve, who had been taught since childhood that "you dance with the one what brung ya." But sometimes, as Steve learned, nice guys do indeed finish last, and blind loyalty is anything but a virtue.

MONEYHUNT
RULE #14

"Don't Look for a Partner in the Mirror"

MoneyHunt *Heroes: Arbuthnot Associates*

It's difficult, if not impossible, to grow a successful business as a one-person operation, yet too many entrepreneurs we see try to play all roles at the same time. They make the decisions, negotiate the contracts, stay up evenings and weekends packing the boxes to make sure the orders go out on time, and clean up the messes when they happen. Sooner or later, it's time to share responsibility with one or more partners.

A basic rule of social psychology is that we tend to gravitate toward people whom we perceive as being like us—it is truly rare to have a close friend with whom you disagree on just about everything. Despite the old saw that "opposites attract," it just doesn't happen all that often in real life. When we look for friends, lovers, and associates, our motto is "send in the clones."

This tendency—which is all too human—has to be resisted in business life. Sometimes the worst thing you can do is start a business with a close friend simply because he or she is a close friend. In picking a business partner, the most important questions are:

1. Does this person have skills that complement your own—that is, make up for your own shortcomings and weaknesses (assuming of course you are strong enough to admit you have any)?

2. Do each of you respect the ways in which you differ? While business partners frequently disagree on how a business should be run, ultimately one partner must defer to the other if the matter lies within the other's areas of strength. Put another way, it doesn't matter a whole lot if you and your partner's skills complement each other if neither of you recognizes and respects that difference.

VISIONARIES, OPERATIONS PEOPLE, AND WHY YOU NEED BOTH IN YOUR COMPANY

Picture an entrepreneurial company (say, in computer software or high technology) in which all the partners are engineers. More often than not, they will end up arguing over technical details, structural points, and bells and whistles in their product development while losing sight of the most important questions: Who will buy the product, and why? Without knowing what the product will be used for, and who will use it, entrepreneurs risk developing beautiful prototypes that will end up in museum displays without making anyone any money. Too many technology companies operate in this fashion; they have the intellectual engines of the QE2 but no rudder to determine the direction, so they keep going in (highly impressive) circles. What is needed in such an organization is a marketing/sales type to balance the engineers' technical prowess and help them focus their activities on projects that will bring in money.

Probably the one thing sadder than the "engineers first" organization is the entrepreneurial company where all of the principals are marketing types who are great at identifying opportunities and strategic planning but lousy at follow-through. While it isn't the most glamorous part of entrepreneurship, for a company to become successful someone has to sweat the details and make sure orders are getting filled in a timely fashion, that products are being assembled correctly, and that project schedules and budgets are being met. Tragically, because marketing types tend to have incredible powers of persuasion and personal charisma, they frequently are successful in attracting venture capital to projects that exist only on paper, without a clue as to how their castles in the sky will actually be built or whether they are even technologically feasible. In such organizations, what is needed are hardheaded operations people with strong budgeting, management, and technical skills.

FACE IT . . . YOU ARE NOT PERFECT

There is one activity most entrepreneurs fear more than failure—focusing on their weaknesses. As we have observed elsewhere, successful entrepreneurs have to have big egos if they are to survive the pitfalls of growing a competitive business in tough markets. To be cognizant of your own limitations requires acknowledging that you can't do everything yourself and that it is often cheaper and more expedient to bring in someone who already possesses a certain skill rather than take the time to develop it yourself.

Many entrepreneurs try to circumvent this rule by:

Looking for partners who are willing to do the things they are unwilling to do, as opposed to the things they cannot do.

Hiring employees to do the things they cannot do rather than business partners (employees, who owe their income to the entrepreneur and who can be fired at will, are less likely to stand up and challenge the entrepreneur's opinions).

Seeking out partners with superficial differences in style that do not really constitute substantive differences in skill.

Obviously, you should remember this whenever you are looking for a business partner, but you should consider it as well when your company forms joint ventures or strategic alliances (which after all are commonly referred to as "partnerships," although not in the legal sense) with other companies.

Strangely enough, if business partners have complementary skills and respect the strengths and weaknesses each brings to the table, it doesn't really matter how communication takes place.

MONEYHUNT HEROES: ARBUTHNOT ASSOCIATES

We don't often have consultants or other service businesses on *MoneyHunt*, but we were willing to make an exception for Arbuthnot Associates. A two-member consulting firm focusing on developing Internet "real estate" for large corporations, Arbuthnot had built up an impressive clientele of Fortune 500 corporations in its three-year history.

Joseph Arbuth, one of Arbuthnot's two partners, was a marketing expert par excellence. Having joined a Fortune 500 corporation as a consumer brands manager right after obtaining his MBA in marketing, Joseph spent twenty years building and managing successful consumer brands in the electronics industry. Then, when he was in his early fifties, a downsizing left Joseph with a substantial early-retirement package and nothing to spend it on. Joseph wasn't planning to become an entrepreneur, at least initially. He in fact started contacting executive recruiters and putting together a résumé for a vice president–marketing position at a major corporation. When Joseph's teenage sons introduced him to some of the senior-executive job-placement search sites on the Internet, Joseph realized the immense marketing potential of this new medium and almost impulsively decided to change course. He read everything he could find (which at the time wasn't much) about Internet marketing, spent every spare minute studying and analyzing successful Internet sites, and put together a blueprint for Web commerce that he knew he could sell to the Fortune 500 corporate market.

What he didn't have was technical expertise, but he found it (through an introduction by one of his teenage sons) in Dick Nottingham, the other half of Arbuthnot Associates.

Dick was the third of seven children in a prominent New England family that traced its ancestry back three hundred years to Nottinghamshire, England. A bad case of acne in high school, however, had left Dick with severe scarring on his face and upper body, which prevented him from participating in athletics (one of his brothers was an all–Ivy League tennis star) or getting a whole lot of dates. Dick, as any sensitive teenager would have, drew inward and focused on his studies, especially mathematics, for which he had an amazing gift. He scored a perfect 100 on his state's mathematics examinations three years in a row, achieved an 800 on his mathematics SAT (compared to a verbal score of below 500), and won admission to a leading university that had, at the time, one of the best and most advanced computer facilities in the world.

Dick became engrossed in computers, to the exclusion of all else. In his senior year of college he was invited to teach computer science as part of the faculty, but turned the invitation down because he realized the money in software was not to be found in academia. He joined a fledgling software company and led the development teams for three of the company's most successful projects, winning awards and write-ups in the major computer software magazines. In his spare time he developed "shareware," which he distributed free of charge on the Internet. One of Joseph Arbuth's teenage sons had gotten hold of one of Dick's shareware applications and had been exchanging e-mails with Dick about other potential applications of the shareware product.

Joseph and Dick did not exactly hit it off at first. Joseph, always a persuasive speaker, talked for hours about the marketing potential of the Internet, about how *Fortune* 500 corporations were mystified by the Internet and needed help developing a Web presence, and so forth. Dick listened, but just barely. To Joseph's teenage son, he admitted he thought Joseph was "one of these slick marketing guys—they promise everything but don't know how to deliver. Guys like him are why you have vaporware." Joseph, on the other hand, told his son he thought Dick was the "typical computer nerd—and, God, did you see those scars? If I do anything with him I don't see him getting anywhere near the customers. His body odor alone will gross them out."

At the prodding of Joseph's son, Joseph and Dick scheduled a second meeting, this time at a personal-computer terminal where Dick was more in his element. Uttering only a few words, Dick demonstrated to Joseph some of the problems in developing the type of Web sites Joseph envisioned, but also suggested possible solutions that would require state-of-the-art improvements to some of the existing programming languages. Joseph seemed disheartened by what was apparently a difficult task, but the two agreed that with the right amount of "angel" financing, Dick could quit his day job and focus full-time on developing the software interfaces necessary to create state-of-the-art Internet sites. The two decided to form Arbuthnot Associates.

We were first introduced to Joseph through an intermediary and decided to interview Joseph and Dick for one of our Internet shows on *MoneyHunt.* Our first clue that this was not your typical business partnership came when Joseph asked that Arbuthnot's accountant be present at the initial screening interview for prospective guests. We thought this odd, as we usually do not discuss financial details at the first meeting with a prospective *MoneyHunt* guest. Still, Joseph insisted that "it would help with the communications. Mike [the accountant] is a key part of our team and would add a lot of value." So we said okay.

Mike the accountant was the first to show up at our scheduled meeting with Joseph and Dick. We knew something was up when he asked us to interview him first. We did, and walked through Arbuthnot's business plan with Mike. "So when do we meet the principals of Arbuthnot?" we asked. Mike replied "Well, Joseph will be here in a few minutes, and I told Dick to show up in a half hour." When we looked puzzled, Mike smiled and explained, "I know it seems a little odd, but trust me, this is how these guys are. You don't want them in the same room together. Let me handle it."

Ten minutes later Joseph arrived, and he and Mike reviewed for us Arbuthnot's marketing plans, client-development strategies, and competitive position. Joseph was, as we expected, extremely verbal, polished, dressed immaculately in a Zegna three-button suit, smiling through a set of perfectly white teeth. Joseph studiously avoided, however, any discussion of the technical side of Arbuthnot's business; whenever we brought up customer-service issues or the timing of product delivery, Joseph would look at Mike, who would respond, "That's more Dick's side of the business. You can ask him about that." About a half hour after Joseph's arrival, right on schedule, our administrative assistant interrupted to say that Dick Nottingham had arrived. Mike excused himself, took Joseph out of the room, and a few minutes later walked in with Dick. We had a pleasant discussion with Dick about some of Arbuthnot's new design types for corporate Internet sites, implementation of Java applets (then a new technology), and other matters relating to state-of-the-art Internet site design and delivery. Surprisingly, Dick was highly articulate in his area of expertise, but whenever the topic turned to the "big picture" of Arbuthnot's business, Mike would interject and furnish the answer without giving Dick a chance to reply. Far from being upset by Mike's interruptions, Dick maintained a stoic calm and seemed almost pleased not to address this side of the business.

After Mike and Dick had left (Joseph, having another meeting in the vicinity, had left our offices after his part of the interview), we both agreed that it was strange to interview separately two guys who practically lived together on a day-to-day basis. Even stranger, our administrative assistant told us that when Joseph left our offices, he passed Dick in the hallway and the two men did not utter a word to each other, not even a greeting.

We called Mike the next day and asked to see the two partners together, as we were considering having both of them appear as guests on *MoneyHunt*. "Oh, no, you don't want that, trust me, please," Mike replied. "If anything, why don't you put me on the show? I think both Dick and Joseph would approve of that." We said "nothing doing" and asked what the problem was with these two guys. "No problem at all," Mike replied. "This is just how they do things. Whenever they have something sensitive to talk about, they go through me. Or the lawyer for Arbuthnot. Or Joseph's kid that brought them together. Anybody that they trust."

"You mean," we asked, "they don't talk to each other?"

"Hardly at all, and only through intermediaries like me. They're usually not even in the office at the same time. Hell, when they do talk to each other they fight like cats and dogs. I don't think they could agree on the time of day if their business depended on it."

"How the devil can they conduct business like that?"

And then it struck us. They really didn't have to. Joseph and Dick each understood what their roles were in Arbuthnot, and each realized that

Arbuthnot could not function without the other's peculiar expertise. They deferred to each other on matters that were within the other's purview. Because the two men were from different generations, had completely different backgrounds and outlooks on life, and spoke entirely different languages in their work, they would have had difficulty communicating directly. Talking through intermediaries, while at first awkward and seemingly bizarre, was probably the most effective way for Joseph and Dick to get the job done for Arbuthnot Associates, the "ships that pass in the night" partnership with annual revenues in the millions and a *Fortune* 500 client list to die for.

LESSONS FROM ARBUTHNOT ASSOCIATES

It is highly unlikely that Arbuthnot Associates would have succeeded if Joseph and Dick had attempted to communicate in a more conventional way than they did. It would have been extremely difficult for a "corporate animal" like Joseph to have to deal with a quiet loner like Dick. It would have been equally painful for Dick to have to deal on a day-to-day basis with a "slick marketing type" like Joseph. Yet both Joseph and Dick realized that together they could go a good deal further in the business world than either of them could separately and that with their unique combination of talents they could make a high-end technology consulting practice feasible. By developing a network of trusted advisers and carrying out their most sensitive communications through these intermediaries, Joseph and Dick overcame their communication problem and created a successful business by staying out of each other's way.

It is difficult for people in different generations to work together, especially if they are not from the same family. For Joseph, a man with sons who were approximately Dick's age, the temptation to play father figure or mentor to Dick was no doubt a difficult one to resist. In such a relationship the senior partner will attempt to use his superior experience to force his opinions upon the reluctant junior partner. Joseph wisely resisted this temptation.

Yet Dick, too, had to learn to be flexible. Having mastered the arcane art of software development, Dick was understandably proud of his achievements and had difficulty accepting that someone with less-than-perfect SAT math scores could add anything of value to a software enterprise. If Dick had been so inclined, he could have engaged in passive-aggressive behavior, throwing computer jargon in Joseph's face and creating unnecessary delays on Web site development projects as a means of gaining leverage in the partnership. "After all," Dick could have said (but to his credit did not), "without me this whole thing doesn't happen. Joseph couldn't write code if his life depended on it. And anybody can do sales if he has the technical knowledge to explain what the software can do."

Dick realized that despite his technical expertise he didn't have the verbal skills to persuade customers to buy an Arbuthnot custom-designed Internet site. As Mike (speaking as Dick's mouthpiece) put it in our interview, "If Dick pitches the customers he's going to talk too much about the problems involved in developing the site, and he's not going to commit to a delivery time he considers aggressive. He doesn't understand, as Joseph does, that sometimes you have to promise something and then work like hell to deliver it. I've always believed that to sell something you have to have a touch of larceny in you, and there's not an ounce of larceny in Dick's body."

Of course, we are not saying that partnerships succeed only when the partners have separate schedules and don't communicate with each other. But our experience has taught us that communication styles and "like-mindedness" among business partners are a lot less important than the possession of complementary skills and a healthy, mutual respect for those skills. When you're looking for a partner, don't look in the mirror.

MONEYHUNT
RULE #15

"Big-Company Experience
Dose Not an Entrepreneur Make"

<u>MoneyHunt</u> Heroine: Julia Cleveland

This is probably the best-known rule in all entrepreneurship, and few books on starting your own business are missing a "horror story" or two that illustrate the rule. Of course, we think we have better ones!

Many entrepreneurs come from corporate backgrounds and start their businesses after chafing under the bureaucratic harness of big business for years on end. Today, corporate America is breeding more than its fair share of successful entrepreneurs because of the many corporate downsizings and rightsizings that have forced people, often kicking and screaming, into entrepreneurial careers in order to survive.

The experience one gets at a big company can be helpful to you when starting a business. You must realize, however, that big-company experience often leaves you unprepared for the hand-to-mouth, turn-on-a-dime, do-it-yourself environment that prevails in small business.

SMALLER NUMBERS DO NOT MEAN AN EASIER JOB

It's important to be aware of this rule because people starting new businesses are often overly confident in their abilities because of their big-business background. Their attitude is best summarized as: "Hey, I ran a billion-dollar division for several years, and increased sales and profits each year! Running a crappy little six-figure firm is going to be a breeze compared to that!" Yeah, right.

The acid test for us, when we interview former *Fortune* 1000 types on *MoneyHunt*, comes when we ask: "Did you have direct profit and loss responsibility when you worked in corporate life? Did you actually run an entire business from soup to nuts?" Most likely, they haven't. Big companies are bureaucratic and specialized in their organizational structure, and they often have to be. Often even seasoned corporate managers have seen only a very small part of the running of a particular business unit.

In an entrepreneurial company, at least initially, you must perform *all* of the essential skills, from making the sales calls, to deciding whether to manufacture in the United States or overseas, to fighting with the distributors over discount strategies, to hiring and firing employees, to deciding which brand of paper clips to buy. In corporate life there were people who took care of things for you. Now you must fend for yourself. You are the boss . . . and also the secretary. You are the marketing, sales, purchasing, finance, accounting, operations, new product development, human resources, and legal department of your new business . . . as well as the janitorial service.

The adjustment is a big one; don't underestimate it, and you should be okay.

BUT BE SURE TO KEEP YOUR ROLODEX WHEN YOU PACK UP YOUR CUBICLE

Of course, we are not saying that big corporation experience is a bad thing. Quite the contrary . . . sometimes big corporate America can mean big corporate contacts and big corporate clients. The networks that people build while working for a large corporation may someday be parlayed into a decent business base. Often, if people have made money on you when you're in big corporate America, they'll be prone to take at least one chance on you in your new job.

Remember That Small Companies Are Very Different When:
- You are sitting in your cubicle reading about all these wonderful little Internet start-ups and how they are making millionaires out of middle managers just like you, and you think you have what it takes to launch a successful business.

- You read the *Dilbert* comic strip faithfully every day and are beginning to sympathize with the animal characters.

- You are reading your business card and discover that it takes you more than thirty seconds to explain to someone just what you really do for the company.

- You have left corporate life to start your own entrepreneurial company and begin to wonder where things like paper clips and legal pads come from.

MoneyHunt Heroine: Julia Cleveland

Julia Cleveland was one of the brightest marketing managers that ever made a run up the career ladder at her company, a *Fortune* 100 soft-drink manufacturer we will call "Fizz Corp." Born and raised in New Jersey, Julia lived and breathed consumer products—both of her parents were marketing managers at large consumer-products companies. When Julia graduated from Rutgers University it seemed natural for her to move on to Fizz Corp., where she quickly gained notoriety for her marketing acumen in everything from corn chips to sugar water.

Julia was popular at work but not threatening. She was meticulous in building her marketing plans and a tactical conference-room infighter when it came to the ongoing battles for budget dollars and market share among the consumer products divisions within Fizz Corp. Although not married, she was very happy living with a significant other, Harvey—an on-again, off-again general building contractor who, most would have guessed, would always be second to her as a breadwinner. Still, Julia loved Harvey—he was easygoing, did chores around the house, and gave her the freedom to do as she pleased with her career and supported her.

One Monday night, sitting in her sweats with Harvey in front of the television, Julia began to analyze the various bags of snack foods they were munching on. Thinking that the number of people concerned about their eating habits was increasing daily, she wondered: Might there not be a successful cross between salty snacks and diet food? She asked Harvey, between quarters of *Monday Night Football*, what he thought of her idea. Harvey mentioned that the house he was currently remodeling was for a caterer who made a unique brand of chips out of a new (to Harvey) type of "potato-type thing" he had seen lying around the kitchen when he was finishing up the project.

They were the craziest looking chips he had ever seen, Harvey recalled, and came in all different shades of crimson and gold. The concept looked attractive, and Julia pressed him for more details during time-outs and commercials. Before the week was out, Harvey and Julia met with the owners of the house Harvey was remodeling, and in a heartbeat she had a contract for the exclusive retail marketing rights for "Slice of Life," a unique brand of chips made from exotic tubers like horseradish, daikon, yams, and taro root. The caterer, it turned out, had been making them to order for high-society parties on a one-to-one basis, but Julia figured she could mass-produce and brand the product and sell it as an exotic healthy alternative to the fried chips she was partially responsible for marketing for Fizz Corp.

The timing was excellent. Healthy snack foods like Robert's American Gourmet were expanding the category dramatically, but larger players like Fizz Corp. were still not in the game. Store buyers were actually receptive to this new category, because the premium prices these brands charged led to attractive margins. Julia's informal polling showed that the category was about to explode, and she wanted a piece of it.

When her research was done, she went into her boss's office at Fizz Corp. for a heart-to-heart chat, and, with a lump in her throat, handed in her resignation from Fizz Corp. She laid out what she perceived to be the opportunity and stressed it was noncompetitive with anything that Fizz Corp. was involved in today, and she would be taking no proprietary knowledge along with her. Her boss acknowledged as much but went on to warn her that if the category continued to grow and she stayed in business, there would soon come a day when she would be butting heads with Fizz Corp. The world of salty snack foods was intensely competitive, her boss pointed out, adding, "You've been a star here but you've had a big support corps behind you—all the resources of a global marketing company. It's not like that on the outside. I don't want to talk you out of your dream, Julia, but if we sit down again in a year I'll be surprised if you are still in business. All the same, good luck. Who knows? Maybe someday we'll end up buying you!"

Business shot right out of a cannon, and Julia opened up new accounts for Slice of Life products, both regionally and nationally. When asked if she was "the" Julia Cleveland from Fizz Corp., Julia played it low key, saying something like, "Sure . . . we made lots of money together." She pointed out that Slice of Life was the salty snack food every health nut wanted but couldn't get from the big companies like Fizz Corp., and she encouraged new buyers by offering hefty discounts and coupon promotions. No one said no to her in the first round of opening accounts. She had been a powerhouse at Fizz Corp.; every supermarket and delicatessen regional buyer had heard of her and was willing to give her a chance.

Julia's efforts with the new accounts quadrupled sales that first year to a level just under $3 million. As her first anniversary in business approached and the big food-industry trade shows loomed ahead, she borrowed money for designing first-class packaging with bright photos of her distinctive products. Since she outsourced most of her production, she was able to keep the rest after her start-up expenses for making a decent marketing show.

Indeed the fancy food show in the Jacob Javits Center in New York City had all the trappings of a Roman triumphal procession for Julia after her first year. Her Slice of Life booth at the show was crammed full of newly designed packaging, the press was having a field day with the uniquely colored chips, and the few accounts that she hadn't opened throughout the year came by the booth to gauge the excitement and to finally capitulate to her Slice of Life marketing machine.

Julia even saw her former boss from Fizz Corp. there. He dutifully made his rounds and came to congratulate her on her first year's success. She had gone further than he had ever expected, he told her, and, as he exited the booth, called back to Julia over the din, "When you're ready to sell it, be sure to call me first!"

Although he never intended it, it was as if Julia's former boss had jinxed everything by uttering those fateful words. Even before the show ended, some of the buyers that Julia had sold first were coming by her booth to voice their concerns about the slow movement of her product. Slice of Life had two hundred customers nationwide who were carrying an average of five of her products each. Her quick penetration in the market had not, however, carried with it a heavy national promotional effort, so store sales were flat or even off slightly.

Her Slice of Life products were premium chips and priced accordingly, sometimes two times that of comparable products on nearby shelves. In the comparative shopping derby, Slice of Life was losing ground. While Julia listened patiently to each of the two or three customers who were telling her the same story, she was prepared to discount the feedback she was getting, at least for the moment. At Fizz Corp. she had reams of data every week to analyze just how fast different products were moving in different stores in different parts of the country. In contrast, Slice of Life had independent distribution routes and no weekly reporting. So rather than having a chance to nip issues in the bud, Julia was now getting the news late, and worse yet, she was getting it from the buyers before she had a chance to analyze the data and propose solutions. When Julia returned from the trade show, she began her second year in business in a "scrambling to catch up" mode. She reacted to the poor sell-through results for Slice of Life products by devising promotions to boost those sales in key markets. She had adopted this strategy several times at Fizz Corp., and it had saved many a fiscal quarter for her. Out went the

coupons and the FSIs (free-standing inserts) and the various other promotions she had launched to goose the numbers.

The situation at Slice of Life was far different, however, than anything
she had faced at Fizz Corp. Julia didn't have the wherewithal to hire a
major promotions agency to pull together the couponing programs. She
had done enough of them herself, and she reasoned she could do most of
the work this time and have a consultant give it the once-over before they
were sent out. At first, the new promotions seemed to be working. Her
first-quarter results were sufficiently improved that some of the buyers
who had first criticized her marketing strategy were gradually coming
back into the fold. They reordered, and she continued to make promises
of promotional support, which now were becoming part of the game.

Unfortunately they missed a crucial point—what people in the grocery trade call "reduction factor." Once you discount something to
increase sales, you have to keep doing it, cutting further and further to
get the same volume. Reduction factors don't come home to roost until
later on, but it soon would be time for the next shoe to drop.

One day the telephone rang. "Hello, Julia? Hi! This is Greg over at
Coupon Promotions Unlimited. I'm just letting you know your promotions are getting about a 15 percent return rate (i.e., for every hundred
coupons mailed, fifteen were being redeemed). Sure hope you have that
in your numbers." Greg certainly had a cheery voice for such a demoral-
izing telephone call. Julia knew exactly what Greg meant. Her coupon
promotions were driving sales, all right, but the discount she had chosen
was too deep, and, because of the large number of coupons redeemed,
Slice of Life's profits were not just eroded. They were gone.

The problem was that Julia's new accounts were expecting her to at
least sustain those sales if not grow them. At Fizz Corp., the answer to
this dilemma had been easy: throw more marketing money at it, more
promotions, more couponing, more advertising. Keep making the fiscal
quarters look good. For a little company like Slice of Life that didn't have
the marketing clout of a Fizz Corp., the high coupon return rate put Julia
into a negative spiral. In order for her to preserve sales, she had to continue to coupon and promote, which only increased the return rate,
which in turn ate into her profits.

Eventually, every new account she opened expected her to do the same
thing. She had to keep the discount high in order to prop up the sales,
but the higher discount kept the redemptions high and her margin in the
same place: nowhere. If she canceled the promotional effort, she was
sure to lose future sales as well as her existing accounts, and it wasn't as
if she could go to the buyers as she used to do at Fizz Corp. and say,
"Hey, you're buying a hundred different items from us in this aisle, keep

us on so we can both make money on it." No way. On this one she was out in the cold. No muscle from other products to bail her out.

Julia was learning the hard way that, like her former boss at Fizz Corp. had predicted, running a business is much more complex than just marketing a product for a major corporate enterprise. It seemed that every issue, however petty and trivial, came to sit on her desk. She didn't have the time for market research. Hell, she hardly had time for any research at all. She was reacting to crises twenty-four hours a day and doing nothing proactive to build her business. The buyers were not giving her second chances, and she had no bottomless marketing budget to draw from. For the next three fiscal quarters it was all Julia could do to prevent her downward spiral from accelerating.

By the time the next annual food industry show at the Jacob Javits Center rolled around, Julia was much less exuberant than she had been the year before. On the contrary, she barely had the funds to afford the booth and transportation to and from New York City to run it. Running a lousy show, dealing with disgruntled customers, and with no new products to introduce, Julia was almost embarrassed to see that the first person to visit her at the convention was her former Fizz Corp. boss. Julia had heard rumors that he was considering getting into the premium-stock business after all.

Without skipping a beat, she was up to meet him at the entrance. "Hey, back again? If you were serious about making an offer for my company, you better do so now before your competitors arrive and start driving the price up." The minute the words flew out of her mouth, she cringed, and thought to herself, "Oh, God, I can't believe I just said that! He's got to know how bad I've been struggling and he'll probably think I'm desperate to get out."

Julia had underestimated something else about the corporate culture that she had come from. They like to buy things that they perceive to be successful rather than start them themselves. In the eyes of her former boss, Julia's company was certainly that: Every time the former boss went to the grocery store, there were Julia's products filling the snack aisles. Without even blinking, he responded by asking, "What is your price, Julia?" "Two and a half million cash and a two-year no-cut contract to run the business," she shot off with hardly a beat to think about it. "Consider yourself bought," her former boss answered. "We'll draw up paperwork and have a deal signed in a week."

That was something else. Stunned, Julia realized something that hadn't occurred to her until that moment. While she had been spending every last cent of her own and Harvey's money to keep Slice of Life running for the past two years, her former Fizz Corp. boss was willing to spend $2.5 million in thirty seconds flat.

Lessons from Julia Cleveland

Julia Cleveland learned the hard way that the rules and systems that worked so well for her in Fortune 500 America would fail her in a small business. Although her former Fizz Corp. boss had warned her, she didn't fully appreciate the multiple disciplines she would need to learn in order to run her own show.

Marketing at a big corporation is much, much different from marketing for a small company. Julia's contacts were good door openers, but her reputation at Fizz Corp. came with the expectation that Slice of Life products would be advertised and promoted, and of course sell through, just like Fizz Corp. products. When that didn't happen, Julia could do nothing to reset the retailers' expectations, nor did she have any leverage to insist that the retailers keep her products together as part of a package. At Fizz Corp., she had the resources and the corporate clout to force retailers to do things they wouldn't normally do, since nobody in the industry wanted to antagonize Fizz Corp. At Slice of Life, Julia was one of dozens, if not hundreds, of small suppliers, and had to beg for even the slightest concessions from the retailers who once cowered at the mention of her name.

The discounting strategies that had worked so well for Fizz Corp. products turned out to be her biggest marketing problem at Slice of Life. Underestimating the redemption in a sales promotion is a big problem whether total sales are in the millions or in the thousands; every point has a big impact on revenue and margins.

Had she not been able to dump the business in Fizz Corp.'s lap at the trade show, she would have been in deep trouble, not just because of her downward sale-discount-and-return spiral and costly sales promotions, but because, as she learned to her surprise, Fizz Corp. was intent on getting in the business. Sooner or later, Julia would have had an eight-hundred-pound gorilla of a competitor in her way, run by a former boss who knew exactly how Julia thought and worked. A formidable prospect, indeed.

MONEYHUNT
RULE #16

"Beware Your Bedfellows"

MoneyHunt Hero: Kwanisha Tyler

I t is an axiom of the late twentieth century that "trust is dead." This is especially true in the business world. Unfortunately, an entrepreneur cannot assume (if in fact he or she ever could) that the people with whom he or she does business share the same goals, objectives, values, and commitment that the entrepreneur does. One of the things successful entrepreneurs must learn to be neurotic about is that their partners have a "hidden agenda" to steal the business, upend their dreams, and make their lives truly miserable.

A GROWING BUSINESS MAKES STRANGE BEDFELLOWS

Once upon a time, business relationships were based upon trust. People lived in the same communities most of their lives, and there was general respect for institutions, organizations, and community in the broader sense. In such a world, you cared very much about your reputation—if you acted in a dishonorable manner, the whole town (or county, or industry) knew about it and you weren't likely to get much business. In forming a partnership with another human being, you relied upon your personal knowledge of the individual (which was usually substantial) and that person's reputation within the communities whose judgment you respected.

In today's faster, more mobile world, the idea of community (some would say the notion of respect as well) has become a quaint and old-fashioned one. Thanks in part to modern technology and in part to the breakdown of traditional institutions, people today are more like atoms—each with his or her own individual orbit, gyrating and collid-ing with other atoms in seemingly random sequence, accepting nothing on faith, questioning everybody and everything. We spend more time on the Internet or watching television than we do participating in civic and political activities. Voter turnout is at an all-time low, and charities, churches, and synagogues have to beg for volunteer help. Relationships and affiliations with other human beings are viewed as "snap on, snap off"—interchangeable at will and more or less fungible.

This is a sad comment, but entrepreneurs must live in the world that exists, not in the mists of nostalgia. In today's world, you frequently don't know your business partners before you form relationships with them—you haven't grown up with them, you weren't roommates in col-lege—why, heck, you may have even met them on the Internet and don't even know what they look like in person! You often do not have the time to check out someone's background and reputation before committing to a business relationship with them, nor do you have the luxury of try-ing things out for a while so you can get to know one another. So very often you find yourself in business with strange bedfellows indeed. In today's world entrepreneurs must daily question, and be very insecure about, the motives and objectives of the people with whom they do business.

IT'S EASY TO MISJUDGE PEOPLE

Forming a business partnership is a little like falling in love. It's easy to see things in people that just aren't there—especially if you like them person-ally. You overlook faults that are plainly obvious to anyone looking at the relationship from a distance, and assume (without any hard evidence) that the person will reciprocate your affection and treat you with the respect and honor you deserve. Such an assumption, of course, can be the prelude to a personal, as well as financial, heartbreak when things don't turn out as you imagined they would. Taking what a person says at face value, not doing your homework on a person's background and reputa-tion, and confusing slick interpersonal skills with professional compe-tence are all ways in which entrepreneurs ignore the negative implications of not trusting their partners.

Of course, it is extremely difficult not to trust your partners when they are friends and family. We have already pointed out that sometimes the most successful business relationships are between people who don't get along personally all that well. Being suspicious of your partners' motives and intentions is just another way of keeping it strictly business between you and the people who share your business life.

It's Time to Check Your "Trust" Level When:

- You start socializing with your business partners to the point where your business and personal lives become intertwined.

- You are tempted to give a significant portion of the equity in your business to a new partner who hasn't yet proved himself or herself.

- You are tempted to make an offer of partnership to someone you've just met at a venture capital club or chamber of commerce meeting.

- Someone offers to become your partner on terms that are just too good to be true.

- You look for evidence that your potential partners have skills and talents that complement your own, and try as you might you really can't find any, but you still like them for some unknown reason.

- Your partners are doing things you really don't like, but you are afraid to bring them up for fear it will upset the applecart.

MONEYHUNT HEROINE: KWANISHA TYLER

When we were first introduced to Kwanisha Tyler through a mutual acquaintance, the words that kept coming up over and over again in the conversation were "force of Nature," and her story was right out of Horatio Alger—the sort of thing that could happen only in America.

A welfare mother of four who dropped out of the eighth grade when she became pregnant with her first child, Kwanisha was introduced at a charity function to Elizabeth Atchison, a blue-haired socialite who was struggling to run a small business distributing children's books in the United States and Canada for publishers in Europe and Asia. Elizabeth was what was commonly known in the book trade as a "packager"—

she traveled throughout the world finding new children's books that she felt would appeal to American children, arranged to have the books translated into English, printed, and then sold in bulk quantities to publishers in North America. Having inherited this old family business from her husband upon the latter's death, Elizabeth was never really comfortable in the business world. Having no children of her own, she merely ran the business the way her husband had done, and was moderately successful.

Elizabeth took an immediate liking to Kwanisha, whose energy and street smarts seemed to complement Elizabeth's own reserve and sheltered upbringing. Elizabeth hired Kwanisha as a part-time clerk, fulfilling orders and dealing with customers. Kwanisha discovered that she loved business, especially the marketing side, which came very naturally to her, and was soon learning German and Japanese in adult-education courses so she could better deal with the overseas publishers. Before long Elizabeth began taking Kwanisha to the publishing industry trade shows in Europe and Asia, and Kwanisha became an instant hit within the industry.

Tipping the scale at 250 pounds, draped in pastel-colored African-style clothing and bronze jewelry that she designed herself, calling every new acquaintance "Honey," and rendering colorful and poetic opinions on every title offered her ("Honey, my kids wouldn't touch that book if you bound it with peanut butter"), Kwanisha soon established herself as a force to be reckoned with in the industry, and publishers vied for her attention. It soon became generally known in the industry that if Kwanisha liked your book, you had the U.S. market at your fingertips.

Within three years of joining Elizabeth's company, Kwanisha was in charge of selecting and marketing new titles for Elizabeth's company, and both sales and profits grew. Elizabeth made it a point to give Kwanisha stock in the company every Christmas, so at the end of three years Kwanisha was a full partner with the title vice president–marketing and sales.

Shortly after their third anniversary as a working partnership, Elizabeth was diagnosed with cancer. Realizing that she would no longer be able to run the business, and that Kwanisha (the only possible buyer) had no money to buy the business, Elizabeth sold Kwanisha her interest in the business for one dollar.

Despite their vast differences in social background and outlook, the two women were fast friends. Elizabeth stayed on as a consultant for one year and taught Kwanisha everything she knew about running the business's operations. Kwanisha visited Elizabeth in the hospital, and eventually the hospice, and personally paid for Elizabeth's funeral expenses when the latter inevitably lost her battle with cancer.

Kwanisha ran the business effectively for several years after Elizabeth's death but hated the paperwork involved. Her strength was in marketing, attending trade shows and picking the titles that drove the business's success. Keeping track of purchases, sales, and inventories did not come easily to her—she hired a part-time graduate student to help out for a while, but when he lost his student visa Kwanisha had to work twenty hours a day for two months to get the business back on track. The business was not generating enough income to bring on full-time help to handle the "back office" functions, so Kwanisha soldiered on.

One year Kwanisha was invited to a friend's celebration of Kwanza— the annual African American holiday that falls at the same time as Christmas and Hanukkah. Looking around for a suitable book to give her friend's little girl as a Kwanza gift, Kwanisha realized that nobody had as yet published a children's book with a Kwanza theme. Kwanisha decided to fill this void, personally persuading a leading author of children's books with African American themes to write a Kwanza book, which Kwanisha then published. As one of the first Kwanza books ever published, Kwanisha's first printing sold out in a few weeks and established her company's successful move into the publishing business. Kwanisha followed upon her early success the next year with another Kwanza book from the same author and a "Kwanza" Advent-type calendar (in which children opened little paper doors each day during Kwanza to reveal a message or image behind the door), which Kwanisha designed herself. Both became instant best-sellers and established her company as "the" place to go in the publishing industry for Kwanza-related products.

Then disaster struck. Kwanisha's company was financed primarily by a revolving line of credit from a local bank, which was guaranteed by the U.S. Small Business Administration (SBA). One day Kwanisha received a telephone call from her banker informing her that the bank would be compelled to terminate their SBA loan. When a shocked Kwanisha asked why, explaining "Honey, you know I *always* make the monthly payments on time!" the banker calmly replied that the SBA prohibits banks from making loans to publishing businesses. While this had not been a problem back in the days when Elizabeth and Kwanisha were merely packaging other publishers' books and reselling them in the United States, it was a major problem now that Kwanisha was publishing books and calendars under the company's imprint. The bank gave Kwanisha thirty days to find alternative financing despite her pleas for more time.

Nothing in Kwanisha's experience had prepared her for a blow like that. She knew she would need more than thirty days to come up with enough money to pay off the SBA loan and keep the business running, and that without an SBA guarantee no bank would lend money to a low-margin business such as Kwanisha's that had few if any hard assets. She needed equity capital . . . and quick!

Having heard from Elizabeth that lawyers and accountants were the first people you talked to when you had business problems, Kwanisha discussed the situation with David, the company's accountant. David said he thought he knew someone who could provide short-term capital for Kwanisha and that he would get back to her in a couple of days.

A couple of days later David called Kwanisha and asked her to meet him in his office later that day. When Kwanisha walked in the door, there were two people in David's office she had not met before. "Kwanisha, this is my father-in-law, Joe, and my brother-in-law Sam. We have been talking about your situation, and we think we can help you. We have been talking for some time about making a family investment in some type of business, and we're very impressed with the operation you've built after Elizabeth's untimely death. We are prepared to buy 48 percent of your company's stock in exchange for enough money to take out that SBA loan. There's only one condition—we want an option to buy all of your shares in two years."

Kwanisha replied, "That's a lot of stock for such a small amount of money. Why do you need so much?"

It was Joe who responded. "Look, Kwanisha, you need this money in a hurry, but what's more important, you need help in running the business. David's been telling us how you have been struggling to run the back-office side of the business, and that's only gotten more complicated now that you are publishing your own stuff. Sam here was just recently down-sized from a major New York publishing house—he knows the publishing business inside and out and would make a good partner for you."

"So, in other words, this is not just an investment; you want me to give you an option on all of my shares and hire Sam too?"

"Yes. He will be your president and chief operating officer. It will still be your business, of course. You will stay on as chief executive officer and handle the marketing and sales side, which you know so well."

Kwanisha said she would think about it. She made it a point to meet Sam for lunch a few days later and "size him up." Sam was a pleasant enough man, and certainly knew the ins and outs of a large publishing company, but in Kwanisha's judgment was not the brightest light on the Kwanza candelabra. "He's no threat to me today," Kwanisha thought to herself, "but in a year or two, once he understands the business and develops relationships with my people?"

Despite her worries, Kwanisha realized she needed the money and that this presented her best opportunity to get it without facing a massive cash crunch at the beginning of her busiest season. She reasoned that with Sam on board she would indeed be able to delegate the back-office work she detested so much and focus her energies on the marketing and product-development side, which was her peculiar strength. She also reasoned that with only 48 percent of the stock her three investors would not be able to force the company to take any course of action unless she went along with it.

Still, there was something about the offer that didn't sit right with Kwanisha. The requirement that Kwanisha hire Sam, coupled with David's insistence that the minority investors have an option to buy Kwanisha's shares in two years, sounded too much like a "creeping takeover" to her. She discussed it with the company's outside attorney, who recommended that she and Sam sign employment agreements with the company, so that if the relationship got rocky down the road Kwanisha could pull out of the company with a large severance package. At the insistence of David, who acted as his own attorney, Kwanisha's and Sam's agreements contained a "noncompete" clause prohibiting either of them from acting as a packager of children's books for two years if the agreement was terminated for any reason.

Within a week Kwanisha closed the deal, admitted David, Joe, and Sam as minority investors, paid off the SBA loan, and settled Sam into an office next door to her own. Sam proved competent in handling the back-office functions of the business, which gave Kwanisha the time she needed to attend the industry trade shows, select new titles for packaging in the United States, and develop new Kwanza-related products. Three months later, Kwanisha was surprised when Sam walked into her office and handed her a notice of a shareholders meeting called by the three minority investors. When Kwanisha asked why it was necessary to call a formal meeting, Sam replied, "We just want to be involved and make sure we agree with how the business is being run. We plan to have these meetings on a regular basis."

The shareholders' meeting turned out to be a shouting match. David proposed the company obtain financing overseas to provide short-term cash, which Kwanisha voted down because of the need to pledge all of the company's inventory as collateral. The three investors criticized Kwanisha for not inviting Sam along to the important trade shows. Kwanisha replied that it was not Sam's job to select titles or decide on new Kwanza products. The minority investors insisted on a three-person board of directors consisting of Kwanisha, David, and a third party whom Kwanisha and David would select. Kwanisha replied, "And who do you think is going to be crazy enough to step in here and act as referee between us? Why don't you just come out and say it—you plan on buying my shares in two years, booting me out the door and making this

Sam's business?" David, Joe, and Sam all denied that was their intention and indirectly accused Kwanisha of being paranoid about nothing, but Kwanisha remained skeptical. Kwanisha did, however, agree to hold regular shareholders' meetings every month to review the company's operating results.

Kwanisha's fears were confirmed later that year when it came to her attention that while she was in the field attending trade shows Sam was answering telephone calls from suppliers and building relationships with key customers and distributors behind her back. When she confronted Sam, his reply was unsettling: "Look, Kwanisha, if I am to function as president of this company I can't just be limited to the back-office functions. The intent here is that I be your number two so if, God forbid, anything happens to you, the business can continue. You have to admit, Kwanisha, you really don't have a succession plan here!"

The relationship between Kwanisha and her minority investors deteriorated over the next several months. It came to light that David was conducting audits of the company's books and records on a monthly basis while Kwanisha was out of the office, and that Joe had sold some of his shares in the company to a friend with connections in the world of venture capital. Clearly it was only a matter of time before Kwanisha was forced out.

At the next shareholders' meeting Kwanisha dropped a bomb. "Look, I'm getting mighty tired of all this bickering and back-and-forth between us. It's starting to hurt the business. It's clear to me that you guys want to run the show. Well, go ahead! I'm prepared to make you an offer you can't refuse, gentlemen. I'm not going to wait the two years—you can buy my shares now for the price we agreed on, and I will introduce Sam to all of my contacts."

"You mean," David said, looking skeptical, "you're willing to hand us the keys now?"

"Yes," Kwanisha replied. "I think it is the best way to preserve Elizabeth's legacy."

"And you will introduce Sam to the right people?"

"Absolutely."

"And you will abide by the noncompete clause in your employment contract?"

"As long as you pay me the severance called for in the agreement."

David, Joe, and Sam looked at each other. "We will find the money."

Within two weeks Sam told Kwanisha the three investors had obtained a loan from one of the company's overseas suppliers to purchase Kwanisha's shares. When Kwanisha asked what the three had offered the overseas supplier to obtain the loan, Sam said that they had offered the supplier 10 percent of the company's shares as an incentive. "I wouldn't recommend that if I were you," Kwanisha said. "Once you go into debt with one of these people, and especially if you give them a piece of the action, they will not want you to deal with any of their competitors. They will want you to deal exclusively with them. I've always resisted those kind of relationships, and I think you're making a mistake here."

Sam admitted, "Frankly, Kwanisha, I understand the risk here. But your offer took us by surprise—we didn't have the money on hand to buy your shares now. This was the only way we could raise the money to do the deal now."

"Well, honey," Kwanisha purred, "you know I know what that's like."

Three weeks later, David, Joe, and Sam purchased Kwanisha's shares in the company, using the money they borrowed from the overseas supplier. Kwanisha stayed on as a paid consultant to the company for two months, introduced Sam to her key contacts, and taught Sam the packaging business. At the end of the two-month consulting period, Kwanisha cleaned out her office and walked out the door for the last time.

A month later Sam opened a publishing industry trade magazine and read a notice that Kwanisha Tyler had been named to head the children's book division of a major publishing house. Furious, Sam called Kwanisha's home, where he heard the following recorded message: "This is Kwanisha Tyler. I will be away from home for three months visiting relatives in the Caribbean. When I return I will be joining [the major publishing house] as head of their children's book division, where I will be developing a line of books and calendars for African American children. To those of my friends in the book packaging business, thank you for all of your support these past several years. It took me a long time to realize my heart was really in the publishing business, but I know I am doing what my late friend Elizabeth Atchison would have wanted me to do. And I have every confidence that you will receive the same service from my successor that you received from me. Please leave your message at the tone."

LESSONS FROM KWANISHA TYLER

Kwanisha Tyler was faced with a tough choice: allow her business to go under, or work with partners she neither needed nor wanted who were intent on taking over the business she and Elizabeth had built from scratch. Other entrepreneurs, faced with her company's desperate financial situation, would have grasped at any straw that would help them stay afloat. Realizing that she had no alternative but to accept a less-than-optimum offer to purchase a minority stake in her business, Kwanisha kept her wits about her and negotiated a package that gave her a graceful exit from the business when her so-called partners showed their true intentions.

On the other hand, David, Joe, and Sam lost out by trusting their business partner—Kwanisha—too much. Underestimating Kwanisha's formidable powers of analysis and judgment, and assuming that they had her over a barrel, they formulated a plan that if successful would have made Kwanisha, despite her majority ownership of the company, virtually their employee. In executing this plan, however, they allowed Kwanisha to write the terms of her exit from the business, including a noncompete clause that permitted Kwanisha to continue her success in book publishing at a higher level while leaving Sam with a low-margin book packaging business.

Once settled in as minority investors, the three treated Kwanisha in a ham-handed fashion, browbeating her during shareholders' meetings, confirming her worst suspicions about their true intentions, and leading her to seek employment elsewhere before Sam was really ready to take over the reins. Ironically, when Kwanisha shrewdly offered to allow the minority investors to buy her stake in the company prematurely, the three investors fell into precisely the same trap they had hoped to force Kwanisha into—acting hastily to line up financing for their purchase of Kwanisha's shares, they entered into an alliance with an overseas publisher that had (as Kwanisha generously pointed out to Sam) the potential to severely hamstring the future growth of the business.

Kwanisha's close personal friendship with Elizabeth Atchison did not prepare her to deal with business partners whose motives were more underhanded and unscrupulous. A less insecure or more trusting entrepreneur in such a situation would have presumed that the company's accountant—a trusted adviser and confidant—would have only the company's best interests in view in offering to bail her out of a tough financial spot. Kwanisha's street smarts saved the day and helped her to recognize David's offer for what it really was—the first step in a creeping takeover of her business.

The most difficult lesson for Kwanisha was, and is, the most difficult lesson for any entrepreneur. It isn't easy to put your emotions to one side and look at a business coldly and rationally, especially where the business has a long-standing history and tradition. Despite the fact that she owed everything to her late friend Elizabeth, and wanted above all to preserve her late friend's legacy by making the business everything Elizabeth would have wanted it to be, Kwanisha reasoned that it was better for her in the long run to leave the book packaging business behind and pursue a new career in children's book publishing—a field in which she became intensely interested after her success in launching her line of Kwanza books and calendars. Kwanisha shrewdly concluded that the best way to pursue her new career goal—and get back at David, Joe, and Sam at the same time—was to give them precisely what they wanted most of all, control of Kwanisha's company.

As Oscar Wilde once wrote, "Sometimes the Gods punish us by giving us exactly what we say we want."

PART FIVE

Show Me the Money!

MONEYHUNT
RULE #17

"Audacity Sells . . . Most of the Time"

MoneyHunt Hero: Chris Sardoni

Successful businesspeople are, first and foremost, salespeople. If you cannot sell, do not, we repeat, *do not* start your own company. We are all comfortable selling ourselves when we are certain we can deliver all of the things we promise folks we can. But what about the times when we're not sure we can deliver? We are told since childhood that it is not wise or ethical to promise something if you know there is a risk you will break that promise. Sometimes, however, being a successful salesperson and getting the big deal that makes or breaks your company requires that you do precisely that.

FAINT HEART NEVER WON FAIR MONEY

There is an old saying in the venture business, "A faint heart never made anyone rich." We are all perfectionists to a certain degree. All of us would like to live in a world of perfect information, one in which we make decisions only when we have thoroughly researched a situation from all possible angles, evaluated the alternatives, discussed it with our friends and business partners, and made the best available decision we can, all of the time.

Unfortunately, more often than not, life does not give us the opportunity to do so. Opportunities often pass quickly and must be grabbed and swallowed before we are completely ready to digest them. Especially in a hot new market, the prizes frequently go to the people who are first to reach the market with something, cleaning up the details later, rather than the folks who wait too long to perfect their products and services. Those of you who have ever purchased "Release 1.0" of a new software product know that there almost always are defects, or bugs, in any new software product. That is why there is almost always a Version 1.1 or Version 2.0 within a year of the launch of any new software product. We are sure you have wondered, as we have, why software developers release products they know are not yet perfected. Yet by waiting until all of the source code of a new product has been debugged, software developers risk missing a promising new opportunity for market leadership to their less efficient but quicker competition.

Several years ago, Cliff wrote a book for lawyers about the right way to interview for a legal job. Once, while speaking at a law school to promote his book, Cliff was asked, "What makes you such an expert on the art of interviewing? Are you a Ph.D. in psychology or something?"

Cliff responded, "Well, there's basically three things that qualify me to write a book like this one. First, I've interviewed for a lot of legal jobs in my lifetime, and I've made all the mistakes you could possibly make. Second, I've made several successful career transitions in my life, so I know the techniques I describe in my book really work. Last but not least, I got my book written and published before anyone else with better credentials thought of the idea."

Sometimes you just have to grit your teeth, cross your fingers, shoot from the hip, get the deal, and then work like hell to make sure you deliver.

Just Don't Start Believing Your Own BS

Selling yourself and your company audaciously involves a certain amount of ruthlessness, and ruthless behavior makes a lot of people uncomfortable. So it comes as no surprise that many entrepreneurs try to rationalize away what they are doing when they sell audaciously.

One way is to let the other party off the hook too easily by hedging during a sales pitch. Investors and clients can tell all too easily when an entrepreneur isn't comfortable in his or her own skin. Believe us, if you don't believe anything else in this book, that if you do not communicate to all people you come into contact with that you believe 100 percent in your business, your products and services, you will not be successful in the entrepreneurship game.

Another way is to make a strong sales pitch but then fail to follow through. When you sell audaciously, as we recommend you do, you are taking a big risk—perhaps the biggest risk of your business life. Except in some extraordinary circumstances, you won't get away with it. In the short term, you can succeed with BS. But sooner or later, you have to prove to the marketplace (and to yourself) that it isn't just BS. Just remember to tell people "I told you so!" when you *do* deliver on time and under budget.

Finally, many entrepreneurs end up believing too much in their own BS. It is difficult for an entrepreneur to be in sales mode all the time without sooner or later believing that the hype is absolutely the gospel truth. It is natural, and probably unavoidable. As Willy Loman points out in Arthur Miller's classic play *Death of a Salesman*, "A salesman's got to dream, boy!" Yet by believing too much in your own marketing literature, you risk crossing the thin and subtle line that frequently separates aggressive marketing from outright fraud (which is precisely the tragedy of Willy Loman in *Death of a Salesman*).

Be Audacious When:

- An investor asks, "Do you think you can show a 22 percent return on investment in two years?" when your best projections call for only 18 percent (do you really want to lose a good deal over 4 percent of anything?).

- A client asks, "Can you turn around this project in two weeks?" when your best estimate is three weeks with the resources you have available (in this case, by the way, a good answer is "Yes, but we will need to hire additional people, which may affect the budget slightly").

- An investor or client seems interested in your company, but says, "I would like the opportunity to think about it for a week or so" (don't let him get away with that).

- You are tempted, during a sales pitch, to give a balanced presentation of the pros and cons of an investment in your company (let your lawyer worry about the cons and bury them in the "risk factors" section of your sales prospectus).

MoneyHunt Hero: Chris Sardoni

Chris Sardoni started his Web page design business right out of college with a rowdy bunch of his former fraternity brothers, convinced they could make a go of it in New York City's "Silicon Alley." With operations in their one-bedroom walk-up apartment on the Upper West Side of Manhattan, things looked surprisingly like they did at college, except now there were a few more computers, some high-speed access lines to the Internet, and a little money.

Before they had even created a single Web page they had pitched and won a project for a major toy company that wanted to build a community of avid game players. Chris had worn his only suit, and his partner Paul bought a new one from a budget factory warehouse clothing store. Luckily there were no other technical people in the room, just marketing people eager to make a big splash in a big way. Chris smelled opportunity, since the lead had come from Peter's brother, who worked at the toy company. Chris knew that the toy company was flush with cash, technologically incompetent, and under pressure to catch up. Still, they weren't committing just yet. A critical moment had arrived: Chris had to shine now, or risk losing it all. It was a spot he would find himself in more and more.

Business negotiations are often like poker games, and Chris had played a lot of poker in his college fraternity. Chris knew well the meaning of the old poker adage: when in doubt, bluff. "I want this to be a big program with a big commitment that would make a major impact on the community," he said. He and his "staff" were busy on multiple projects, Chris said, and had to manage their time diligently. So if the client said no now, they may lose the opportunity to work with Chris and his design team for up to twelve months. Chris referred to projects that he and Peter had worked on, failing to mention the fact that they were in college at the time and didn't truly deserve credit for the creation. He even listed as current commitments a few projects that his technical person was thinking about doing someday but hadn't really started. The client started looking interested: No middle manager in a large corporation wants to be known as the person who had the opportunity to work with the hottest up-and-coming Web design team but turned them down because they looked like kids.

Chris had them hooked, and they were just waiting to be reeled in. So the master poker player upped the ante. He told the prospective client he was going to sketch out the terms on his computer then and there for their review, because he had meetings that afternoon and the next morning and would not have the time to focus on details. The toy company took the bait and signed a memorandum of understanding that very afternoon.

Chris's design team worked evenings and weekends and developed an award-winning Web site for the toy company. Soon Chris was getting telephone calls from other companies who wanted "the same people who did that wonderful site" to do their Web site design work. Chris struck fast, making the same promises he had made to urge the toy company to sign: "We're very busy right now and we're looking at a lot of projects. To ensure that we will be able to give your site the time and effort it deserves, we need a commitment from you right now." Very soon he had project commitments capable of supporting a staff of almost a hundred people in creative, programming, design, sales, marketing, and executive. The only problem was that Chris's entire design team consisted of only a dozen programmers, who were soon overpromised, overcommitted, overworked, and overwrought.

Chris did the only logical thing. He upped the stakes and began forming a new division with newfound agency accounts. Chris had a blowout party, renting out one of the hottest loft-style restaurants in Manhattan's Greenwich Village, stocking the bar with potent drinks and serving dim sum and sushi on plates carried by lively short-skirted women from the local modeling agencies. Needless to say, an invitation to one of Chris's parties was essential if you were to be considered a "player" in Silicon Alley. Each party was chock-full of Silicon Alley dealers, Wall Street hitters, and clients present and future. Chris must have had a dozen investors approach him with offers to get involved with money, expertise, referrals, and offers to go public.

Chris played coy, knowing that anyone foolish enough to make such overt advances at a party would make the effort to do things Chris's way. True to form, he received calls from each and every one of the investment bankers he met at the party by noon the next morning. He had meetings set up on his turf for those interested in reviewing his business plan.

Chris continued the brinksmanship that he had learned in winning new clients. Except this time he did deliver a complete business plan to each of the twelve would-be investors that came calling. As he sized them up, he realized each one of his suitors was desperate to be in on the new wave of Internet companies, seeing the potential for huge returns on their investment even before the company turned a profit (or even had revenues). Within two weeks of his networking parties, Chris has commitments for over $2 million in venture capital. In typical Chris Sardoni fashion, he overpromised, pressured his investors to complete their transactions in ridiculously short time spans, and insisted that they not only invest but also bring the institutions they often did deals with along with them. Late at night, however, after the last party and the last meeting with his first-round investors, Chris wondered how long it would be before all his promises came home to roost.

Soon Chris found himself overwhelmed by his company's lack of organizational structure, constant changes in corporate direction, and outright failures. Two out of their last three major projects were out of control technically, and Chris's company was behind on virtually every deadline. Worse, Chris's company hemorrhaged money. The estimates that they had made to their clients, which seemed so grandiose and laden with profit margin at the time, actually became ball-and-chain projects of undeliverable expectations that weighed down the already under-staffed programming department with numerous corrections, changes, and improvements. The only good part of the bleeding was the fact that Chris could now draw an outrageous salary and benefits befitting a new media titan with an Internet-content empire and a tremendous buzz in the press.

The irony was not lost on Chris. He had begun to use parts of his sig-nificant income to open trading accounts with the very firms that invest-ed in his company. It was one grand, if indirect, circle that made him very popular with his broker, who, favoring Chris with early market tips and warnings, allowed Chris to create a personal fortune in the market for Internet start-ups while Chris's company burned.

Soon enough he needed a second round of financing, as he saw clearly that the money he had raised in the first round would not last but two more quarters at his current burn rate. Soon after his appearance on MoneyHunt, he met separately with almost all of his first-round investors and tried to explain the numerous reversals, blown deadlines, and unful-filled promises, both in terms of the business and its profitability and in investor expectations.

Surprisingly, no one was particularly upset at his explanations. As a matter of fact, many of them shrugged them off, ascribing no personal blame to Chris, but rather to the vicissitudes of the rapidly changing new media market. But . . . those investors who had heard the promises before and who had been fooled by both the market and by Chris were not at all interested in throwing bad money after good. Chris had burned all his bridges and was becoming increasingly desperate with each old investor he met with. His new story and new opportunities would forever be viewed through the lens of what he and his investors had already been through.

With only two months of cash left at his present burn rate, Chris's des-peration grew. He fairly jumped at the chance to meet with a new investor who had seen him on MoneyHunt and was interested in doing business. Chris began the conversation with a respect befitting the fragility of his situation. He treaded ever so softly in making his initial pitch, fearing that the loss of this opportunity might well spell disaster for his company, leading to the inevitable downward spiral of a dying business—mass firings, account losses, reduced revenue, collection difficulties, and cash shortages. Chris could hardly imagine facing it.

When the deal progressed more slowly than he would have liked, Chris resorted to the threats that had worked so well for him in the past. "We have thirty days to complete a deal or I'll be forced to revalue the opportunity based on this booming market," Chris thundered. Immediately, and quite shockingly to Chris, they snapped into action. So he tried another threat. "You must sign a letter of intent within two days, you must complete your due diligence within two weeks, and you must post a nonrefundable 5 percent earnest payment to an escrow account should you decide, after signing the letter of intent, not to proceed with the transaction," Chris demanded.

Chris's onerous terms only served to make the new investors push harder to get the deal done, because, Chris realized, they now had come to the conclusion that they had to be in the Internet business. No timing threat from a founder, no questions raised of due diligence, no valuation issue was going to get between them and a major piece of an up-and-coming brand in the Internet marketplace. To the astonished delight of each of his first-round investors, Chris raised enough money to give him a second chance at finding the ever elusive revenue stream, to avert layoffs for a few months, and to pay his princely salary. He now had accumulated $400,000 in cash and stocks to add to his paper net worth of $2,200,000 from his share in his company.

Still, late at night, in the privacy of his (newly purchased) penthouse condominium on the Upper East Side of Manhattan, Chris wondered . . . where will the next round of financing come from?

LESSONS FROM CHRIS SARDONI

There's an old saying, "If you want something badly enough, you will get it . . . badly enough." The person who wants or needs a deal more than the other person will end up doing the deal on the other person's terms, as Chris Sardoni shrewdly realized. By promising clients more than his design team could deliver, Chris won important contracts that gave him the operating revenue he needed to hire the extra developers who could get the jobs done. By promising investors a return on investment that he knew couldn't be justified by his firm's revenues and profit margins at the time, Chris capitalized on the "Internet fever" of the time, knowing full well that in a hot market stocks often rise or fall based on people's perceptions and emotions, with total disregard for the hard numbers that should (but don't) drive investment decisions. His investors, who were no fools, were willing participants in a con game whose only victim is . . . the next person to buy into the company.

Chris's first lesson in audacity came during his initial meeting with his first prospective client, the toy company. Realizing how desperate the company was to develop a strong presence on the Internet, Chris sold his company aggressively and insisted the company close quickly with him to avoid losing the opportunity to work with a hot Web page design team. Frequently, when selling yourself or your business to a prospective customer, you don't know with 100 percent certainty if you can do the job—there is a certain leap of faith required on both your and your customer's parts. Fortunately, Chris's design team did a terrific job for that first client—the client's Web page alone was the best advertisement Chris could have placed for future business.

Chris later realized that the same aggressive selling techniques would work with investors as well as clients. Despite their sophistication and expertise, Chris's investors were as blinded by Internet fever as were Chris's clients, and Chris took advantage of that.

It may seem surprising at first that, despite the poor performance of Chris's company, his investors did not rip Chris's liver out during their periodic meetings. Once an investor signs on the dotted line, he is inevitably "on the hook" and must, at least for a time, follow the entrepreneur's plan for growing the business for fear of admitting to himself (or to the people who put money into the deal) that he has made a mistake. In the words of a great entrepreneur and dealmaker, "If you owe your investors $10,000, your investors own you; if you owe your investors $1,000,000, you own your investors." Chris was surprised that his first round of investors let him off so easily when he made full disclosure of his company's operating difficulties, but he shouldn't have been so surprised. Nor should he have been so surprised that they would not invest additional money in his business. Or that his first-round investors were "extremely grateful" that somebody else's money would support Chris's future operations.

Chris's strategy, while extremely successful, comes at a high price. Even though Chris is technically a millionaire and has survived two successful rounds of venture financing, he must ask himself every night, "When will the bubble burst? When will people start demanding performance from my company? When will the chickens come home to roost?" While overpromising is sometimes the only way to build a business in a tough market, sooner or later you must live up to those promises. The money that comes from hype is very often a short-term loan—the longer term financial security a company needs to grow is based on solid performance for customers, investors, employees, and other constituencies of a growing company.

The line that separates aggressive marketing from outright fraud is an extremely thin one. As Abraham Lincoln wrote, "You can fool all of the people some of the time; you can fool some of the people all of the time; but you can't fool all of the people all of the time." Sooner or later someone realizes the emperor is naked, and that's when it all comes undone.

MONEY HUNT
RULE #18

"Don't Judge a Deal by How It Lands on Your Doorstep"

MoneyHunt Heroine: Denise Chao

Sometimes opportunity doesn't arrive the way you might expect; judging a book by its cover can be fatal to the success of a growing business.

Sometimes entrepreneurs form an image of the perfect investor for their business and become fixated on that image, so that when the perfect investor shows up looking more like a toad than Prince Charming, the entrepreneur foolishly turns his back.

Money can come from just about anywhere. If the terms are right and the people check out, play your cards.

AN INVESTOR IS ANYONE WITH MONEY TO INVEST

Entrepreneurs can ill afford to pass by any opportunity for funding, no matter how far-fetched it may seem at first. Yet many pass on perfectly good opportunities.

Sometimes entrepreneurs don't recognize an opportunity because they never seriously considered looking for money from that particular source. A supplier or customer, for example, can also be a source of funds in time of trouble. We even know of one well-publicized instance where a company made a $100 million investment in its arch competitor, which was failing and desperately needed a cash infusion. Of course, the company's motives for shoring up its competitor's finances were far from altruistic. If the competitor had been allowed to fail, the surviving company would have had a virtual monopoly in its industry, which would have made worse the company's already serious exposure to liability under the federal antitrust laws. By propping up the competitor, the investing company was able to keep the antitrust regulators at bay while at the same time gaining access to information that the competitor only shared with its insiders.

SOMETIMES PRINCE CHARMING DOESN'T LOOK LIKE THE GUY IN THE DISNEY MOVIES

Sometimes investment opportunities don't look the way they should look in an entrepreneur's eye. Most entrepreneurs have an image in their minds of the type of investor they feel would be most appropriate for their business. Any investor who does not conform to the ideal model in the entrepreneur's mind is passed over, without further analysis or examination. While it is true that there are different types, or "flavors," of investors, and it is important to know the right type of money you are looking for (debt versus equity, SBA loan versus venture capital), in our experience money has, and has always had, one color and one color only. As Gertrude Stein would have put it, money is money is money.

You may not always be able to recognize the right type of investors for your business until they've been your investors for several years, so it pays to judge every prospect innocent . . . until they prove themselves guilty. Then walk, unless you are desperate for cash.

WHEN AN INVESTOR ALSO PLAYS OTHER ROLES

Often entrepreneurs convince themselves that what they need is something more than an investor. "Well, yes, Joe is willing to put in $100,000 of his own money, but we really don't need someone like Joe as an investor. We need someone who can open doors for our company in the industry. . . ." That may be true, but will the door openers be interested in a company that's not already attracting investor interest?

Sometimes, entrepreneurs pass over an investment opportunity for fear that it will alter other business relationships. "Well, sure our key supplier wants to invest $1 million in us! If we take their money they will own us and will want us to carry every product in their line to the exclusion of their competition. . . ." This is a real risk, of course, when a supplier becomes your investor, but it can be managed by making it clear in the investment contract that you are free to deal with other suppliers.

As a practical matter, every investor you bring on board should be treated as if he were your business partner. On our *MoneyHunt* television show, we frequently talk about the "personality" of money. A bank behaves very differently from a venture capital firm, which in turn behaves very differently from an "angel," or wealthy individual investor. A wealthy angel who has experience in your industry will behave very differently from an angel who doesn't. And so forth. It's very important to make sure you understand the personality of the money you are attracting the same way in which you would size up the personality of a prospective business partner.

Remember Not to Judge the Book by Its Cover When:

- A venture capital firm wants to make a $5 million equity invest-ment in your company, but the partner in charge is a former boyfriend from high school who jilted you in order to date the captain of the cheerleading squad (don't laugh—we actually saw this happen once).

- You have a regular golf foursome with three investment bankers, and when your company gets itself into a cash crunch you can't think of anyone you can turn to for help.

- You need $250,000 for expansion capital, and you hear from your mother that cousin Irma in Iowa just hit the state lottery for $2 million.

- You graduated from an Ivy League college, and the millionaire angel you are introduced to at the country club didn't complete high school.

MONEYHUNT HEROINE: DENISE CHAO

Denise was early, as was her custom, for her initial *MoneyHunt* interview. She prided herself on preparing completely for big moments like this. Long before she arrived at the *MoneyHunt* studios, she had rehearsed her appearance and researched the implications thoroughly. It was her way. Preparation gave her confidence, which allowed her to kick into her sales spiel and avoid the slow starts and long pauses that often made her seem nervous.

Denise was good when it came to her product and pitching it. Listening to her in full-pitch mode, her love of the product was clear. Her hand gestures, the way she displayed it tightly at her shoulder, so that a head shot would include the product's packaging at shoulder level, was nothing short of masterful.

When Denise came through the spinning compass door at MoneyHunt for the first time, it seemed to us she wasn't the least bit afraid of the cameras, and the lights, and the controlled chaos. Perhaps because of appearances on cable television's shopping channels, she was used to the dynamics of a live television set. As she settled into her chair, she looked perfectly at home, relaxed, but with that same nervous energy, about to jump. She purred through her presentation, especially at the point where she displayed her own product, just like on cable television. She hit high points, deflected tough questions, and redirected them to point out the opportunities her product presented. Neither of us, nor our MoneyHunt Mentor that day, could argue much with the product. It addressed a rare market need, was well packaged, well merchandised, and of course with Denise, well pitched.

Soon after her appearance on MoneyHunt, she received a call from a man named Mohammed Saldun, who congratulated her on her MoneyHunt appearance. Mohammed had first seen her on cable television's Home Shopping Network and had introduced himself as the son of a Pakistani beauty-products magnate who was here in the United States scouting out new investment opportunities, particularly those run by overseas Asian immigrants.

In their first conversation, Denise instinctively peppered him with questions and diligently checked out his story. The results were somewhat mixed. His father was wealthy enough, but their relationship was not exactly a cozy one. He probably did have access to money but couldn't name one deal that he had completed since his father sent him to the United States two years ago. Denise kept putting off Mohammed, nervous about dealing with someone whose style and method of doing business were so different from her own. Still, Mohammed continued to pursue Denise, taking every opportunity to congratulate her whenever her company received favorable publicity. Denise never considered Mohammed as a potential investor . . . frankly she thought of him as a good-natured pest.

Despite her reservations, when Mohammed suggested a meeting to discuss a possible business relationship, she agreed. What greeted Denise as she walked into the restaurant was a young man barely out of his teens, dressed in traditional Pakistani clothing, polite to the point of embarrassment. Once the conversation turned to business, her instinctive sales mode kicked in, and she was as passionate as ever about pitching her product and her company. Mohammed showed a surprising amount of sophistication, asking relevant questions, pressing for more detail, and finally indicating he was authorized by his father to make an offer of a significant investment in her company. Clearly the young man had been well coached. "Put it in writing and call it a term sheet," Denise said, recalling the advice she had received from other entrepreneurs who had done the same.

Quite surprisingly, the next day, over the fax she got just that—a term sheet offering to buy $1 million in preferred stock of Denise's company, with a respectable but not overbearing dividend, repurchase and management rights that were not onerous, and a promise to close within sixty days. Clearly Mohammed was talking to his father, who had probably dictated the term sheet paragraph by paragraph, so there was keen interest in this deal back in Pakistan.

Denise resolved it was time to start doing some in-depth homework, and in her research she was able to identify the "hot buttons" that might motivate Mohammed to actually complete his first deal in two years. When she signed the term sheet, she pushed hard to get the contracts in place, on time and on schedule. There was no question that Mohammed was far from Denise's dream investor. He was basically a rich kid from Pakistan, trying desperately to prove his worth to his father, yet hopelessly out of touch with standard business practices in the West. She doubted his credibility and was certain that he would not add much to the business in terms of contacts, connections, or industry knowledge. But one thing was clear to Denise: Mohammed's family had money, money, and more money.

Denise resolved that if she was going to go through with a deal, she was going to do it right. She spent countless hours with Mohammed over coffee at a diner near Denise's offices, answering his questions about the business and volunteering items of due diligence that were not on Mohammed's checklist—the latter to make him more familiar with the business and make his report to his father that much more credible.

It didn't hurt that the business itself was taking off like a rocket ship on steroids. She had secured distribution to over 2,200 retail outlets since her appearance on *MoneyHunt*, bringing the total to more than 3,000 nationwide. The product was beginning to move, which meant that the business would become desperate for capital soon, which added to Denise's anxiety about dealing with Mohammed.

The day of the proposed closing, Denise stopped by her local branch bank to make a small withdrawal. After months upon months of being served perfunctorily by the stony-faced tellers and ignored by the assistant vice presidents who sat behind the walls, today for some reason three of the tellers were beaming and glowing as she approached the window. The assistant vice president made his way from behind his cloistered office to extend his hand and welcome Denise to the bank, insisting he was available six days a week to help her in any way she pleased.

This made no sense. So, after making the withdrawal, Denise asked the teller to write her company's checking-account balance on the back of her withdrawal slip. Miraculously Denise suppressed a smile and the blush she felt coming to her face when she read the numbers: $1,000,945.67. Mohammed had made a ridiculous, lucky mistake. In his anticipation to close the deal he had instructed his counsel to wire the funds the morning of the transaction, which in Pakistan was a day earlier. Mohammed did indeed have the money he had said all along he had. Now, so too, did Denise and her company.

It was a sweet victory for Denise, and she savored every long step from the teller window to the ladies' room and then out again to brush by the senior vice president and inquire what kind of corporate account benefits he could offer. When he brought out a portfolio of options to review with her, she waved her hand, smiled, and said, "Pull together your best package and visit me at my office."

Lessons from Denise Chao

First impressions are lasting impressions, but Denise almost rejected a very worthy suitor indeed because she stereotyped Mohammed as a rich kid in search of a green card, which was actually far from the case. Fortunately, she overcame her reservations about Mohammed and worked with him in order to secure an investment from the real investor, Mohammed's father in Pakistan. Throughout the process, though, she did her checking to make absolutely sure that Mohammed was the genuine article.

If Denise had relied on her first impression of Mohammed, nothing would have happened. If her background checks on Mohammed did not reveal access to money or revealed an unsavory background, she would have dropped Mohammed right then and there, as well she should have.

As Denise became better acquainted with Mohammed and with his family's background in Pakistan, she began working with Mohammed instead of against him, to the point of teaching him about the due-diligence process so that he would provide accurate and favorable reports about the company to the real source of funds overseas. In the course of doing this Denise was able to control the content of those communications, to her ultimate advantage.

As it turned out, Mohammed was a little sloppy (for wiring money before the investment paperwork was signed), but his sloppiness was certainly something Denise could work with!

MONEY**HUNT**
RULE #19

"One Bidder Makes a
Short Auction"

MoneyHunt Hero: Francis X. O'Shaughnessy

The one-bidder rule comes into play primarily when you are pitching your company to financing sources that can provide every penny of the investment capital you need. It does not normally apply with high-income individuals, or "angels," each of whom will take only a small portion of your offering. If they are not capable of writing a check for the entire amount, the negotiation of the valuation with each individual investor will simply drive you crazy. Once you reach a deal with your first investor, you'll have to change it for the second and the third and the fourth until you have enough money rounded up to meet your needs. It is much better to pick a value and stick with it when raising funds from individual investors or anyone who can't do the whole deal.

It's not difficult to understand the logic here. When a company is in play it's a little like a piece of art at an auction house. When there are two or more bidders involved, they invariably chase the price higher and higher. The mere fact that someone else likes the piece seems to draw others out of the woodwork, egging each other on. It's a true marketplace environment and usually one that favors the seller. On the other hand, if there's only one bidder, he tends not to bid against himself and the gavel comes down fairly quickly, the single bidder getting his price. When marketing a business, an entrepreneur is often put in the spot of being auctioneer and object simultaneously. This has to be handled delicately and fairly, lest any of the bidders suspect favoritism or foul play.

The alternative is to set an asking price for a business and accept the first offer that comes close. Of course, you'll never know the true market price, the true market valuation for your company, unless you can conduct an auction between at least two qualified bidders.

TRY FOR AN AUCTION, BUT DON'T OVERDO IT

You have an auction going when your suitors are picking up cues and respecting your rules of play. For example, informing all suitors that term sheets must be in by the following Friday or they will not be accepted sends the signal that more than one term sheet is expected and that theirs should be as competitive as possible from the outset.

But beware overworking a deal—pushing the buyers so hard that both of them suspect they are not playing on a level field. Some entrepreneurs have abused the auction rule so much that some buyers will not read an auction book—a business plan they know competing firms are looking at. Stick to your word in terms of the rules of the auction and in awarding the winner.

THERE'S A LOT OF FISH IN THE OCEAN

When you are seeking your first round of financing, it is easy—way too easy—to jump at the first offer that comes your way. If you are at all insecure about your company or its future prospects, you may be tempted to think, "Oh, thank God! An investor! I'd better not lose this opportunity because God only knows if I'll find someone else if this person walks away." Thinking this way not only does you a great disservice as an entrepreneur but practically guarantees that you will sell your company for much less than it's actually worth.

Some entrepreneurs develop a cozy, complacent relationship with their existing investors, such that the entrepreneurs feel it would be unethical for them to betray these early-stage investors when they need more money. The fact, however, is that many early-stage investors (including many well-meaning ones) are not in a position, financially or otherwise, to help a company grow to the stage where it can launch an initial public offering (IPO) or be sold to a major corporation. Smaller investors tend not to have the contacts, connections, and clout in the marketplace necessary to forge a new public company. It is not betraying an investor when you successfully negotiate second-, third-, and fourth-round financings, take your company public, and enable them to cash out at a huge return on their investment!

TRY FOR AN AUCTION WHEN SELLING OUT

You should remember the auction rule as well when you are selling your business. If your company is in the $1,000,000 to $10,000,000 range in sales, what we call the "middle cap" market, you may find yourself dealing with auctioneers, agents, or so-called business brokers who will help you find prospective buyers and manage the auction. Be careful when dealing with these folks, as many of them have abused their reputations to the point where many sophisticated middle-market and small-cap (under $1,000,000 in sales) buyers will not look at their deals for fear that the prices will be sky high. Agents are, however, adept at finding new buyers in the market who don't have deep-set prejudices against auction environments.

MONEYHUNT HERO: FRANCIS X. O'SHAUGHNESSY

When Frank O'Shaughnessy arrived at our studio for his initial *MoneyHunt* interview, it seemed as if he had visualized it in quiet meditation for weeks in advance. Frank seemed to relish the one-upsmanship of *MoneyHunt* and had a quick-trigger response to every question, often adding a snide remark to demonstrate he was, or at least considered himself, the master of the situation.

To some extent, Frank's self-assurance was the product of his elite social standing and education. A Boston Brahmin and former star athlete at Phillips Exeter Academy and then Stanford University, Frank had a long-standing reputation as stubborn, self-centered, and a control freak. Fresh out of Harvard Business School he developed the idea of starting a service to enable people to order corrective lenses over the telephone. Before he even began working on his business plan, he had the foresight to reserve an easy-to-remember toll-free telephone number, 1-800-4CONTAX.

Because of the peculiar dynamics of the corrective lens market, his sales boomed. People loved the convenience of phoning their contact lens orders, especially as the new disposable lenses hit the market in the early 1990s. Most people hated showing up at the ophthalmologist to be overcharged for lenses and reminded that a semiannual exam was due. It was much easier to phone it in, give a credit-card number, and expect to receive the lenses by mail in the next few days.

At first, Frank worried that the ophthalmologists would not cooperate, fearing the loss of such a lucrative and high-margin business. He need not have worried, however, as the ophthalmologists, while not happy about Frank's new toll-free service, were more worried about the legal and other ramifications if they tried to organize to fight it.

The inbound telemarketing side of the business was relatively simple: take the order, confirm the credit, and ship the right lenses. Sales continued to grow at a rapid pace, roughly doubling each year until they reached the current rate of $26 million annually.

Then along came the Internet. Realizing early the potential of this new medium, Frank created a Web page to permit on-line orders of corrective lenses. Because of its ease of use, Frank's Web site generated more business than the toll-free telephone number.

Frank looked as if he was about eighteen months from a possible initial public offering, or IPO. So he had begun to build his management team, with a director of operations and a chief financial officer. While Frank initially was not happy about bringing his accounting team in-house, he knew that no respectable investment banking house will take the risk of an IPO unless the company has a management team that has credentials and experience in "worshiping the numbers."

Of course, Frank had plenty of models to choose from in developing his toll-free ordering business. 1-800-FLOWERS, the pioneer in the field, had been in business at least twenty years when Frank started his company. Paper Direct had done much the same for preprinted brochures and announcement papers. These and other toll-free ordering companies were carrying huge valuations in the marketplace. So it was easy for Frank to draw comparisons when first valuing his company, normally a difficult task for an early-stage company.

To understand the significance of this, think of an art auction. If the last painting in similar condition by the same artist has sold for X, his next painting (at least in theory, all things being equal) should sell for X as well. So using comparative ratios such as price to earnings, price to sales, and growth rate and comparing these to those of similar companies such as Paper Direct and 1-800-FLOWERS would result in a favorable valuation range for Frank and 1-800-4CONTAX.

Despite the overwhelmingly favorable marketplace response to Frank's business, 1-800-4CONTAX bumped along for quite some time with no real financing options other than those offered from his existing investors, who were mostly wealthy individuals. Despite the fact that his growth was meteoric, his bottom line was anemic due to high overhead (operating toll-free telephone banks is, after all, a labor-intensive business), and he had to keep raising capital to "feed the beast."

Frank's one sure source of funds was Farnsworth Group in San Francisco, a medium-sized venture-capital firm with several solid investments in consumer-products companies, but not one from the top tier of Silicon Valley. Representatives from Farnsworth sat on his board and were well aware of the issues facing Frank and his company. A letter of intent from Farnsworth for every penny (and more) Frank needed to finance his operations for the next three years was sitting on Frank's table. The Farnsworth people emphatically discouraged him from looking around for capital.

Farnsworth's motives in discouraging Frank from seeking additional capital are easy to understand. As Farnsworth had enough money in their coffers to finance the next round of financing for Frank's company, they wanted that round to be a one-bidder auction (with themselves as sole bidder). If John were to open it up to others, Farnsworth could be paying a higher price for their next round of participation.

Frank wrestled with the issue. Were the Farnsworth people undercutting him? Were they trying to hide his deal from the market—from other bidders? What was the real market? Frank would never know unless he went around Farnsworth and hired an outside agent to find out.

Frank put out feelers for second-round investors and was encouraged by the response. He mentioned the results of his informal research to the Farnsworth delegate on his board of directors and got a severe tongue-lashing for his efforts. The board member insisted that Farnsworth could never approve relations with an agent, which could make a financing look shopped. Why, the board member insisted, did Frank need an agent when Farnsworth's offer was on the table?

Frank resolved to pursue the prospects anyway and resolved not to tell the Farnsworth people what he was up to. This, of course, was a dangerous move. Rather than dealing above board with his existing investors, he went behind their backs in the hopes he would not be caught. He still controlled a majority of the issued and outstanding stock of the company, he thought, and so could easily overrule the Farnsworth people if it came to a vote. So he authorized a search for new investors without the consent of his other board members.

Frank quickly learned an important lesson about the venture-capital business, and that is how small the community is. For no sooner had Frank had his first conversations with these new prospects than news of the opportunity got back to the Farnsworth Group, who exploded, threatening to oust Frank from his management position.

Frank waited out the storm. He knew the honeymoon with Farnsworth was over; from now on they would be breathing down his neck, questioning his every action. But again, Frank reasoned, the

Farnsworth people held only a minority interest in his company. Why not see what else is out there and arrange the cheapest financing he could?

In short order, Frank had two attractive offers on his desk, one from Beta Partners, another medium-sized California venture-capital firm, and one from Centurion Capital Corporation, a "mezzanine lender" based in Michigan. (A mezzanine lender is one that provides preferred stock and/or subordinated debt financing to growing companies—their interest tends to fall midway between senior lenders such as banks and equity investors such as inside angels, management, and private investors, hence the term *mezzanine*).

Frank obtained term sheets from these two new players and shared them with the Farnsworth people, who acknowledged how attractive the terms were, particularly those for the mezzanine financing. Farnsworth agreed to match most of the terms offered by Centurion for the mezzanine financing. Nonetheless, they pressured Frank to take less of this new money and more of theirs. Frank shrewdly insisted that the Farnsworth people put their offer in writing.

No sooner had the Farnsworth proposal landed on Frank's desk than he orally shared the contents with Beta Partners and Centurion Capital, asking them to sweeten their respective offers. Frank knew that every large investor wants to invest as much money as possible in each company they deem an attractive prospect, because small investments often take as long to complete and monitor as large investments. So to a venture capitalist, getting squeezed out or making an investment as only one member of a syndicate of investors is not as attractive as having the lion's share of the offering.

Frank effectively played Farnsworth off against Beta and Centurion, and Beta and Centurion off against each other. Indeed Beta's term sheet eventually became so attractive Frank informed Centurion and Farnsworth he was about to sign it and set a closing date for one week from the signing of the term sheet.

Farnsworth was not, however, ready to quit. Having the inside track on Frank's company because of their nominee on Frank's board, the Farnsworth people reviewed the terms of the Beta deal and hinted that they might have a first-tier venture capital firm, Everest Partners, interested in making a serious investment in Frank's company.

Farnsworth sold Frank aggressively on the value of Everest Partners' expertise and its intimate relationship with the investment-banking firms that launch IPOs. The Farnsworth board member insisted that Everest would be instrumental in helping Frank build his management team by "salt and peppering" the group with talent already known to the underwriters and thereby increasing the likelihood of a successful IPO.

Interested in pursuing a relationship with Everest Partners, Frank returned to Beta Partners and asked for a few changes in their term sheet. Beta reluctantly agreed but only if the closing date—now only five days away—remained unchanged. By this time Everest Partners arrived at the offices of 1-800-4CONTAX to begin their due-diligence investigation. Frank took his latest offer from Beta and outlined it to Everest Partners, saying that he would need Everest to at least match this latest offer to consider Everest as a participant in the auction.

Surprisingly, Farnsworth, who had introduced Frank to Everest Partners, felt the new terms were too rich and exited the auction. This was an important development, as Farnsworth would have gained much more control of the board had they participated in the second round of venture financing. With a new investor coming in, however, Farnsworth's power and influence would have been diminished, leaving Frank with the largest block of stock in the company.

Everest Partners agreed to match Beta's latest offer. No sooner was the ink dry on Everest's offer, a mere two days before the scheduled closing with Beta, than Frank had his CFO call Beta and explain that 1-800-4CONTAX had selected Everest Partners as its lead investor for a second round of financing. The CFO explained that Everest was a tier-one venture-capital firm willing to match the best offer on the table and deliver excellent connections with the investment-banking firms that launch IPOs.

Frank closed the deal with Everest Partners on the day that he was supposed to have closed the deal with Beta. 1-800-4CONTAX ended up with financing, at a higher valuation than Farnsworth had used in calculating its offer, with a tier-one venture-capital firm that could introduce new managers and position the company for an IPO.

Frank's victory did not, however, come without a price. Frank had exhausted his troops in keeping three balls in the air. His CFO had been keeping the folks from Farnsworth at bay while working the numbers and entertaining Beta's, Centurion's, and Everest's dealmakers. The CFO had been the one who had given the word to Beta that their deal was on with a few changes in the term sheet. As icing on the cake, Frank assigned him the pleasure of delivering the bad news to Beta, only days before the closing. As successful as the auction was, Frank was to lose both his CFO and chief operating officer within three months.

Of course, when the prospectus for the IPO came out a year later, chock-full of management talent provided through introductions from Everest Partners, it looked like any other IPO deal. To the company's former CFO and COO, and to the auction "losers" at Farnsworth, Beta, and Centurion, Frank had abused the auction process and would never again be involved in any of their transactions.

LESSONS FROM FRANCIS X. O'SHAUGHNESSY

Frank was a master at the high-stakes game of running an auction, but he missed the fine points of dealing with integrity. It's important to generate interest in your company and play potential bidders off against one another in order to maximize value for your company, but do not overdo it or your business reputation will suffer dearly.

By taking a minority stake in 1-800-4CONTAX, Farnsworth Investors left themselves open to just the sort of manipulative behavior that Frank ultimately exhibited in order to reach his goal. Frank went behind his investor's back, risking a lawsuit for breach of fiduciary duty in the process, to find out how the market truly valued his company.

Once Farnsworth realized that it was in an auction with Beta and Centurion, it brought in a heavy hitter to improve its position with Frank, but then abruptly changed course and bowed out of the auction. The reason is not as surprising as it looks at first. Had Farnsworth stayed in the bidding war, it might have come out in a stronger position than before, with much more leverage over Frank. By bringing in a tier-one venture-capital firm that they knew (or should have known) would realize Frank's cherished dream of launching an IPO for his company, Farnsworth brought about its own exclusion from the bidding process as the tier-one firm took over the negotiations. We suspect that Farnsworth exited the auction because it decided that Frank, because of his manipulative behavior, was no longer someone they "wanted to get in trouble with," and accordingly cut their losses, bringing in the tier-one venture-capital firm to preserve the value of their investment.

Although Frank successfully negotiated the best deal he possibly could for his company with Everest Partners, his victory came at a great loss—his two most trusted senior managers (who may have suspected that Frank would shortly replace them with people recommended by Everest), his early-stage investor (who almost certainly would bad-mouth any new venture Frank chose to launch in the future), and his reputation in the venture-capital community. If it had not been for Frank's strong stock position in his own company, Frank's behavior might have had disastrous consequences for him. Instead, it had disastrous consequences for everyone around him. If you were Everest, what sort of conditions would you impose upon an investment in Frank's company?

MONEYHUNT
RULE #20

"Learn from Every No"

MoneyHunt Hero: Orrin Schimmel

So much of being successful at the capital-raising game is getting to the right person at the right time. You can scratch for weeks, even months, at the door of an investor who you think is a perfect fit for your business, but if the stars aren't aligned in your favor, you'll never see a nickel. Perhaps the investor is looking for larger deals than yours, or maybe he's looking in other industries. He may have just been burned by a recent investment in your industry. He may be out looking for a new pool of money for himself. The possibilities are endless. A no from an investor today might have been a yes six months ago, and may be a yes six months from now.

We guarantee you'll never know unless you ask.

YOU WANT TO START A BUSINESS, AND YOU'RE AFRAID OF REJECTION?

Often investors know what other investors are looking for and can refer you on. They're willing to pass you along in hopes of hearing back from the other investor on the next deal. They give and take constantly and sometimes work together. So if you're really dedicated to the hunt, don't be bashful about asking for directions here and there.

We all get tired of hearing no all the time, but it's important to realize that rejection is endemic to entrepreneurship. You must use those nos in your next pitch and preempt the questions that expose the weakness in your presentation. Nos allow you to reposition your pitch the next time and turn old weaknesses into new strengths. Each time you hear a no, don't put your tail between your legs before you've asked why. If the investor has invested the time to read the plan, he'll certainly invest a few minutes to tell you his thoughts. Although it may hurt because it was your work and you put a lot of time and energy into it, you can improve it by asking something like: If we did this differently, would it have been better? Be sure to let him know that you're not doing this to change his mind. You're doing this to improve your presentation next time and move on with this knowledge. He of course can help, and if he gives you a few references of folks that may be interested, be sure to not only thank him but to use his name when calling your new prospects.

BUT DON'T FORGET THAT WHERE THERE'S SMOKE THERE'S OFTEN FIRE

Be aware that hearing too many emphatic nos may be a sign that shouldn't be ignored. At a certain point, if you're not able to reposition around nos to improve your presentation, you may well have a bloody "no-hoper" on your hands that isn't worthy of outside financing. At that point it's worth considering saving the house and the family harmony. It's one thing to pull in others on a risky venture, but when all the risk is yours, it's a whole new ball game.

WHEN YOU DON'T GET WHAT YOU WANT, GET AN EDUCATION

Entrepreneurs dodge this rule all the time, usually in two ways. One way is simply to ignore nos without getting to reasons why you are hearing them. Many entrepreneurs say to themselves, "Well, I guess the fit just wasn't right here. Oh, well. Better luck next time." There may well not be better luck next time if you don't ask precisely why the fit wasn't right. Sticking your head in the sand in the interest of bucking up your self-esteem may make you feel good in the short term, but long term you're going to wonder why every time you look in the palms of your hands, there's nothing in them.

The other common way entrepreneurs dodge this rule is to take nos too seriously and interpret them as a definitive judgment on their business plan. Sometimes no is no merely because of the timing of the sales pitch, because it is uttered by an investor who has no cash on hand to make new investments, because it is uttered by a junior partner who doesn't have the authority to tie his shoelaces without writing an interoffice memo, or because it is uttered by a person who is having a bad hair day. Walking away from a perfectly sound business plan because you take no as a personal indictment is pretty silly, in our humble opinion.

MONEYHUNT HERO: ORRIN SCHIMMEL

Orrin Schimmel's company was in the computer-security software field, a quite interesting and valuable little niche in the multibillion-dollar computer software market. For multiple-terminal computer installations (such as personal-computer networks), Orrin had invented a piece of software that sat on a server terminal and inventoried all of the terminals on the network. If a terminal was removed, it would be the equivalent of an open switch, and an alarm went off, silent or audible as the user chose. It sure beat the hell out of locks and reinforced wire, which were never much of a match for a hacksaw.

Orrin introduced his product at a time when theft of computers from multiple-terminal installations such as universities, laboratories, and corporate headquarters facilities was escalating out of control and costing millions of dollars a year. Yet, there never was any software to monitor security on these networks.

Despite the huge losses major corporations face in lost computer hardware, Orrin had an uphill battle in persuading information systems (IS) executives at large companies to buy his software solution. Orrin had to first graphically demonstrate to each potential customer the need for his product and then attempt to make the sale.

At first, Orrin admits with a chuckle, he was "something of an ambulance chaser," researching computer-hardware thefts from major corporations and universities and conveniently making a call shortly thereafter, when awareness was high. Luckily, Princeton University happened to see Orrin's appearance on MoneyHunt and made a major purchase, which gave his company credibility and led to several other sales.

Investors, however, were a little more skeptical than customers. Orrin's first pitch was to a group of angel investors in town. His business plan was fairly well developed, and his presentation was by all means quite compelling. But he ran into an incredible string of nos. It started with doctor friends of his father who were polite but had a host of excuses. It then moved on to the country club. Again, his father's suggestion. Again, nos. Orrin then moved his quest for capital to the alumni association of his business school. Thumbs down, again. At the recommendation of one of his business school professors, he did a presentation to three or four members of a local angel group (an informal club of high-income individuals who regularly make investments in small start-up and early-stage companies). He seemed to have their interest until time for the big question. Then they all scurried away, changing the subject and making excuses. No again.

Nearing exasperation after three hard months of pitching his software concept, Orrin cornered one of the angels in the hallway on the way out of a "no-no" meeting (as he came to call them). Orrin was firm, saying that he had heard enough nos and at this point wanted to know why.

Surprisingly, the investor was quite candid and more than willing to help with advice, although not with dollars. "Your company needs more money than we can provide," the angel said. The angel explained that most angel groups are good for amounts between a few hundred thousand and maybe up to a million or so. Orrin knew that if his business was going to be successful, he was clearly going to need three to four million dollars in capital in relatively short order. The angels, for their part, were faced with the prospect of having a successful, growing business run out of money that they couldn't pony up.

Orrin drove home with mixed emotions. He had spent three months pitching his company at investors and only recently had learned that he was barking up the wrong tree. So he set his sights on several large-capital funds in the area, knowing that it would take a little more detail in his business plan. He spent an extra month, now his fifth, to fine-tune the marketing section and the financials. Through an introduction from the last angel who had given his input, he set up meetings. Through his sixth and seventh month he thought he had generated some interest from a few of the venture capitalists in the area. After sending in his books, he got called in for meetings, pitched, and had calls back with follow-up questions. These were all good signs. But the communication began to get strung out and broken down after that.

Orrin could see the writing on the wall. He called back and pressed each of them for answers and wasn't surprised to get four successive nos in a row. As with the angels, Orrin felt he couldn't take it anymore and began asking what was needed to make the plan financeable. The first venture-capital firm's reaction was short and crisp—"You need a more professional management team." Orrin had never run a business before. Orrin accepted that and did not press for further information. He then went to the second venture-capital firm and asked, "If professional managers were brought to the table, whom would you like to see?" Then the third: "What exactly is needed on my management team—sales experience, operating experience, product development?" Finally, after conducting information interviews with the venture-capital firms that had said no and wanted to get Orrin off the phone, Orrin deduced the following: Hiring a professional manager with prior operating experience in a venture-backed company with industry experience in technology and software would dramatically increase the likelihood of finding financing at this level.

Orrin resolved that he needed a "gray head" with operating experience. His search for that individual was just as challenging as pitching to the venture-capital firms. Résumés were easy to get, but the responses came back fairly quickly:

- No, the company is too small, I'm more accustomed to managing more people.

- No, I want to be sure I can draw a salary day one.

- No, I need the security of a larger company that's backed by a major venture-capital firm before I will risk my time.

This was a critical juncture, and Orrin began to put two and two together. He could provide the security of a venture-backed company if indeed he had the entrepreneur with the operating credentials to assuage the venture-capital firms' concerns. So he zeroed in on his top candidate, Mark, and explained the situation. Orrin felt there were two or three venture-capital firms in the area that would be interested in the property if it came along with the résumé of an entrepreneur with operating credentials.

When he returned to the same venture-capital firms that had once said no and announced that he might have a solution, there was some interest. As a matter of fact the partner of one firm volunteered that if Mark had some significant equity in Orrin's company (the exact phrase he used was "if Mark had some skin in the deal"), he might well consider the plan to have new merit.

This is an important point. Having a talented executive with real risk in the deal besides his time is a compelling sign for other venture capitalists to consider backing the company. So Orrin returned to Mark, mapped out the venture-capital support that he thought he could gain with Mark's presence, and cut a deal. Now he returned to the venture-capital firms that had said no so emphatically four months ago. But this time he returned with his new soon-to-be chief operating officer, Mark, in tow. Orrin, with Mark's coaching, had practiced their presentation over and over again and had clearly mapped out responsibilities so there was no confusion about who would be doing what.

The presence of the new talent with excellent operating credentials was enough to gain the interest of the one venture-capital firm that had helped point Orrin in the right direction. Eleven months after writing his first business plan and making his first pitch, Orrin closed the financing with the venture-capital firm for two million dollars, an extra half million thrown in by his new chief operating officer, Mark, and an extra quarter million by the angel that had said no eight months earlier.

Orrin didn't need that last quarter million, but he figured he owed the guy.

LESSONS FROM ORRIN SCHIMMEL

During the nine months from his first business plan to the closing of his first investment, Orrin heard more nos than many of us hear in a lifetime. It would have been easy for him to throw in the towel, and indeed he almost did. Orrin was close to being utterly frustrated with financing his business and was considering going back to school for a Ph.D. or going to work for someone else.

A combination of factors turned him around, but it was ultimately his belief in his product that led him to finally get up the courage to ask about all of the rejections. He quickly learned it wasn't personal—that investors see deals every day and can't afford the time to mentor everyone who comes along. Orrin also learned that they were willing to help and refer him to other places as long as he didn't pressure them to do so or pressure them to invest once he had corrected the perceived negatives.

Orrin also had to be willing to give up control of the operations of his business relatively early in the game. For many entrepreneurs this is a difficult pill to swallow, but Orrin truly believed that his business needed more capital than he was able to raise and that bringing in a partner with excellent credentials would allow him to raise that money. Orrin learned well from each one of the nos he got and improved his presentation and his chances each time.

Rejection is so much a part of entrepreneurs' lives that it's in the air they breathe every day. Given that, it's best to learn from it and make yourself stronger or it will bury you.

Note, for example, the way in which Orrin overcame sales resistance from his prospective clients. Selling a new solution to an old problem is often a difficult sell, especially when the customer is a large institution—such as a major corporation or university—that is slow to accept change. Orrin's "ambulance chasing"—waiting until a widely publicized theft occurred and then calling the affected institution to pitch his software—may have been crude, but it was effective. It was hard for an executive facing a room full of cut wires and empty terminals to argue that he didn't need a better antitheft solution for his computer equipment.

Orrin eventually realized he could ask questions about the rejections he was receiving without getting his head bitten off. Quiet and unassuming by nature, Orrin found it difficult to ask these kinds of questions because he was afraid of wasting a prospective investor's time. Far from perceiving him as a time waster, most of the angels and venture-capital firms he asked for advice freely gave it. Most of us like being looked up to, and it's a turn-on when someone honestly and sincerely asks us for advice. As one of our grandmothers once said, "If you don't ask, you don't get."

Once you understand what the market wants, you have to give it, even if you don't agree with it at first. The unanimous feedback Orrin received from the venture capital firms—that he needed to bring on more qualified management—was at first difficult for him to swallow, as it meant giving up some control of his company. Calculating that the opportunity for financial growth far outstripped any dilution of his equity, Orrin bit the bullet and did the right thing.

PART SIX

The Legal Side of Business

MONEYHUNT
RULE #21

"In Litigation There Are No Winners"

Money Hunt Hero: Herbert Sperry

W hen someone has done you wrong, it's very tempting to "sue the bastards!" You may think that in every courtroom case there is a winner and a loser. Wrong! There are two losers. Getting involved in a lawsuit saps time, energy, and money and can affect your market reputation, even if you are completely in the right, and even if you ultimately win the case. Avoid lawsuits whenever possible or, if you can't avoid them, push for a quick settlement that allows you to fight another day.

IT'S TOUGH TO SWALLOW YOUR ANGER, BUT YOU MUST

It's difficult not to react emotionally when somebody has "done you wrong" in the business world—breached a contract, committed a fraud, swindled you out of your hard-earned cash. It's even tougher not to react emotionally when a strange-looking fellow shows up at your doorstep one day and serves you with a summons and complaint—the documents that tell you that you are being sued because someone else thinks you have breached a contract, committed a fraud, or swindled them out of their hard-earned cash. Most entrepreneurs fly off the handle, especially if they feel they are in the right, and especially if they correctly believe they are in the right. Being fighters by nature, too many entrepreneurs call their lawyers and say something like, "We are fighting these bastards to the very death!"

Emotional reactions, however, can kill successful businesses. This is one place where being emotional can really put an end to your success.

A FAMOUS CASE INVOLVING TWO COUNTRY SQUIRES

In the first year of law school, most students read a famous case named *Pierson v. Post*. Set in bucolic upstate New York in the early 1800s, the case involved a local aristocrat who, with several inebriated friends and a pack of bloodthirsty dogs, were chasing a fox across a neighbor's land. The neighbor, himself in charge of an inebriated crew of horn-blowing hunters in red coats and barking beagles, caught and killed the fox. The issue in the case, believe it or not, was: Which of the two aristocrats was entitled to keep the fox pelt? The first aristocrat—who flushed the fox, raised the "hue and cry" (it's amazing how many common everyday terms had their origin in fox hunting), and gave chase? Or the second aristocrat—who cornered, caught, and killed the fox? The first aristocrat argued that the fox was a "wild creature" and did not belong to the owner of any land. The second aristocrat argued that the first aristocrat was trespassing, that the fox's burrow was located on the second aristocrat's land, and . . . well, you get the picture.

The important thing in the case of *Pierson v. Post* was not the outcome, however. It turned out these two neighbors never really cared for each other much anyway, and the fox pelt case gave them the excuse to really go at it. The case dragged on in court for almost twenty-five years, forced one of the litigants to sell his property to pay the legal fees, and drove the other into bankruptcy. Each litigant spent the equivalent of over $250,000 in today's money to determine the true ownership of a fox pelt worth, at the time, about $10. By the time the case was settled both litigants were resting uncomfortably in their graves, and the people showing up in court to fight the case didn't even know who the people on the other side of the room were.

Things in the legal world have only gotten worse since the days of *Pierson v. Post*. In America today, it's the easiest thing in the world to start a lawsuit. All you need is a dollar and a lawyer willing to take the case. Once started, though, lawsuits develop lives of their own, and it's often next to impossible to stop them without running up large bills.

DO YOU REALLY LIKE LAWYERS ENOUGH TO WANT TO MAKE THEM RICH?

Some entrepreneurs are so indignant and vindictive they will launch into commando mode at every wrong, or perceived wrong, they suffer in the course of building their business. They are a lawyer's dream client, and an investor's nightmare. People who feel the need to "fight for the right, without question or pause," who are willing to "march into hell for a heavenly cause" (in the words of the Broadway musical *Man of La Mancha*) end up making no one rich except the lawyers.

Sometimes entrepreneurs pretend that lawsuits don't exist. It's hard to believe, but some entrepreneurs have difficulty acknowledging and accepting the fact that they are being sued. They figure that if they just put it on a "back burner" and let the lawyers seek postponement after postponement, deposition after deposition, sooner or later the bloody nuisance will just disappear. Meanwhile the legal bills keep coming in every month, slowly increasing in amount, until the entrepreneur needs to go to a full-blown trial and a judgment just to recover the legal fees he's paid over the years.

Sometimes, even when you are in the right, it is best to confront a lawsuit directly and seek a quick settlement out of court that will save face for both sides and, most importantly, stop the legal meter from running.

Get It Behind You Quickly, at All Costs

Remember this rule at the first sign of legal trouble, be it a thinly veiled letter from a lawyer accusing you of this or that or the realization that someone may be ripping off one of your patents. Whatever the thunderbolt, get on it. Get to the bottom of it, learn whether your legal position is a strong or a weak one, and use that information to forge a settlement at the earliest possible time.

Whenever bad things happen to your company, count to a hundred, or even a hundred thousand, before you call your lawyer. Weigh carefully the pros and cons of litigation and look for a business solution to the problem. When there is no other alternative, swallow your pride and get on with your life.

Most importantly, if you absolutely must spend money on lawyers (Cliff has to make a living somehow, after all), spend it on finding ways to avoid legal problems before they happen. Many business lawyers actually hate litigation as much as you do and will work with you to develop internal procedures and disciplines that will minimize the risk of lawsuits in the early stages of your company's life.

MoneyHunt Hero: Herbert Sperry

Herbert Sperry was probably the first entrepreneur we'd ever seen at the studio who didn't come with a type A personality, but Herbert's cool demeanor in the studio belied the trouble his business was in back home. Many years ago, collaborating with his then wife, Herbert had designed a unique line of bed-and-bath accessories that soon found their way into upscale catalogs and upscale bedrooms throughout many of the affluent communities on the East and West Coasts. One product in particular, a bedside light that allowed someone to read a book while their spouse slept calmly in the same bed, was a natural solution to a real market need.

Herbert had obtained a patent for the light and was the first out in the marketplace with this product. This gave him a tremendous advantage, and soon his reader's nightlight was a smashing success. The marketing of the product was fairly straightforward. From his days as a flight attendant for a major airline, Herbert knew that the upscale passengers in first class and business class (an attractive demographic for any entrepreneur) were a captive audience who read their in-flight magazines cover to cover, including the ads. So he inserted ads for his book light in in-flight magazines, and, sure enough, his return came to almost twenty times his investment in the medium.

Herbert also made his way into bookstores, discount stores, and a variety of other retail outlets. The product was well received everywhere and sold through much better than one would expect from a first product. Barnes & Noble, which had ordered 100,000 units initially, was reordering 25,000 units a month to restock, and sell-through (the number of units ordered less returns) was three times their expectations. Surprisingly, the book light product also did well at computer stores, including CompUSA and Egghead Software.

Life was great. After having started the business on credit cards, it looked as if Herbert was building something that could sustain his relatively modest lifestyle and his family in a way that he had only dreamed of before. But it wasn't just the profits. The benefits of being in business, especially when traveling, made trips much more enjoyable than traveling as an individual. His frequent trips crisscrossing the country gained him valuable frequent-flyer miles, and his overseas trips were rarely taken in less than business class. He got to see a lot of different cities in the United States and many different countries in the world that he would never have imagined being able to visit. It was all part of doing business and, best of all, it was all deductible (you can bet Herbert was looking at the magazines other people were reading during the flight, to determine how to best position his product).

It was during one of these business trips to Hong Kong that Herbert quite unexpectedly came across the product that made him break out in a cold sweat.

One of his overseas manufacturing representatives had asked to meet him in his hotel and review a couple of other potential products that he might sell in the United States. They met in the hotel lobby and, after the customary Oriental greetings and small talk, Chin Yueh-shih (pronounced "yr-shr") pulled out the sample case that he wanted to show to Herbert. By accident, Chin Yueh-shih's briefcase also yielded a low-priced Taiwanese knockoff of Herbert's now world-famous book light.

When Herbert saw it and picked it up, he wasn't shocked, thinking it was his own. But when he realized it was a knockoff, something snapped inside Herbert. He confronted Chin Yueh-shih then and there, and the latter, having lost face, came clean immediately and admitted that this actually was produced from a mold that had been stolen from the plant Herbert used for his manufacturing and combined with schematic drawings pilfered from the same factory.

As it was his last day in the Far East, Herbert decided not to confront immediately the Asian manufacturers who had allowed this to happen. He returned home, but he soon regretted his decision. Within the next six months his newly formed Taiwanese competition had dramatically undercut the market with poorly packaged book lights sold at 50 percent of the price Herbert had been offering. Herbert's suppliers were up in arms that he could be charging so much for something that was available for so much less in such huge quantities.

Herbert attempted to describe the situation to each one of the major distributors who carried his book light, explaining how he was being undercut in the market and how his patent was being infringed upon. The distributors clucked in sympathy, but the bottom line was that there was a comparable product available to them at half the price in good quantity.

Herbert started losing business almost immediately upon the release of the Taiwanese knockoffs in the United States. Because Herbert did not have a diversified product line, the loss of business spelled disaster for his company.

This unfortunate incident also had the effect of whipsawing his efforts to raise additional funds for expansion. He had originally pulled together his business plan expecting to raise more dollars for additional product development and additional marketing for his existing product line, but soon money raising became a monumental struggle. Herbert saw a stream of potential investors, many of whom were introduced to him during long flights in business class to Asia and Australia, and everything went smoothly until he talked about his need to pursue the Asian knockoffs in court. Lawsuits or potential lawsuits against patent infringers are simply not a good use of proceeds for an investor, and the investors told him so.

Eventually, Herbert realized he could wait no longer. He took some of his own working capital and filed patent-infringement suits against the Taiwanese companies that were ripping off his product. The litigators he hired advised him that it would take a minimum of two to three years unless the case was settled out of court. Herbert, relying perhaps too much on his principles and not enough on the pragmatic issues of running a business, pushed forward with the lawsuit as a first business priority, using up his precious working capital. Herbert regretted not having taken money earlier in the process at lower valuations, but at the time things looked good and he felt he could hold out for higher prices.

One important question Herbert forgot to ask was the financial wherewithal of the Asian defendants. It turned out that the two principal companies that were knocking off Herbert's products were start-ups themselves, poorly financed and even more poorly managed, that could not have afforded to pay a judgment even if Herbert won the patent-infringement suits quickly and decisively. Had Herbert known this he could have pushed for an early settlement and a face-saving agreement that would have preserved the integrity of his principal product without forcing the Asians into bankruptcy.

Herbert hunkered down to a long, hard fight with no excess cash in the business and barely enough to pay his lawyers to keep the case going. It kept spiraling downward from there. Legal fees mounted, his time shrank, he advertised less and less, which meant fewer sales, less margin, and of course less money for his legal bills. He had no idea what he had started, or how draining the whole process would become.

Within a year and a half of first discovering the book light knockoff in Chin Yueh-shih's briefcase, Herbert had shrunk his sales by 50 percent, was doing virtually no advertising, barely had enough to draw a reduced salary, and seemed to be sending twenty cents on every dollar to his lawyers. He had all but given up looking for money from outside investors and had just resigned himself to hanging on for as long as it took to win a case, in the hopes that the attendant publicity of a big win against Asian knockoffs would jump-start his operations and get him back on track again.

The last time we looked, Herbert was still waiting.

LESSONS FROM HERBERT SPERRY

The world of entrepreneurship frequently presents you with hard choices. It is hard to envy the choices Herbert had when he discovered his book light was being knocked off in violation of his patent. On the one hand, if he didn't defend his rights and pursue the Asian knockoff manufacturers in some fashion, the latter would take over the market and force Herbert's company out of business. On the other hand, by defending his rights and pursuing the Asian manufacturers, he risked declining sales and mounting legal bills, which would eventually threaten to bankrupt his company. In deciding whether or not to sue, Herbert was truly damned if he did and damned if he didn't.

A third choice was open to him, although it would have been difficult for him to accept. This would have involved approaching the Asian manufacturers directly, notifying them of the infringement, and working out some sort of strategic alliance with them so that they would become suppliers or contract manufacturers for Herbert's products. Given that the Asian companies were themselves poorly financed start-ups, such an offer of a guaranteed American market for their product would have been very attractive to them and could have been a win-win solution for both sides.

Accepting such a solution, however, would have required Herbert to put aside his anger at having been knocked off. That is hard to do, for any of us.

Consider, first of all, Herbert's decision (whether consciously or through inertia) not to diversify his product line. Relying for his entire revenue and margin on a single product that did not involve high technology, Herbert took a huge risk that someone, someday, would find a way to circumvent his patent and compete with him. Sure enough, somebody did.

Next, Herbert assumed that everyone hates knockoffs and would gladly join him in his fight to regain control of his markets. Herbert learned the hard way that when customers see a significant discount being offered by a competitor for a commodity product with no value-added services attached, even a poorly manufactured knockoff, customer loyalty frequently goes out the window. Ask any local hardware-store owner who's had to go head-to-head with Wal-Mart or Home Depot.

Next, Herbert decided not to meet the Asian knockoff manufacturers immediately, on their turf. Bad mistake. Doing so would have given Herbert the opportunity to craft a win-win solution, something his pleasant personality and easygoing manner might have handily accomplished. By giving the Asian manufacturers time to establish an American beachhead for the knockoff product, Herbert undercut any advantage he may have initially had in light of the Asians' poor financial condition.

Finally, Herbert's decision not to build a "war chest" before embarking on the infringement suit gave him no alternative but to use up his precious working capital fighting a battle that could ultimately have no winner. Although it would have been difficult, Herbert would have been better advised to use his dwindling cash to develop or buy a new product whose sales could make up for the revenue loss from book light sales.

MONEYHUNT
RULE #22

"People Make Agreements, Not Vice Versa"

MoneyHunt Hero: Peter Tcherakis

When you are starting in business for the first time, it is easy to assume that once you have a written agreement with someone, that agreement will govern your working relationship. While sometimes that is true, often (we would say most of the time) written agreements have nothing to do with the way you will actually do business with someone.

To have workable agreements with other people, you need to be on solid ground with the other people, and there need to be commitments and benefits that run both ways, for the more one-sided a deal (even if it's one-sided in your favor), the more likely it is that the other side will starting looking for ways to exit the relationship gracefully.

TICKETS TO A COURTROOM

In our live presentations around the country, Cliff often refers to written contracts as "tickets to a courtroom"—great insofar as they clear up ambiguities and detail points in the relationship between two or more companies, but lousy if you expect them to enforce themselves. "A contract, even a well-drafted one, is only as good as your willingness to spend years of your lives and tens if not hundreds of thousands of dollars in treasure making them stick," Cliff points out.

Cliff adds, "Whenever I close a deal, almost the very last thing I say to the parties (before collecting my check, of course) is a little benediction—'May you never look at these pieces of paper ever again.' People laugh when I say this, and they sometimes ask, 'Yeah, right—so why did we spend all this money having a written agreement in the first place?' My response is simple: 'Think of it this way. When you leave the conference room today, you are going to put these pieces of paper in a drawer, where they will gather dust and nothing else. Don't tell me you plan to look at them to find out how you should be conducting your business affairs! When it comes time to make decisions you will do whatever seems right at the time, and you won't even glance at these contracts.

"The only time," Cliff continues, "that you will ever even look for these pieces of paper and call me on the telephone is when one of you, or perhaps both of you, decides it's time to get out and you want to know how to go about doing that with a minimum of legal liability."

BREACHES OF CONTRACT ARE PART OF THE BUSINESS

Aside from the fact that good contracts do not make good business relationships, it's important to recognize that breaches of contract are part of the business world. Suppose you do have a written agreement with someone who then brazenly violates one of the terms, taking the risk that you won't sue them? Well, contracts are not self-enforcing. You have a terrific cause of action, but you will have to spend thousands of dollars and years of your life getting a judgment in your favor. Without any guarantee you will indeed get one. And then when you do get your judgment, you may have to enforce it against someone who doesn't have two nickels to rub together. If someone across the country buys something from you for $100 and his check bounces, most lawyers will tell you it isn't even worth the time and bother to try to collect it.

Our legal system does not put people in jail for breaches of contract. On the contrary, judges since at least the 1700s have recognized that it is sometimes necessary to breach a contract to avoid economic disaster. When someone breaches a contract, your recourse is to sue for damages—the difference between what you actually got out of the contract and what you would have gotten if the contract had been fully performed on both sides. Rarely will you get punitive damages, or recovery of your legal fees, in breach-of-contract cases.

If you are planning to start a business, you will have to get used to the idea that some of the people you will deal with will not honor their contracts, even the ones in writing.

MoneyHunt Hero: Peter Tcherakis

We heard it from our female staffers long before he walked into the green room for our initial interview: Peter Tcherakis was "Hollywood handsome." Tan, tall, with a pearly white smile, he struck us as a cross between Ted Turner of CNN and Roger Moore in the James Bond movies of our youth. Except better looking. He was the sort of guy you'd expect to step off a hundred-foot yacht on the Costa Smeralda wearing an ascot and $500 Bermuda shorts.

We had heard that, true to his image, he lived quite a carefree life and had settled in the media business only when he was in his late thirties, in a sales capacity. It was clear, in the two minutes we spent in the green room, that Peter played at the highest level. He went first class all the way, from his suits to the quality of his videotaped product demonstration, and Peter made one hell of a presenter.

Peter's business was an exciting one, especially for a media-driven, sports-crazed society like ours. His company, Golf TV, was the ultimate how-to television network for those who love the game of golf—part instructional (tips from the pros), part travel (the one hundred—no, make that two hundred—best golf courses worldwide), part entertainment (celebrity interviews, golf trivia game shows), and part sports (live telecasts of every major U.S. and international golf classic, with repeats during the graveyard hours for those who videotape first and read the results later). Peter was capitalizing on the golf craze and the growing desire among affluent Americans in pastel-colored pants to shave strokes off their scores.

Peter had developed a series of thirty-minute television shows to provide the initial programming for his new network. But television was only the tip of the iceberg. Peter realized, as surprisingly few media entrepreneurs do, that television is more profitable as a marketing medium than it is as an end product. Soon Peter launched a very successful Web site structured around the show, with magazine and newsletter sections (strictly pay by subscription, of course), golf-related travel sections, instructional clinics, and on-line chat communities of golfers.

To Peter's credit, and our amazement, Peter had put the whole thing together on a shoestring budget. In the early 1990s this type of business was just beginning to find favor with the investor community, as new niche media companies with CD-ROM and Internet products were starting to extend their brands across the landscape and reap tremendous profits through the domination of their respective niches. Martha Stewart was fast becoming the how-to maven for homemakers worldwide. Bob Vila had done it and done it well for the home improvement set. Millions and millions of dollars were being made through the launches of these brands, and it was easy to see how Golf TV might have a chance to do the same.

While the concept may gross out some of our more delicate readers, investors have a pet nickname for companies like this—"saliva pump"—meaning that all you have to do is get your idea across and hard-to-sell investors start falling like dominoes in a Tampa Bay hurricane.

Now we knew that in a business like Peter's distribution is key. No matter how good your Nielsen ratings, no matter how many cable awards your programs garner each year, no matter how instructional, no matter how "must have" the information, no matter how large the potential audience . . . if no one sees it, you are dead in the water.

Beyond that, a continuous stream of programming is crucial to building an audience and a community. You don't just launch one program and see how it flies—you must build a pipeline of at least two seasons' worth of shows. (Are you beginning to see, by the way, why we were probably the toughest critics this guy ever faced?) It was a big boys' game, and big boys had come to dominate the business.

Peter had built his distribution on the back of a loose affiliation of regional cable television stations. His launch had gone better than expected, but he was looking to move up to a higher level and thought he had found the perfect partner for doing so. Ever mindful of the tight community of broadcasters, where everyone knows everyone else and gossip travels fast, he first asked consent from his existing distribution partners to proceed. Having obtained it with little trouble (again, those teeth), Peter was soon meeting with the vice president of the largest cable station group (called a multiple system operator, or MSO) in the country.

Richard Schechter was oddly detached for someone who was the decision maker of a large media group. At his first meeting with Peter, Peter noticed that Richard's eyes shifted nervously throughout the room whether he was listening or talking. He seemed always to be looking for the reaction of others more than listening to what was being said and by whom. Richard was well informed for the meeting, having clearly done his homework on Peter's business plan, but eerily soft-spoken.

Accordingly, Peter interpreted him as someone who would play everything safe. Peter's staff took its cue from Richard and proceeded with caution as well. Little did Peter realize that this was the modus operandi for the entire group—the culture in which this particular organization operated—and it would be a critical factor in future developments.

Peter was at his best during that initial meeting. He was able to draw out the fact that there was currently no golf programming at all in Richard's group besides coverage from live events, which Peter pointed out could easily be programmed into the new channel. Peter deftly outlined how the derivative business—merchandising, the Internet site, CD-ROM golf instructional products, books, and audiotapes—was promising.

Peter knew, as did Richard, that the demographics of golfers are among the most desirable in the entire world of advertising. There are golfers and would-be golfers (called hackers by those who don't consider themselves part of the group) who would be prone to buying books, magazines, CD-ROMs, instructional videos, and planned vacations to the great golf courses, all organized or sponsored by Golf TV, which would collect a few pennies every time the cash register rang.

Since Peter was walking into Richard's station group a proven commodity because of the well-publicized success of the cable channel in its trial season, a deal was quickly arranged and a term sheet drawn up. Peter still had some misgivings about working with Richard, but everything was proceeding and he chalked up his anxiety to just the personality differences that make the world go round. Shortly after the term sheet was first put on Peter's desk, Peter looked at it quickly and within a day or two, after a cursory legal review by an attorney and avid golfer friend of Peter's, the contract was signed, sealed, and delivered.

Buoyed by his success, Peter left on a brief vacation, confident that Golf TV was going to take off and make everyone rich.

All was not as it had seemed. In fact, the very stations that Peter had first worked with—the ones whose consent Peter had sought to make sure they would stay on board if Golf TV moved on to the next level— realized that Peter would actually not be staying with them. They began shooting down Golf TV at cable television conventions and media gatherings, in a classic case of sour grapes: "If I can't have it, you can't have it either."

Sure enough, the marketplace venom made its way back to Richard and rattled him. He valued his relations with the other stations above anything sacred in the media world and wondered quietly whether his new deal with Golf TV would ruin his relations with all these people. He called in the others who had been in the meeting with Golf TV to feel them out on the issue. Richard's head of sales expressed his concern that Peter had been selling advertisers for three times the rate that his sales force could ever get. Richard called in his head of distribution and realized he could do no better than Golf TV had already done in its first season.

Richard was quickly realizing that no matter how well he performed under his agreement, he was up against the specter of overpromising and underperforming and never holding the trump cards (such as exclusive access) that so many distributors hold when seeking to control the destiny of programs. There and then he realized he had to get rid of the deal, and get rid of it any way he could.

Peter was snorkeling in the Bahamas, getting his head together for the challenges of the oncoming season when he got an urgent fax message delivered to his beachside cabana. It was from Richard on company letterhead, and it said, in brief, "We have decided to terminate our contract because we were not fully informed of all the circumstances regarding Golf TV at the time we executed."

Peter was beside himself. A new partner was trying to terminate a written contract for reasons with no basis in fact or law. He ran over it a thousand times in his mind and each time could come up with nothing logical to explain Richard's actions. The one thing that was clear was the fatality of the blow. Without distribution he had no program. With no program he had no brand. Without a brand he had no business. He was finished. At this point Peter could have let it lie and spent his time developing alternatives, but it's very difficult to be so objective after being in the middle of the negotiations and having been so ecstatic at the completion of the contract. So he did what he felt was logical, hiring first-rate lawyers with extremely powerful connections in the telecommunications industry who immediately began ranting and raving and preparing a lawsuit for service to Richard and his company.

Despite entreaties from Peter for a follow-up meeting, Richard wouldn't budge from his position and wouldn't listen to Peter's warnings of what prolonged litigation could do to Richard's company. Richard wanted out of the deal—that was it—no explanations or arguments. When pressed by Peter, Richard did mention one or two grounds for termination, but Peter replied that in anyone's view they were not "material" breaches of the contract and could have easily been resolved with a little bit of due diligence or a simple telephone call to his new partner. Peter accused Richard of wanting to take the easy way out, and Richard did not deny it.

Nothing Peter had said in his several earlier meetings with Richard was a misrepresentation. Richard simply hadn't done his homework. Richard also had been surprised by some of the realities of the deal when these were pointed out to him by his in-house attorney. So if Peter sued and won, Richard's caution might well cost him his job and his company some $50 million. Richard, though, was taking a calculated gamble that Peter would not sue. To do that, Peter would put himself out of business. News of the lawsuit would spread like wildfire throughout the tightly woven television broadcasting community. Who would broadcast a pro- gram—much less an entire network—from a producer who sued its dis- tribution channel? It would mean hundreds of thousands of dollars in legal fees for Golf TV, and years of time trying the case and hearing the appeal. It would be a mess. Peter would be out of business, owing hun- dreds of thousands of dollars to his lawyers and probably would be locked out of the TV business forever. "Not worth the risk," Peter muttered over a mai tai at the bar (the first of several) as he pondered the outline process and imagined scenarios of what might happen next.

So the deal had become one Richard no longer wished to honor. Although, legally speaking, Richard had signed his name and committed his company, no argument—moral, legal, or financial—would dissuade him. Walking away from the agreement would put Peter and his compa- ny back at square one, since in addition to selling his concept, Peter now would have to explain what happened at Richard's media group.

Peter's alternative choice—enforcing the contract in what lawyers call a "specific performance action" where, if successful, Peter could have forced Richard to honor the contract as written—was even worse. Such a lawsuit would make Peter's company a pariah in media circles through- out the world. Even in the remote chance that Peter won and the judge told Richard's media group to comply, Richard's compliance would not bring with it the enthusiasm and commitment that Peter had hoped his new partners would bring to the deal—Richard's media group would do only the bare legal minimum required to avoid a contempt citation from the judge.

With pain in his heart, nursing the hangover of all hangovers, Peter dropped the entire matter and returned to the United States to fight another day.

LESSONS FROM PETER TCHERAKIS

People make agreements, not the other way around. When people want to, they keep the agreements they sign. As an entrepreneur with a grow- ing business, you shouldn't think that a piece of paper will keep some- one sharp if they don't see a win for their side to motivate them. A piece of paper requiring someone to perform in a certain way is only good if a judge says it is—written contracts are enforceable only to the extent the parties are willing to throw good money and years of their lives at win- ning a favorable judgment.

Integrity and a moral code are much better binding factors in a deal than any lawyer's clause anywhere. Be sure you feel that way about the people you sign contracts with, because no piece of paper will keep you together if you both aren't 100 percent committed to making the relationship happen. Breaches of contract are a part of the business world.

Believe it or not, although Peter's troubles were caused by Richard's breach of a written agreement, Peter neglected to get a written agreement he needed to have. When Peter approached his existing cable "carriage" stations and asked if they would mind if he looked for greener pastures for Golf TV, the stations clearly told Peter whatever he wanted to hear. In their hearts, they believed that Peter would not be successful, so it would be a no-lose proposition for them to humor Peter and say, in effect, "Oh sure, go ahead. We realize you're a growing company and need to move on. We'll tell people someday that we knew you when." Yeah, right. Peter could have given himself more leverage by getting a simple, one-page agreement from each of the stations giving their consent in writing and including a "no disparagement" clause that would prevent the stations from badmouthing Peter's company in the marketplace down the road. With such an agreement, Peter could have threatened legal action against the individual cable television stations if he even heard rumors that one of them was badmouthing Golf TV. Even though you don't really intend to enforce it, a threat of costly and time-consuming litigation can be effective leverage to make the bad guys behave the way you want them to.

When Peter signed the agreement with Richard, he should have asked himself (or his attorney, who gave the agreement only a cursory review at Peter's request), "What happens under this thing if Richard gets uncomfortable and wants to head for the exits?" As Cliff points out, that is the only thing in a written agreement worth caring about—the rest is only so much "spinach." While Peter suffered a setback, he successfully resisted the strong—almost compelling—temptation to "sue the bastard." Instead, he offered to forgive Richard's default and excuse Richard from further performance under the contract if Richard gave him a letter of recommendation and supported Peter's efforts to obtain carriage elsewhere in the cable television community. Peter even went so far as to have his attorney draft the letter, to make it easier for Richard to say yes. While not as good as having a deal with Richard, this informal settlement did preserve Peter's reputation in the tightly woven television community and enabled him to live to fight another day.

MONEY HUNT
RULE #23

"Always Read Before You Sign"

MoneyHunt Heroine: Maura Halbrook

Although contracts are not as important as lawyers and others may make it seem, it is a *huge* mistake to assume that contracts don't mean a thing. Strange as it may seem, plenty of entrepreneurs sign documents that they really shouldn't.

Whenever we read legal documents, we both have a funny habit: We put our pens down, put the telephone on hold, and read through the document page by page. We do this because we feel holding a pen in our hands implies a certain finality. "Let's get this *over* with!" is the very last thing one should think when signing on the dotted line. Especially after a lengthy negotiation, the temptation to sign with a big flourish and get on to the next deal is sometimes irresistible to the inexperienced entrepreneur.

ONCE YOU SIGN, YOU'RE STUCK

The fact is, once terms are agreed to and signed, they're very difficult to negotiate away, so invariably it ends up costing you, or worse yet, getting you into serious trouble. Never, ever commit yourself or your company to something in a letter of intent that you can't or don't want to deliver at closing. Technically, a letter of intent is nonbinding—heck, it even says so. Everything is subject to "definitive legal documents satisfactory to the parties and their legal counsel." That is not altogether true, however.

While items that are not addressed in a letter of intent are easy enough to negotiate during the definitive contract stage, God forbid you ever agree to something in the letter of intent and wish to have it changed later. Your negotiating power on that point is forever gone once the ink is dry. For example, an innocuous clause that usually appears at the bottom of a letter of intent says, "The company will deliver audited financial statements within 45 days after each quarter." Now this doesn't sound crazy. Usually you do prepare your financial statements within thirty or forty-five days of the close of the quarter. So what's the big deal?

Well, if you don't audit your books today, you've just signed up for a major step-up in accounting fees. The letter of the law in this case calls for delivery of *audited* statements. That means your accountants will have to review and opine on your quarterly financial statements as well. Not too many private companies audit on a quarterly basis, and those that do spend a load of money to get it done.

Here's another one. Every legal document contains a clause, usually near the end in the "miscellaneous" section (which most entrepreneurs skim over—bad mistake!) that says something like "this agreement represents the entire agreement of the parties and supersedes any and all prior and contemporaneous agreements between the parties relating to the subject matter hereof." Sounds straightforward enough, right? There's only one agreement anyone has to look at, and this is it. By signing a clause like this one, however, the entrepreneur says, in effect, "Anything the other side's people may have told and promised me about this deal is totally irrelevant now, and I'm not relying on any of that in signing below." Everything the other side said . . . including all those promises about when the stuff will be delivered and the condition in which it will be delivered. All gone now. If the stuff turns out to be worthless garbage, you are now prohibited from going back and saying, "Well . . . they told me it would . . ."

SO WHICH IS IT, GUYS—ARE CONTRACTS IMPORTANT OR NOT?

We very often hear entrepreneurs say, "What's the big deal, it's just a term sheet! We can clean it up later." Term sheets may or may not be binding, depending of course on what they say, what your attorney says, and what some court of law says after a bloody horrendous lawsuit that you never wanted to get into.

Some entrepreneurs rationalize by saying to themselves, "Hey, I know it's a contract, but a contract is only as good as the parties' willingness to enforce it, right? I just read the last chapter of this book, and I buy it! I am comfortable this guy is never going to sue me because we have a relationship, so it doesn't matter what I sign." In the words of Gilbert and Sullivan, "never . . . well, hardly ever????" You can never assume that even your closest and most trusted friend won't sue you if he or she gets mad enough at you. Some people are just crazy enough to bring lawsuits even though they know they won't win in the long run. Never say never.

Many entrepreneurs mistakenly believe (as do some lawyers) that the written word is sacred and will protect them in case the Velveeta hits the fan. You can easily tell this type of entrepreneur because they nitpick every detail of a contract—fighting over every dependent clause in a two-hundred-page agreement, asking "what if" questions that have little to do with the realities of the relationship, and saying things like "If we don't have this in the contract, here's how I'm afraid you will screw me."

At the other end of the spectrum, some entrepreneurs are too lack-adaisical about contracts—they take a quick glance at the first draft, turn to the last page, and sign on the spot, saying something like "I trust you, and this demonstrates my trust." Such conduct has two negative effects— it may tempt you to do the same thing in return, saying to yourself, "Oh, what the hell—this guy has faith in me, so I should demonstrate the same to him" and overlooking the little clause on page 4 that gives him a lien on your firstborn child.

As a famous entrepreneur once said, "Oral agreements aren't worth the paper they are printed on." Just because you can't count on written agreements to protect you against someone who is determined to breach them and has the leverage to do so doesn't mean you shouldn't even the playing field by getting everything in writing and forcing the other guy to make concessions when he feels like breaching.

Be Sure to Read (Twice or More) Before You Sign When:

- Someone insists on a written agreement before the first meeting with you.

- Someone insists on not doing business with you without a signed, twenty-page agreement in place, even if the deal involves only a few thousand dollars.

- You find yourself worried about the way certain little paragraphs in the "miscellaneous" section at the back of the agreement are drafted.

- You really don't want the deal unless you can get a killer, pull-out-the-stops, one-sided agreement with the other party.

- You are asked to sign anything under deadline pressure.

- You are asked to sign something that is represented to you as "standard legal boilerplate—don't worry about it."

- The other side sends you a revised draft of an agreement and hasn't marked it to show where the changes were made.

- You are told that if you show an agreement to your attorney to be reviewed before you sign it, "That means you don't trust me, and I won't do business with anyone who has to get lawyers involved every time we shove a piece of paper back and forth across the table."

- You are told "read this quickly but get it signed—it's not legally binding anyway."

- Anytime you are asked to sign something by someone who has breached his obligations to you under a previous agreement.

MoneyHunt Heroine: Maura Halbrook

Maura felt a tremor shock of excitement as the fax machine rang. She knew it was the document she had been waiting all day for, and fairly ran down the hall to watch it come through the machine. The documents for her much-needed financing were now coming through page by slow page. As she read them, still warm from the heat of the thermal transfer, she knew she was at a crossroads in her business venture. Consumed by the legalese in front of her, she hardly heard the phone ring, and the caller ended up on her voice-mail recording.

She played it as she was rereading the fax she had just received. "Maura, this is Henry. The attorneys are faxing the documents through to you now. Everything is exactly as we had discussed." Then something she couldn't make out: ". . . something . . . something . . . so let's finally sign the thing and get prepared for the big launch date on Monday."

The knot in her stomach twisted tighter.

Maura had felt that knot before. Trained for ten hard years as an investment banker, she had worked her way up the ladder of Wall Street by being a people person. With a killer smile and a cool confidence, Maura was the type of person you knew was in the room, even if you didn't see her. She had presence.

Winning clients on Wall Street is not all fun and games, however, and Maura had her share of great opportunities that came along from unsavory people. Like the initial public offering (IPO) she steered through the firm despite the fact that the founder and chairman was an admitted womanizer, bore children out of wedlock, had been bankrupt three times, and gambled incessantly. She swallowed hard and showed the good side to the brokers—100 percent year-to-year growth, sustained margins, great new products. The deal came off without a hitch, but Maura felt the knot in her stomach. She didn't get burned that time.

She left Wall Street after ten years and began her own media business—a producer of how-to children's programming with some unique properties. Her first show, *Jeffie*, was kicking Barney's ass in focus-group tests, and the licensing deals were just beginning to roll in. Product development and promotion seemed to be her strong cards, but she needed someone to run the company on a day-to-day basis.

She met Henry just as Henry was about to meet her. She had clipped an article from the *New York Times* about a business angel who went in to manage companies and help them grow. Operations was his specialty. The article seemed to imply that money came with the deal, but fell short on the details. Never one to let opportunity lie, she picked up the phone and left a voice-mail message for him. Henry didn't answer because he was on the telephone with a local investor who knew Maura and was recommending her to him.

By the time they actually spoke, they felt they knew a lot about each other and were on a fast track to a deal. Good thing too, because *Jeffie* was about to debut on national television in a few weeks. Henry sensed the anxiety in Maura's voice. Things were about to bust out, and her company needed muscle.

Henry always liked a deal that had no other alternatives. Since selling his business a few years ago, he had hobnobbed with Baltimore's business elite and often heard his cohorts brag about "shooting fish in a barrel." They, of course, had much more money than Henry, but most outsiders lumped them all together as men with money. Henry thrived on the misconception. The *New York Times* article only served to further the perception: The week it hit the newsstands he had over fifty entrepreneurs calling seeking his help.

Maura quickly rose to the top. She had an excellent business plan, a compelling pitch, and an exciting industry. The fact that her show was about to debut on national television did not hurt things. Henry quickly snapped into action and began laying out ways he could add value to the business. As Maura and Henry's discussion got more intense, Maura began to notice that many of Henry's ideas were retreaded versions of ideas that were in her business plan. He asked the questions with a hard Baltimore style, but there was nothing new under them. No matter, she felt stronger when she had to answer something for the umpteenth time.

Finally, they began grinding toward a deal. Henry proposed that he be given a large part of the company for nothing, that he come to work for a salary, and that he control the company. He wanted to be an equal partner and treated with the respect he deserved. "Get real," Maura countered, "or get lost." She ticked off the number of accomplishments the company had achieved since she had started it. Henry was willing to come around and offered more cash for less stock. So she began checking his references.

Maura had always been a stickler about references. It was how she had turned up the infidelity and gambling thing about that investment-banking client ten years ago. Henry did not have that long a list of people to check with, but Maura kept digging. All she was able to get was a lot of "he's a straight shooter" and "he's a go-getter." None she could find could tell her "Henry is a great operating guy, and can make a major positive impact." Except Henry, of course. He discoursed on his prowess at every turn, used language laden with financial jargon, and came off as either determined, crazy, or both.

With a deal on the table, Maura was still antsy about the references, so she went for the acid test. Dinner at home. Henry walked in late. Maura's dog growled at Henry. Bad sign. She introduced her husband, Evan, and Henry went out of his way to buddy up with Evan, leaving Maura to put the finishing touches on dinner. The meal went fine, and the three adjourned to talk more deal details late into the night. Evan wasn't involved in Maura's business, but she respected Evan's judgment. When Maura finally turned in, it was well past 1:00 A.M. As she turned out the light, her husband whispered three words: "He's a fake." She sighed.

Next morning, Henry was up before dawn, made the bed in the guest room, worked out in Maura's makeshift gym in the basement, and was going full stream on the final deal details when Maura got downstairs. Like him or not, it looked as if Maura would have her investor and operator in time for the big launch—now only five days away.

The deal they had agreed on had two very specific clauses that made Maura more comfortable. One required Henry to invest a minimum of $100,000 at a set valuation. The second was a bonus clause that gave Maura the option of giving Henry a windfall bonus, based on a formula, if the business was ever sold. She made Henry repeat them both so there would be no misunderstandings later.

Henry left for Baltimore and his attorneys, who would be drafting the papers. Evan asked Maura if they had come to terms. "My terms," she replied. "Only on my terms . . ."

The fax she held in her hands could not have been a mistake. She thought the attorney had something wrong at first. In the clause that was to say "minimum investment of $100,000" it now read "up to $100,000." The optional windfall now read as if Henry got the windfall at his option. The deal described on the fax allowed Henry to invest nothing, sit back, and enjoy the windfall whether he contributed or not.

She was about to call the attorney and chew him out for getting the deal wrong when it all came rushing back to her. She grabbed the *New York Times* article out of the file. It never said he made an investment. She rechecked her notes from the references. He had never given the name of the company he had sold "for a small fortune." She looked at his first offer. It now looked strangely like his final one. The dog hated him. Her husband called him a fake. Now there was a voice-mail message from him saying the contract was perfect, please sign it and let's get started.

She hit replay. "Everything is exactly as we had discussed. Something . . . something . . . so let's finally sign the thing and get prepared for the big launch date on Monday." *Something . . . something?* What *was* that? She hit replay again. "Everything is exactly as we had discussed. . . . *You don't even need to review it* . . . so let's finally sign the thing and get prepared for the big launch date on Monday."

Looking back, it was the easiest deal Maura never did. She called Henry and left him a voice-mail message, the substance and tone of which cannot be reprinted here.

LESSONS FROM MAURA HALBROOK

Reviewing the fax from Henry's lawyers, Maura realized that neither she nor the attorneys had made a mistake. Henry was trying to squeeze Maura into giving him a richer deal than she ever intended to give him. Had she signed without reading the fax, she might have been able to back out of the deal before contract time, but not without considerable expense.

Although Maura had been meticulous about checking into Henry and hadn't turned up any negatives, what she knew about him suddenly reinforced the opinion she had now formed about the changed terms in the fax. She also refused to succumb to the rationale of, "Well, it's too late."

Maura's investment-banking background made her suspicious by nature, and in her dealings with Henry that suspicion really paid off big-time. Her decision to check references, and her suspicions when none of the references would do anything but damn Henry with faint praise, raised her suspicions.

Her decision to invite Henry over for dinner at her home was an excellent one. Business partners usually spend a great deal of time together, to the point that they become part of the entrepreneur's family. Getting the opinions of Evan, to say nothing of the unsolicited reaction of Maura's dog, helped her solidify her vague, nagging suspicion that something was not altogether real regarding Henry.

Fortunately for Maura, Henry's voice-mail message garbled the part that pushed her over the edge, when Henry said "you don't even need to review it." Had Maura heard that part of the message the first time around, she might have been tempted not to read the letter of intent Henry's attorneys faxed over. Instead, it made her repeat the message several times until she understood Henry's meaning . . . perfectly.

MONEYHUNT
RULE #24

"Good Housekeeping Can Save Your Life!"

MoneyHunt Hero: Carl Rzewski

W hat lawyers like to call "corporate housekeeping" is usually at the very bottom of most entrepreneurs' priority lists. It isn't much fun, involves mostly mind-numbing details, and doesn't add a dollar to the bottom line. In fact, it costs money, because you usually have to pay lawyers, accountants, and other professional folks to handle these matters for you.

There's only one problem. If you don't handle housekeeping chores when they need to be done, you risk making a fool of yourself when venture capitalists and other professional investors start demonstrating an interest in your business.

THE DUE-DILIGENCE PROCESS

When a venture capitalist or other professional investor is interested in an entrepreneurial company, it performs "due diligence" before making the decision to invest. This due diligence is conducted in three phases:

Accounting due diligence, in which the investor retains independent auditors to tear apart the company's books, records, and financial statements looking for trouble.

Business due diligence, in which the investor's team of analysts lives at the company's headquarters, talks to suppliers and customers, second-guesses the entrepreneur's marketing research (sort of like what we do on MoneyHunt), and generally "kicks the tires" to make sure the entrepreneur's business lives up to the business plan the investor has reviewed.

Last but not least, legal due diligence, in which the investor's lawyers examine and assess the company's legal risks and liabilities.

When a company first seeks investment capital, the founding entrepreneurs are usually ready for the accounting and business due diligence. In preparing a business plan, after all, it is necessary to look at how the business is actually conducted, and there is usually time to fix any minor operational problems before the investors begin their diligence. Similarly, most entrepreneurs involve their accountants in preparing the cash-flow projections, financial statements, and other number-related information in the business plan, so any issues are usually ironed out before the plan is presented to investors.

It is a different story with legal due diligence, however. Few if any investors seek to involve their lawyers in the process of drafting a business plan, which is a big mistake. Sometimes the company's lawyers are asked to draft the risk-factors section of the business plan, in which the risks and liabilities of the business are disclosed. As entrepreneurs are trained to be marketers who accentuate the positive and spin everything that happens in a positive direction, it is difficult if not impossible for many entrepreneurs to even include a risk-factors section in their business plan for fear the reader will focus on negative information and outcomes. Accordingly, there are frequently unpleasant surprises when the legal due diligence is conducted, and they are very difficult to correct on short notice.

NOBODY EVER GOT RICH BECAUSE HE HAS MINUTES OF ALL HIS BOARD MEETINGS

Many entrepreneurs fail to keep up with their legal housekeeping chores, figuring that "I can always get my lawyers involved when the time comes, and they will clean up any problems then." Some legal issues and risks require lots of lead time to be solved properly, and even the best lawyers money can buy will have difficulty putting your legal house in order for a fee you can afford. To say nothing of what it will take the lawyers you *can* afford to fix any problems.

More commonly, many entrepreneurs delude themselves into thinking that they have no legal issues just because they've been in business for two or three years and nobody has sued them. Even if the wolves are not beating down the door with subpoenas and court writs, a company can have legal problems simply by doing nothing.

Remember to Keep Your Business House Clean When:

- You have been in business two or three years and you cannot recall ever receiving any "junk mail" from federal or state government agencies.

- You do not have written agreements with any of your employees or independent contractors.

- You cannot remember who owns stock in your company.

- Your director of new product development has announced his intention to leave your company and join a competitor, and you can't remember in whose name his thirty-six U.S. patents are registered.

MoneyHunt Hero: Carl Rzewski

Ever since he was a kid, Carl Rzewski liked things that glow in the dark. In college, where he majored in biology, Carl wrote his senior thesis on bioluminescence, the process that makes some animals and plants produce small amounts of light in totally dark environments. In engineering school he developed a wafer-thin strip of light-sensitive film that, exposed to a small electric charge, could make anything printed on it glow in the dark in full, three-dimensional color.

Carl dropped out of engineering school, obtained a patent for his luminescent strip, and, together with his father, who supplied the seed capital, formed a corporation in his hometown of Willamette, Oregon, which he named BioSign Corporation. Madison Avenue, always looking for new and exciting ways to deliver advertising messages for their clients, fell head over heels in love with Carl's invention, and soon BioSign's electroluminescent strips were being used to light up print advertisements on billboards, trash receptacles, taxicabs, buses, and other advertising media that until that time had been restricted to daytime use. Within three years of its formation, BioSign was making over $1 million a year on $5.3 million in sales.

Carl realized that to grow the company any further, he would need capital to expand BioSign's manufacturing capacity overseas and develop an international network of distributors for their electroluminescent products. Carl prepared a business plan and shopped BioSign to venture capitalists. Within a month one of the top venture-capital firms in San Francisco sent him a letter of intent to make a $3 million equity investment in BioSign.

We badly wanted Carl to pitch BioSign on *MoneyHunt*, because it's exactly the type of technology company we look for. BioSign's product line involves state-of-the-art technology with many different applications, yet is easy to explain to viewers who are not well-versed in technology. After his initial interview with us and the *MoneyHunt* producers, Carl called and told us that he didn't need to be on the show anymore because of the $3 million deal waiting for him in San Francisco. Three weeks later, a bashful Carl called and asked if we would still be interested in giving him a slot on *MoneyHunt*, as the deal had fallen through. What happened between those two telephone calls is the subject of this story.

When Carl first received the letter of intent from the venture-capital firm in San Francisco, he was on top of the world. At first, it looked as if BioSign would survive the due-diligence process. A team of junior people from the venture-capital firm swarmed over BioSign's offices and manufacturing plant for several days, poking holes in BioSign's manufacturing processes and quality-control systems. They came back with a glowing report on Carl's operations.

Next came the accountants, who conducted a thorough audit of Carl's books, records, and financial statements going back to the formation of BioSign. They even reviewed personal financial statements for Carl, his father, and another relative who was serving as the company's chief financial officer. The accounting team, like the business due-diligence team, came back with a "thumbs-up" recommendation for investment.

The next step in the process came as something of a surprise to Carl. The senior partner of the venture-capital firm asked to meet privately with Carl and his dad in the firm's downtown San Francisco offices. When Carl walked into the partner's office for the meeting, there sat in a high-backed chair a man Carl had not met before. Tall, thin, with a protruding Adam's apple, the man parted his hair in the middle and wore tortoiseshell horn-rimmed glasses and a rumpled three-piece suit the likes of which Carl had not seen since the Reagan administration. The partner introduced the man as Clement Hopkins III, a lawyer in the San Francisco law firm that represented the venture-capital firm.

The partner in the venture-capital firm then announced the purpose of the meeting: "It is our policy to conduct the legal portion of our due-diligence investigation in private, as some of the problems that frequently surface in legal due diligence are highly . . . shall we say sensitive? Clement has been doing this for us for some time now, and we value his judgment highly."

"Well, let's get on with it then," Carl said, a trifle impatiently. "We certainly have nothing to hide. Our record is squeaky clean, and we've never been sued."

"Oh, I'm sure you haven't been," Clement piped in a high-pitched voice, "because we would have found out about it when we searched your company on our Lexis/Nexis database." Carl looked at Clement's ashen white complexion and wondered when it was this guy last had a good night's sleep.

Glancing over at his client, the partner of the venture-capital firm, Clement continued with Carl. "There are just a couple of things I need to ask you about," he said.

"Fire away," Carl replied, sitting back in his chair and folding his hands across his lap. Whatever Clement was going to ask, Carl was confident he had nothing to apologize for.

"Do you realize," Clement asked, "that your company, BioSign Corporation, no longer exists?"

You could cut the silence in the room with a knife. At first Carl and his father thought Clement was joking. "BioSign doesn't exist?" Carl squeaked, "Surely you are kidding!"

"Wish I were," Clement continued. "But I'm not. We checked with the Oregon secretary of state's office, and BioSign was dissolved two years ago."

"Dissolved?" Carl and his dad responded in unison.

"Dissolved. It seems that you failed to file your annual report two years in a row, and when that happens the secretary of state dissolves your company. You and your stockholders have been operating as a partnership the past couple of years. Good thing you haven't been sued . . . you all would have lost your houses."

Carl couldn't believe his ears. "But . . . but . . . we received no notice of this!"

"Oh, you usually don't," Clement went on, continuing to look at the notepad on his lap. "They publish something in the 'Legal Notices' section of the big newspapers, but nobody ever reads those. Your statutory agent should have sent you the annual report to be filled out each year."

"Our . . . what?"

"Your statutory agent. When you form a corporation, you designate someone to act as your statutory agent. He or she is responsible for sending you your annual report and other documents from the secretary of state's office."

Carl and his dad looked at each other. "The attorney who formed

BioSign is no longer practicing law. We did receive a letter from him about . . . was it a year ago? He retired and moved to Florida. Come to think of it, there was some kind of legal form in that letter . . . I don't recall . . ."

"It was probably a change of address form," Clement droned on. "Too bad you didn't look at it. You could have designated yourself statutory agent. Because BioSign didn't have a statutory agent the secretary of state didn't know where to send the annual report."

"But this is ridiculous!" Carl complained. "We pay our taxes every year. The state of Oregon certainly knew where to find us!"

"But when you file your taxes you send the returns to the Oregon Department of Revenue Services. This is the secretary of state's office we're talking about. Amazing, isn't it? In this age of modern computer technology you still have government agencies that don't talk to each other."

"Okay," Carl said, pulling a handkerchief from his pocket and wiping his upper lip. "We obviously were unaware of this. As soon as we get back to Oregon we'll call the secretary of state's office and clean this up."

"I'm afraid it won't be that simple," Clement intoned.

"What do you mean? It was an honest mistake."

"No doubt about that. But under Oregon law if you haven't filed your annual report for more than two years, you cannot reinstate the company simply by filing the two annual reports. At this point you will have to get a special act of the Oregon legislature to reinstate your business."

Carl and his father both went white. "You mean . . . we have to petition the legislature? That will take months! Can't we . . . just incorporate the business all over again with the same name?"

"Sorry," Clement said. "That will only make things worse. And I'm not sure my client is willing to finance a start-up company. May I continue?"

"You mean . . . there's more?" Carl whimpered.

"Afraid so. You list in your business plan seven or eight people who own stock in your company. I will have to confirm that they are indeed the only stockholders. Can you please send me your corporate minute book and copies of the signed stock certificates when you get back to Oregon?"

"Minute book? . . . Stock certificates?" Carl sputtered.

"Surely you have a minute book," Clement looked up, removing his glasses, "and the stock certificates are those little green pieces of printed paper . . ."

"I know damn well what stock certificates look like!" Carl blurted out. "Our . . . old attorney . . . the one who retired . . . he kept the minute book. We meant to ask him to draft stock certificates but . . . but . . ."

"You never got around to it?" Clement asked, again not raising his head from the notepad on his lap.

"We'll take care of it," Carl said. "I'm sure we can find out who has our minute book."

"And since you don't have your minute book," Clement added, "may I assume you don't have minutes of your directors' and stockholders' meetings?"

"Directors' meetings? Stockholders' meetings? Dad and I are the only directors, and the stockholders, they're all relatives and employees! We see these people every day! We don't need meetings!"

"I'm afraid you do, at least under Oregon law," Clement droned. Carl was beginning to truly hate this man. "You are supposed to have stockholders' meetings at least once a year, to elect the directors, and you should have director's meetings once in a while to make the big decisions. I'm sure you and your dad have voting control of the company, although without the stock certificates we cannot be sure. . . ."

"You can be sure," the partner of the venture-capital firm added, "that once our firm has seats on your board, there will be regular directors' and stockholders' meetings . . . with minutes."

"Sure . . . fine . . . whatever you say." Carl thought for a moment he was going to have a seizure. Everything was going so smoothly up to this point.

"Now let's talk about employment agreements," Clement said. Carl noticed for the first time that the notepad on Clement's lap contained a checklist—a list of documents. With each question Clement was putting an X next to each item on the list. Carl wondered if Clement used this same list every time his client was thinking of making an investment.

"Employment agreements?"

"Yes. Agreements with your key employees. Such as—what's his name, Fred?—the scientist who has his name on a couple of your patents."

"Yes, yes, Fred. He's helped us improve some of our products. What do you mean, though, that he's put his name on patents?"

Clement handed Carl two patent documents with Fred's signature on them. "Looks like your man Fred is getting himself some employment security."

Carl exploded. "He can't do this! He's an employee! He's working on company time!"

"Show me the agreement that says he can't," Clement added, returning to his checklist.

The due-diligence meeting continued for two hours. At the end Clement made a copy of the checklist for Carl. As the partner in the venture-capital firm escorted a dazed Carl and his father out of the door, he said, "Don't worry. We like your company. When you've addressed some of these issues, call us and we'll consider whether it makes sense to renew our offer to invest in your company. Of course, we may have to adjust the investment amount . . . and we will insist that you bring a general counsel on board. . . ."

When the partner returned to his office, Clement said, "You know, I really hated doing that to such nice people. It's really a terrific line of products they've got, and a solid management team. Shame they didn't get a lawyer involved sooner. A lot of these problems could easily have been solved."

"Yeah, that's because everybody loves you lawyers and the stuff you dig up . . . they just can't wait to work with you!" the partner laughed, as he offered his friend Clement a cigar. "But don't worry, old friend, you know I love the legal profession . . . you guys keep me from making investments in half-assed companies that haven't got their act together."

Lessons from Carl Rzewski

Carl learned the hard way that legal details can kill a hard-won deal with an investor. Confident that the legal due-diligence process would be a breeze, as there was no pending or threatened litigation against his company, Carl was completely blindsided by his meeting with Clement the attorney, who correctly pointed out that if Carl had been more awake to his legal environment in forming and running BioSign during its early years, the legal due diligence would have gone just as easily as the business and accounting due-diligence investigations had.

Nobody enjoys paying legal fees, just like nobody enjoys paying taxes. An attorney we know, however, puts it very well: "You can either pay me a small fee now to keep you out of trouble, or you can pay me a large fee later when the mess has been made and I have to clean it up."

Carl's errors were, as the lawyers say, errors of omission, not errors of commission. Carl lost his financing not because of things he had done but because he had neglected BioSign's legal compliance for so long that several "easy fixes" had become intractable problems requiring months of time and thousands of dollars in legal fees to solve.

At the beginning of BioSign's existence, Carl failed to establish a long-term relationship with an attorney. Very often the attorney that forms your corporation is not willing or able to act as general counsel to the company going forward. In such a case it is important to develop a relationship with an attorney who can draft and negotiate contracts, oversee your patents and other intellectual property filings, and help you comply with government regulations in your industry.

When Carl received notice that the attorney who formed the company was retiring and moving to Florida, that should have been a red flag to Carl, warning him that certain information on file with government agencies (such as the secretary of state's office) would need to be changed. At the very least, he should have named himself or his father as the company's statutory agent to receive copies of the annual report and other documents from the secretary of state. Filing that document each year would have taken all of fifteen minutes of Carl's time and would have prevented his company from being dissolved without his knowledge.

It must have been embarrassing for Carl to learn about these problems for the first time from Clement, the venture-capital firm's lawyer. Had Carl met with an attorney at the beginning of the due-diligence process, he would have been forewarned of these problems and could have put off the legal due-diligence meeting until he had had a chance to develop a strategy for dealing with them.

Carl failed to learn that good agreements make for good business relationships. By adopting an informal management style with little paperwork between the company, its shareholders, and employees, most of whom (as Carl correctly pointed out) were relatives and good friends, it would have been difficult for Carl to insist upon formal written agreements now that BioSign was ready to enter the big leagues. The time to get a written agreement with someone—anyone—is at the beginning of the relationship. Once the relationship exists for a period of time, a "course of dealing" is created that makes it awkward—if not totally off-putting—to insist upon a written agreement later on.

We are sure that Carl's employee Fred thought he had every right to file patents in his own name, and we can only imagine how Carl dealt with that very delicate situation. Put yourself in Carl's place. Do you fire Fred, one of your key technical employees, sue him in federal court for patent infringement, and petition the U.S. Patent and Trademark Office to reregister the patent in BioSign's name—a lengthy and expensive process? Or do you require Fred, as a condition of his continued employment, to assign to BioSign all rights to the two patents he filed? As Fred was probably well aware of the pending $3 million investment from the venture-capital firm, we wonder what he would have asked for in return for that patent assignment.

PART SEVEN

Getting Out—And Moving On

MONEYHUNT
RULE #25

"It's a Business, Not a Baby"

MoneyHunt Hero: John Thibodeaux

E motions don't mix well with businesses, but, ironically, many of the best entrepreneurs are emotional people. Entrepreneurs have a way of becoming attached to their companies, sometimes letting their infatuation with their progeny cloud their vision.

To a point, that's okay. Too many entrepreneurs aren't passionate enough about their businesses to do the (sometimes) crazy things you have to do to succeed. But identifying *too* closely with your business has its downside as well. When we see an entrepreneur who's clearly too close to the business to stand back and take an objective look at what's going on, we tell them, "It's a business, not a baby."

THE BUSINESS DOESN'T KNOW WHO OWNS IT

Entrepreneurs need to be passionately committed to their business. They also need to be cold, cynical, and ruthless, which requires a certain amount of objectivity and distance. Put another way, the business doesn't know who owns it. It does not get mad if you sell a piece of it for too little. It does not blush if someone offers too much. It's just a business, which in the end gets bought and sold like any piece of meat.

Practically speaking, why is it important to remember that your business is not a baby?

For starters, getting emotional about your business can cost you a lot of money. For example, let's say the founder of a business wants to find an investor for a planned expansion. Being a perfectionist, he begins mapping out what the ideal investor would bring to the table, in terms of both valuation and personality. He refuses to compromise on terms, even minor ones. After all, it's the business *he* founded. Several investors come and kick the tires. Some almost fit the bill. He keeps playing the field.

Meanwhile, his competitor allows his business to be acquired by an investor with a good fit, albeit not perfect. The competitor is now gaining market share with his added capital, forcing our hero to reduce his margins in order to stay competitive. The lower margins become an issue with new investors looking over the company. It gets harder to keep their interest. Valuations once considered too cheap are now being revised downward because of the extra competition. He decides rather than give a piece away at these low prices, he'll wait it out without the capital.

His well-capitalized competitor crushes him.

"I Don't Want to Do It, So It's a Strategic Decision"

Entrepreneurs try to rationalize their way around this one and pretend their business is not a baby when to them it really is one. For example, watch out for the entrepreneur who rationalizes an emotional decision by dressing it up as a business strategy that others will find more acceptable. "Dear family shareholders . . . despite our previously stated desires to acquire capital to expand sales of our newly developed product, we have elected not to take on additional capital. Because of the low valuations offered by potential investors we have decided to grow more slowly with our own internally generated capital." If the competition does not crush them first, that is.

Another time when it really pays to watch out for the baby/business dichotomy is when you are selling or financing a business and it comes time to value the bloody thing. The owner's expectation of value is almost always influenced by how attached he is to the baby he created. Professional managers suffer a little less from the problem because they weren't around when the idea was hatched. They may not have risked home and family harmony to get it up and going. They won't feel too much of a sense of loss after it's sold. We once worked with one seller who insisted he was willing to crater a $10,000,000 deal over a $500 plane ticket—if the buyers wouldn't reimburse his airfare to corporate headquarters, he would back out. And don't you know they wouldn't? And he did? He actually left the investors with their pens poised in midair over a $10,000,000 check over a handful of frequent-flier miles. Our hero's reaction? "Hey, it's great to still be king."

He did sell it, by the way. Even babies have their price.

MONEYHUNT HERO: JOHN THIBODEAUX

I f he weren't an executive in the new media rush of the mid-1990s, you would have sworn John Thibodeaux lived a past life as a card sharp aboard a Mississippi paddlewheel 150 years ago. Soft blue eyes, a thin mustache, and a soul patch (for the hirsutically challenged, this is a growth of hair between the lower lip and chin, midway across, with everything around it shaved off; if not done right it makes a long division sign out of your face) complemented his polite mid-southern drawl and a nimble mind. Underneath the skin, we suspected he was all ice water. His company was barely nine months old and he had never raised money before in his life. He was still in college.

John's business was not all that unique, but his timing was good. Give us the choice between good timing and a good idea, we go for the timing every time. At the tender age of nineteen, a freshman at a large southern university majoring in computer science with minors in game theory and Kentucky bourbon, John had come to the sudden realization that his parents had already paid his tuition in full. However, student loans were more than available. Putting one and one together, John was somehow able to pull together a credit line based on his paid tuition and to start buying computers, co-opting roommates and neighbors in the hall into doing HTML and Java script programming for the Web sites he would produce.

The sites were small at first—school projects, athletic organizations, and some local restaurants. Quite by chance, through some of the work he did at the restaurants on Bourbon Street, John landed the mother of all accounts—a not-for-profit organization (which even without profits managed to make a lot of money) that wanted John to produce dozens of Web sites for its affiliated organizations. Pressed to give a name so the contracts could be drawn, he came up with Galactic Interactive. Full of sound and fury, it signified absolutely nothing, but would a big account commit its Web presence to "College Kidz' Really Cool Web Sites"? Wouldn't bet on it.

Galactic Interactive's first project was called "A Taste of New Orleans." Headed by the city's department of commerce, the site's objective was to promote the restaurants, jazz clubs, and other attractions of Bourbon Street and greater New Orleans, tied together by genre, and fully searchable. "A Taste of New Orleans" was to become the interactive promotion machine that drove local customers and visitors alike to gather more information and plan their every move on Bourbon Street.

With this, John's life was quickly becoming dazzling. Every restaurant, nightclub, and blues hall on Bourbon Street got to know John. Everyone in New Orleans knew John, and if they didn't, they wanted to. He was the toast of the New Orleans after-hours society. He got the best seats in the best clubs on Trudeau Street. And come Mardi Gras time? Fuhgeddaboutit.

Among this whirl of activity, John met someone who expressed an interest in buying a big chunk of his business (not an uncommon occurrence when things work; as the Chinese say, "Success has a thousand fathers"). John was certain that the videotape of his appearance on *MoneyHunt* would just seal it.

This potential partner was a straitlaced military man who had latched on to the New Orleans advertising community back in the 1950s, when many of his air force comrades had migrated to New York. The offices of S. Perkins & Co. were as dull as the business. Sam was proud that almost everyone in the firm had a computer on his desk, though Sam hadn't the faintest idea how to use his. He even consented to upgrading and buying new machines to install Windows on his IBM-compatible personal computers. The fact that 99 percent of the advertising community functioned in the Macintosh world didn't seem to cross Sam's mind. The graphic and creative demands of his clients were so basic, people rarely complained that S. Perkins was functioning on the wrong platform.

When your company services the likes of the New Orleans Sugar Bureau and the Southern Louisiana Petroleum Exporters Association, most of the decisions upon who wins what account are made at the local country club, of which Sam was a long-standing member. But Sam also liked jazz. Though married to the same woman for thirty years, he had somehow managed to finagle one regular weeknight where he could stay out past midnight in the smoky clubs of Bourbon Street and return home without reproach. Wednesday nights, though, were out of the question. That was reserved for Bible study, and Sundays for church and evening get-togethers. It was late one Thursday night on Bourbon Street that Sam happened upon an Internet café that had an okay blues band and ten terminals hooked up to a T-1 line. Curious, Sam dug in.

His first stop, a curious Web site called "A Taste of New Orleans," featured all the best restaurants and all the best jazz clubs, just the way Sam had once dreamed of doing, before he gave up the idea. Having never been on the Internet before and never seeing a sight like this, Sam was blown away by the depth of relevant information, attractive graphics, and local information paths that the Web site had. He spent the better part of four hours on it, returning home uncharacteristically late and unable to sleep. The excitement of the Internet had hooked him, and hooked him right in the gut.

He spent the next few weeks studying the Internet and what it could mean to his insular, parochial, stodgy advertising agency. The playing field was being leveled, the barriers to entry brought down. Sam soon realized that S. Perkins & Co., if it were to survive through the millennium, needed an interactive presence. But he was in no position to start one himself, nor would he know who his first hire should be. So he went back to the site that started the whole train of thought and dropped an e-mail to John, who was conveniently linked to the bottom of each "Taste" page.

John had just returned from another chaotic night on the town, visiting the jazz clubs and restaurants that were members of his "Taste" site. Hard work, but somebody has to do it. Now the memo section of the e-mail on his screen caught his attention:

To: JohnThibodeaux [Sweet@Taste.com]
From: sp202@compuserve.com
Subject: Personal message from S. Perkins.

I am impressed by your work.
I would like to discuss possible collaboration.
Call me if interested.
Sam

Personal message from S. Perkins. John knew exactly who it was. Though his eyes could barely focus, he instinctively clicked on the message, and read what amounted to an appealing overture. *Impressed by your work.* Since "A Taste of New Orleans" was the default home page at all of the downtown cybercafé locations, it wasn't hard to find. Maybe Sam had stumbled upon it there. John had become an expert at reading between the lines of e-mails. The fact that S. Perkins was even looking at a Web site was a major sign of change. It was a sign that the early adopters time was over. The mass market was about to make its presence felt.

"I would like to discuss opportunities" meant one of only two things. Mr. Perkins, over drinks, would try to determine whether he could get into the business himself, and if he couldn't he would flatly make an offer to buy what he perceived to be the top company in the field in New

Orleans. If the offer were rebuffed, he'd repeat the process with #2, #3, and #4 until he had acquired talent that could service the market direction that Sam perceived. *"Call me if interested"* spoke volumes of how Sam preferred to proceed. Ironically, he was e-mailing but requesting that they speak by phone. He probably had sent it from a cybercafé and didn't know how to open up his own e-mail at the office. John made the call and agreed to a meeting.

When he arrived at the offices of S. Perkins & Co., John was surprised how quickly he moved through the phalanxes of protection on his way up to the boss's inner sanctum. He fairly breezed into Sam Perkins's office, shook hands, had a seat at a small side table that Sam had motioned to, and waited for him to finish his phone call. When he did, Sam hastily moved around his giant desk and fussed over John, asking him if he would like a cool drink, tea, or coffee. John deferred with a polite thank-you, and Sam yelled for his assistant to bring him in lemonade with ice. By the time Sam's assistant arrived with the lemonade it was clear to John that Sam had done his homework. He had researchers look up every element of John's career, including the fact that he hadn't quite yet graduated from college, business being as good as it was, what Web site he had worked on, how well regarded his crew of eight programmers and designers had become, and the impressive client list they had already developed. He also had the skinny on John's flashy reputation on Bourbon Street. It seemed all Sam wanted to know about, at first, was John's take on different jazz clubs in the area.

John kept redirecting the conversation to the issue at hand, and his slow, deliberate honesty nullified any anxiety Sam would have had about their culture gap. The technical knowledge John had was significant enough to impress Sam, although John only knew the basics, often delegating the programming and creative details to members of his team. When the conversation turned again to jazz, John realized that Sam had already made up his mind, so John decided to pile it on. He spoke of the tremendous synergy between the two companies. How John's team could be moved almost immediately and become a core squad, powered by Macintosh and ready to deliver high-end creative, interactive programming to Sam's existing clients, as well as use the Perkins name to win many new clients coming on board in the Greater Bayou Area.

The conversation turned to jazz again, but John kept redirecting it. He knew that five minutes after he walked out Sam Perkins's door, Sam would have another phone call and another opportunity and forget most of the conversation he'd had with John. That being the case, John preferred not to be remembered as someone who knew everything about jazz but someone with whom S. Perkins & Co. could do business.

As he sat there in his tailored suit, and his coifed hair, he was tempted to drift into a dream state. Even this meeting, sitting in this chair, next to this table was terrific fun for John. It was all a matter of perspective. Two years ago, he was a relatively homely looking, poorly dressed computer nerd with taped glasses and crooked teeth parking cars at one of the low-downest clubs on Bourbon Street. Now, he drove a fancy new Acura Legend with all-leather trim and a giant CD player that could hold ten of his favorite jazz clips. He had been on national television. He was running his own million-dollar business. And he felt certain that he was about to get an offer from the guy sitting across the table from him. Sure enough, Sam's next words were just that. He made an offer to buy the company lock, stock, and barrel, accounts included, for an amount fifty times what John had originally put into the business nine months previously. And to sign multiyear, big-dollar contracts with the key creative and programming people, as well as with John.

Knowing this was his moment, John struck. His gambler's instinct told him now was the time to put his chips on the table and run for everything he was worth. So as not to appear too eager, he put up token objections to several of Sam's deal points. But by the time the hour was up, they had spent forty minutes hammering out the elements of the term sheet, which Sam then dictated to his assistant and promised to send to John as soon as it was done. Knowing better than to leave the task unfinished and risk market forces changing the terms, John politely asked to wait around outside Sam's office while Sam's assistant finished up the term sheet, so that each of them could sign it then and there. Sam applauded John's initiative and asked his assistant to hurry up, so as not to keep this busy young man from his business. The twenty minutes that the assistant took to type the term sheet seemed an eternity to John, who tried to pass the time making calls from his cellular phone, then scribbling notes about who would handle the transaction and how he would spend the money. The assistant interrupted him with a smile and announced that her work was done. They both returned to the small desk adjacent to Sam's work space and signed off on the term sheet that would put $700,000, after tax, in John's pocket only nine months after his initial $14,000 investment.

LESSONS FROM JOHN THIBODEAUX

John, whether by instinct or by preternatural wisdom, knew not to "baby" his business. His riverboat gambling–style instincts told him when to put his chips on the table and roll the dice hard. When the crowds arrive (in this case, every Tom, Dick, and Chauncey doing Web sites out of their spare bedrooms), it's time to get out. Of course, John hardly had time to get attached. Nine months, even in his industry, is not a long time. He was probably also pushed by other emotions, like fear, which helped him do the right thing.

When John and Sam finally met, Sam kept trying to turn the conversation to jazz and other irrelevant matters, while John casually but firmly kept redirecting the conversation to his company and its potential as a future investment. This was an important step in the courting process. Successful investors are very busy people who make snap impressions. Their minds often work on multiple tracks. By constantly refocusing the conversation, John was able to make his impression and control the script.

Once John had Sam's undivided attention, he did not let go. He kept pressing his point, quietly but firmly. Taking a wait-and-see attitude with someone so interested in the industry could lead to Sam checking out Galactic's competition for a better deal.

It would have been easy for John, or any first-time entrepreneur, to ignore the casual e-mail message Sam sent him (from a cybercafé, no less). After all, most people think big deals cannot begin so offhandedly. Had John ignored the advances of S. Perkins, he could very well have been competing against the know-how of the number two company in the market and the resources of S. Perkins. It's amazing how frequently the company that jumps out of the starting gate and grabs the number one market-share slot loses out to number two, number three, or number four, who gets the big money first and develops the brand name. That is not fair, but hey, neither is entrepreneurship.

When Sam indicated an interest in buying John's business, John asked for a term sheet *right at that moment*—no delays, no lawyers, no accountants, no second-guessing over brandy and cigars, just put up or shut up and I'm not going to the bathroom until I get it. It was a risky move—Sam could have interpreted it as overanxiousness on John's part. "Hmm, if he's that anxious to sell, what's he hiding? There's something in his plan I should know more about." Or worse—Sam may have sensed inexperience, naïveté, or just plain weakness in John; the wrong kind of investor (we think it's the right kind) would then declare "open season" and go for the entrepreneur's jugular. "Okay, kid, you want to sell? Great! 80 percent of the company for two weeks' payroll."

As it turned out, it was worth the risk for John. He calculated (lightning fast and on his feet, like any casino card counter) that it was better to appear a little overanxious than to risk Sam forgetting the deal after the excitement of the moment had passed. Or maybe John was really overanxious, inexperienced, and naive, and just got lucky—catching the right investor at the right moment with the right pitch.

Does it really matter?

MONEYHUNT
RULE #26

"Be Sure the Reward Is Worth the Risk"

MoneyHunt Heroine: Amanda Rubinstein

Studies show that 80 percent of new companies fail in their first year, another 10 in their second, and by the third only 5 are left standing. With that kind of risk, you should be getting a reward that is significantly higher than you can get from a passbook savings account at your local bank. Much higher!

Most books on entrepreneurship emphasize the emotional and non-monetary rewards of starting and owning your own business. We do not discount these rewards, of course—they are very real, and sometimes they are the only things that keep you going.

Yet sooner or later there should be monetary rewards as well in an entrepreneurial company. When these rewards fail to materialize within a reasonable time, it's time to get out and do something else with your life.

BIG RISKS DEMAND BIG REWARDS

There's no doubt about it: Running your own company is one of the riskiest things you can do in life. Here are a few examples of the risks that entrepreneurs take when starting a business. First, your personal savings and capital will be chewed up, often before the business gets off the ground. You may eat into your home equity and put the house over your head at risk. You may dissipate your savings, raid the 401(k) plan, draw down the individual retirement account despite the penalties. You may hit your family and friends up for dough, you may max out your credit cards. You may do all manner of things financial in order to start and keep feeding your growing business. It's a life on a tightrope.

But the tightrope is not just financial. Growing a business is an all-consuming avocation, especially in the formative years. You would be wise to prepare yourself to sacrifice time with your spouse or your kids, to be nervous when you go on vacation, if you take them at all. Prepare to have a difficult time communicating your challenges at home unless your family runs businesses for themselves.

Make no mistake about it, when you start a business you risk your family harmony as well as your money. Ironic, isn't it? The whole reason you leave your corporate job and take the risks you do is because you wish to be your own boss, set your own hours, chart your own directions, and see your efforts bear fruit. Yet the most common occurrence of a risk-reward ratio being out of whack is when an entrepreneur gives up too much of his company to secure financing and begins to wonder "Who exactly am I working for?" Like the song says, meet the new boss, same as the old boss (the one with the money). And that financing may not adequately compensate for the risks you continue to take, financially and with your family, if it means diminished stakes in the company that you helped birth and causes you to call into question why you grind away at work each day.

Finally, while the romance of owning your own business is very seductive and very real, it doesn't pay the bills. It never fails to surprise us how many entrepreneurs spend years of their lives working eighty hours a week and more for a return that comes to less than $30,000 a year (pretax). We point out to some of these folks that they could do better, financially speaking, by taking a job as a manager at the local burger joint. You should hear some of the answers we get back:

- "Yes, but what I do is so fulfilling!"

- "I really feel like I'm making a difference here."

- "I could never go back and work for a boss—it's just not me."

- "Yes, I know, but I really feel that this thing is going to take off if I hang around just another couple of months. . . ."

Please don't get us wrong. We are not saying that the only rewards of owning your business should be monetary rewards. We merely suggest that the rewards you receive from your business—*whatever* they are—be commensurate with the amount of effort you put into the business. We can think of a lot less stressful ways to make $30,000 a year than owning a high-risk enterprise in a tough market.

KNOW THE PRICE OF "BEING YOUR OWN PERSON"

Entrepreneurs have an overwhelming desire to avoid a return to corporate life. They want to become "their own person"—the masters of their own destinies. Career freedom comes, however, at a large price, and most entrepreneurs (especially but not exclusively first-timers) discount or overlook these costs, figuring failure won't happen to them despite the long odds of success. Faith is a wonderful thing, as long as it's backed up by hard analysis.

Far too many entrepreneurs ignore the financial realities of a start-up business, focusing instead on the romance of it all. Few people will doubt that there is a certain mystique about successful entrepreneurs— those brave, heroic souls who have bucked the odds and find themselves at the top of the *Forbes* 400 list of the wealthiest people on earth. No one who has stayed up all night to make sure an order is shipped properly thinks of himself or herself as glamorous, however. No one who has skirted bankruptcy to keep a declining business alive views himself or herself as a hero. Romance is great, but it doesn't pay the bills.

Get rich first, and the glamour will come. We do not know of too many successful entrepreneurs who have difficulty getting dates for Saturday night.

Weigh the Risks and Rewards of What You're Doing When:
- You have been working on an entrepreneurial company for five years or more and your brother-in-law, a middle manager of a large corporation, makes more money than you.

- You are the toast of the small-business speaking circuit in your locality, but you have trouble paying your utility bills at the end of the month.

- You win a prestigious small business award from the local chamber of commerce and find yourself wishing that some money went along with the commemorative plaque.

- You look around for your friends and family, and they are no
  longer there.

MoneyHunt Heroine: Amanda Rubinstein

Amanda saved a lot of cats from untimely deaths. At first, she saved them one at a time working in a highly regarded holistic veterinary practice. But now, with her new company, she was literally saving them millions at a time. When we saw her in the studio for her initial MoneyHunt interview, her cold knowledge of the marketplace impressed both of us. Her undying enthusiasm for her new product and for the positive results it could have gave her a sparkle that played right through all the hard challenges she had faced.

Amanda could have been an old-time movie star. Her great looks were mellowing in middle age, her smile as bright as it was sincere. She wore classic clothes, even if they were a bit frayed at the edge and probably had seen better times.

Amanda had invented and patented what was essentially a color-coded kitty litter. Approximately six million cats die each year from urinary tract disorder—something very easy to treat if diagnosed early, but extremely expensive and almost always fatal if diagnosed later in its development.

The simplicity of the product was beautiful. To the classic household variety of clay-based cat litter, Amanda had added a color dye, which was an indicator of the presence of uric acid. Cats are fairly predictable animals, and so trips to the kitty litter box can be monitored. A change in color means a change in status and a quick trip to the vet. An important part of Amanda's strategy was that she educated the marketplace to the dangers of this disorder and the high rate of fatality among late diagnosis. It was a great story for the media, especially those publications about household pets.

Before long, Amanda was making the rounds of each of the television talk shows, being interviewed by the major news weeklies, and appearing as a special guest at many animal-rights-oriented events. This helped add awareness to feline urinary-tract infection, which buoyed sales of her product. Although the cost of adding the dye forced the retail price of the product higher than conventional clay-based kitty litter, and the distribution channel experienced slower sell-through initially, sales took off. If you love an animal, you will spend money to ensure its continued health.

Strong sales do not, however, necessarily translate into strong profits.

Amanda had, within her first six months in business, mortgaged her house, withdrawn her entire individual retirement account proceeds, and maxed out her credit cards. She was only beginning.

The hard hours and constant public appearances were putting great strain on her family life, as she hardly saw her two sons and husband, but she knew she needed a big push to continue to move product and attract investors for the next round of growth. So she gritted her teeth, did her best to fulfill her family obligations, and worked like a dog.

Luckily, at one of her public appearances at a black-tie benefit in New York City, she was introduced to a very wealthy individual who happened to be a cat lover. Within two weeks Amanda had secured a three-and-a-half-million-dollar equity investment from the investment vehicle of one of Canada's wealthiest industrialists, who also happened to be (you guessed it) a cat fancier.

These highly successful financings did not come without cost. After the second round of financing, Amanda had given up control of her business, owning less than 50 percent of the stock. Nonetheless, she continued to run it as president and put in ungodly hours to see her "baby" grow into the dream she imagined for it. You didn't know Amanda long before you realized just how passionate she was about cats—you began to suspect after a while that she was on a one-woman crusade to wipe out feline urinary-tract infections.

It wasn't long before the retail channel for Amanda's products began to sell through more quickly. International expansion looked like a possibility. Product-line extensions (other products directed at the high-end kitty litter market) began to be developed, and more capital was needed. The next round of five million dollars reduced Amanda's stake to below 5 percent of the entire company and, because of the dollars at risk, a new president and chief operating officer were appointed by the investors.

Amanda quickly began to realize that her original goal, to save cats from a horrid disease, was rapidly on its way to being accomplished. As her stake in the company shriveled, the amount of money she expected to receive in a sale or initial public offering (IPO) was becoming smaller and smaller. Yet the hours she was putting in were not shrinking. The number of public appearances was only growing, the travel was becoming intense, and her relationships and her treasured family time were getting more strained with each day.

When it came time for the third round of financing for her company, Amanda requested that her partners buy out her small remaining equity stake and allow her to remain as honorary chairman and founder of a charitable foundation sponsored by the company to help eliminate feline urinary-tract diseases.

LESSONS FROM AMANDA RUBINSTEIN

Amanda was in complete harmony with her goals and understood only too well how risk-reward works in practice. Had she stayed on as president of the company, owning just a sliver of the company's stock, who was she really working for? After weighing the costs and benefits of being her own boss, Amanda decided that the costs had far outweighed the benefits. Her capital was still in the business, her family and friends had not seen her in two years, and she was exhausted. The hard work she could take, but in the end, things that she did no longer had a measurable effect on the business. Like it or not, she had a new boss. It was time for her to leave.

Amanda was a passionate cat lover from her childhood—saving cats from the pain and suffering of urinary-tract infections was a lifelong crusade for her. Successful businesses usually "do well" and "do good" at the same time. For Amanda, however, doing good was far more important than doing well—she enjoyed being the official spokesperson for feline urinary-tract infections far more than she did the day-to-day drudgery of building a successful business. Someone who was less committed to the feline world and saw the business only as "just another business" would have had an easier time than Amanda in handling the conflicting emotions that come with a successful business.

Although in most venture financings the company founders must accept a certain dilution of their equity stakes in the company, too much dilution makes them employees of the companies they founded, sapping their energy and watering down their passion and commitment for the business. To Amanda's credit, her commitment and passion for the business never wavered, even after she awakened to the fact that her ownership was more like a vested employee than a founder-owner. Still, one cannot escape the feeling that she should have negotiated a bit harder to preserve her percentage ownership of the company at a level that would keep her motivated and driven to build the company's success by tying it to her own.

Ultimately, Amanda realized that there was more to life than business. Although her investors were anxious for her to stay on board, as she knew the products and marketplace better than just about anyone else in the organization, Amanda knew that every decision in business life involves weighing the costs against the benefits. Amanda did not like the way the balancing act was coming out, and she had the strength to say so to some very powerful people.

MONEY HUNT
RULE #27

"Shoot Ducks When They're Flying"

<u>MoneyHunt</u> Hero: Harlan Baxter

F rom time to time in the entrepreneurial world, opportunities will pass directly over your head, whether you are ready for them or not.

Miles learned this early in life from his brother, an accomplished duck hunter accustomed to the hours that would pass between opportunities. Duck hunting, like sailing and some other outdoor sports, can best be described as "hours of boredom punctuated by moments of sheer panic."

Sometimes the solitude of sitting in a duck blind waiting for something to happen can lull you to sleep, while at other times, if you are fortunate enough to have a battery-powered television, a decent football game can jar your attention away from what is happening in the sky overhead. If you're a duck hunter, and there are ducks in the air, everything else becomes secondary. You can watch the game later, you can go to the bathroom at another time, you can look for a more appropriate gauge shotgun. Whatever you've got in your hands at the moment the ducks are overhead, you need to be throwing up in the air or nothing's going to come down. Set aside the fact that your team is on the four-yard line or that your feet are cold or that your bladder is full because, when ducks are in the air you should be firing whatever you've got and not leave one round in the chamber. Under no circumstances would you let a fly-by pass and an open shot at your prize go unattempted. God knows when those ducks will pass this way again.

By now you have probably figured out that in our duck-hunting metaphor the ducks are "opportunity" and your weapon is . . . your "pitch."

You Can't Always Predict When Opportunities Will Arise

Opportunities come up just as unpredictably as the ducks themselves. Investors and buyers and deal propositions come from anywhere. We have met investors at softball games, buyers at Broadway musicals, and venture capitalists while walking the MoneyHunt mascot, a rottweiler named NetScape. It could just happen anywhere.

Also, keep in mind that sources of funds come and go. The criteria constantly change. Buyers pop up when none existed before. For example, a few guys with an investment concept may be out for nine months shopping their company with institutional investors that are never too eager to look at investments. Until . . . they hit upon a pool of funds and then they're out spending money like drunken sailors.

With all this constant change, consider that there are really two opportunities to sell a company: when you are ready or when the investors are. Now make no mistake. When they are ready you have an excellent opportunity to get your price. Investors and buyers on the hunt are happy to pay top dollar when something meets their criteria. However, if you wait until you are ready, be prepared to get only what they're giving. Because the fact that you finally pulled your act together has no bearing whatsoever on how interested the market is.

"Thanks for Your Generous Offer, but We're Just Not Ready Now"

We have seen plenty of companies say that they're "just not ready now"—not ready to go through what it takes to pull together a deal, not ready to make sacrifices, not ready to go into auction mode. Well, if a buyer or investor is ready, we often suggest to clients that they get ready as well, and darn fast.

Entrepreneurs also complain that they're too busy running the business to go through the deal process, with the intense demands for information and quick turnaround that can be taxing on organizations, especially small ones. If you are too busy running your business to run down an investor who flies overhead, well . . . you may be running the business forever.

We have actually heard entrepreneurs complain about "having too many suitors to handle." Can you imagine! There is a name for that. It is called . . . an auction. If you have too many bidders it's not a problem. Appoint someone your agent and have them run the deal and maximize the value of your business assets.

Be Sure You Have a Fully Loaded 12-Gauge in Your Hands When:

- You spot a market opportunity but you are so busy keeping your existing customers happy that you say to yourself, "I can't handle that now. I'll wait for the next one."

- You are handed the opportunity to do something that will make you a household word in your industry, but it comes at a time when you were planning a long-cherished vacation.

- You see an opportunity that will help you significantly grow your business, but you fear you haven't the education, training, or skills to take advantage of it.

- You find yourself focusing on things that are "urgent and not important," as opposed to things that are "important and not urgent."

MoneyHunt Hero: Harlan Baxter

Harlan Baxter had made it out of Brooklyn many, many years ago but, as they say, Brooklyn had stayed in Harlan Baxter. Harlan was a super salesman who relished the opportunity to launch into selling just about anything. He was just as happy to sell you on going to one restaurant over another as he was selling his relatively mundane corrugated boxes and vinyl organizers to anyone in his path. He was relentless when he wanted something, or wanted to sell something.

It was also interesting to note that Harlan appeared the master delegator. We had heard through the grapevine that there was nothing on the man's desk. When he received a fax or a memo or a piece of paper, he read it, ripped it, and dumped it in the trash barrel. "Why keep it around?" he would say, "I know it now." Keeping his desk clean was important to Harlan's self-image. His delegation was a two-edged sword, however, as Harlan could also be a control freak when he wanted to be. As much responsibility as he delegated to his subordinates, he would snap it back instantly if he perceived they were about to make the wrong step. If they did do the wrong thing, he treated them brutally. His half-hour harangues behind closed doors in his office—the penalty for making a bad decision or failing to fill an order on time—were feared by everyone in the company.

It was a little surprising that so large and successful a company was on MoneyHunt, but Harlan had a new idea for an exciting new product category and was considering raising outside financing to launch it.

Harlan's company, Box-Rite Corporation, distributed a variety of corrugated storage products, hangers, and vinyl organizers. It was the type of low-tech business that bounces along in the housewares industry for generations, making decent money but not making too many splashes. Harlan had been about the most exciting thing to come along in corrugated organizers when he designed a line of nicely colored "decorator" boxes that his customers, usually single women living in an apartment, would use for underbed and closet storage. Any brown box would have done the job just fine, but the floral patterns made things a little more acceptable, and the long, low-cut boxes were especially ideal for sweaters and the like being stored for the winter.

Soon Harlan added products to round out the line, including color-coordinated vinyl storage bags for shoes and the like, specially padded hangers for delicate garments, and bags of cedar chips to keep the moths out of the game. The fact that these could all be coordinated with colored prints and sold as a set through the major discount chains such as Wal-Mart, Kmart, and Target Stores allowed Harlan to carve a niche in the organizer business and become one of the most profitable small companies in the American housewares industry.

Being essentially a distributor in the housewares business, his profitability came from the efficiencies built into his operations. Distribution companies must remain very nimble, and Harlan had taken all the waste out of the ordering and shipping process. Most all of his accounts were on electronic data interchange, so the orders came in automatically via the company's computer network. The warehouse ran like a racetrack and used the most sophisticated tracking software available to coordinate shipments coming in from hundreds of suppliers, which were repacked and reshipped to Harlan's customers within twenty-four hours.

Harlan was turning his inventory twenty-five times a year, and his maximum churns of inventory allowed him to achieve maximum efficiencies and tremendous cash flow on a very low asset business. Like the most successful distributors, Harlan ran his company like a spinning top.

Somewhere along the line the housewares business decided it should start consolidating itself and each week brought new announcements of dramatic combinations of plastic, canvas, vinyl, and corrugated container companies merging with and acquiring each other to form a few eight-hundred-pound gorillas combining salesforces, marketing efforts, design, and distribution. More importantly in a consolidated industry, larger companies gained economies of scale on their smaller competitors. When wild fluctuations in resin and corrugated raw materials costs hit the housewares market, they caught the smaller companies off guard and unable to raise prices swiftly enough to preserve margins. Thus weakened, many sold out or simply went under.

Meanwhile, Harlan was large enough to anticipate these trends and lock up long-term supplier agreements before the fluctuations could hurt his precious profit margins. His company was not quite an eight-hundred-pound gorilla, but it was large enough to demand stability from its vendors. In an effort to further diversify his product line, Harlan was working on launching a new expanded cedar-products division that would complement nicely his other storage activities. It was this new cedar-products division that prompted his appearance on *MoneyHunt*.

Shortly after Harlan's appearance on *MoneyHunt*, out of the blue, he received an offer to buy his entire business. To Harlan's way of thinking, at least initially, the offer could not have come at a worse time. His launching of the new cedar-products division was going to make his profit margins shrink. He had been feuding with a nonactive partner about their future together, and their feud was spilling over, entangling negotiations with his main corrugated paper source, which it happens was owned by his partner.

Add to these concerns the fact that the company was hitting its heavy selling season and he had no current business plan developed, there seemed like a hundred reasons not to do the deal or even respond to the inquiry. Just before Harlan ripped up the offer and dumped it in his wastebasket, however, a news flash hit his desk. The headline, in an industry trade magazine, described the trials and tribulations of a Chicago-based investment firm named International Consolidated Investment Partners, or ICIP. The article reported that ICIP was beginning to get pressure from its investors because the $200 million fund it had raised to consolidate companies in the housewares industry had not yielded one investment in its first eighteen months. Two deals had recently fallen through, and it was safe to say that at this point ICIP's money was burning a hole in its pocket. ICIP's managers would have to spend it somewhere in the housewares industry, or soon face giving it back to their investors.

The article went on to say that ICIP also had a tremendous banking relationship with a major middle-market senior and subordinated lender in Chicago. Harlan realized that the banking relationship, coupled with ICIP's equity, could allow ICIP to pay top dollar for companies. This was definitely worth a telephone call.

Harlan checked with an agent he knew and found out ICIP had been offering five to eight times pretax earnings for core businesses in the housewares industry that could lead ICIP to a consolidation plan. Both the deals that had fallen through had been in that range. A major factor in their not closing was the lack of management talent at each of these targets.

Harlan read on, which meant that he actually had two separate pieces of paper on his desk at one time for the first time in perhaps years. This is one hungry buyer, he concluded, and, smiling, he knew he had one perfect company for them to use as their core vehicle for consolidating the industry. Now, three times pretax earnings was all Harlan ever thought he could get for his business. On the average day he was probably right—companies with low asset bases relying on meteoric growth don't often get much more than five times pretax earnings in the crowded market.

This was the crucial time for Harlan to realize a tremendous windfall, and despite the timing not being optimal, Harlan jumped. He could have thought of a thousand excuses not to pursue the opportunity, but here was the chance to get twice to three times what he ever could have expected for his business.

If Harlan had been a duck hunter at this point, the sky around his blind would have been full of 12-gauge iron shot. He met with his sales team to pump up sales in the corrugated box and vinyl divisions of the company. He hatched a plan to give his large customers promotional programs that would lock in higher sales, despite the effect this had of pinching his margins slightly. He delayed launch of the expanded cedar-products line for another quarter, and—a crucial move—he visited the nonactive partner/supplier with whom he was squabbling and got him to give Harlan his irrevocable proxy to his shares in Harlan's company if Harlan received a bona fide offer of $10 million or more for the company. This would save Harlan a lot of time later.

Harlan roused his senior management team and let them in on the opportunity, offering them a small equity piece in the deal if it went through. Harlan insisted that they give their all to the company and do whatever it would take for the next three months in order to get the deal closed. He would rework his equity piece later to his advantage. He prepared a flawless business plan, which he designed to look very much like he was going to shop his deal to the highest bidder, when indeed he was focused on just one buyer. Thus he avoided the flaw of an auction with only one bidder.

Harlan "allowed" ICIP to make a "preemptive bid" which, if high enough, would preclude Harlan from going anywhere else to shop the deal, and he attached onerous conditions in terms of timing, due diligence, and financing, which, ironically, made ICIP all the more interested.

ICIP desperately needed to buy a core company to drive its consolidation strategy in housewares, and Harlan's company looked like the quickest, best building block to start with. A week later an offer came through to Harlan of eight times pretax earnings, or $25 million cash, a number almost obscene for the housewares industry. Harlan smiled, and asked for more.

Since Harlan already had his partner's proxy to sell the company for anything above $10 million, he worked out a way to keep a small equity stake in the new company in addition to his cash price. Once ICIP agreed to that, Harlan turned around and effectively resold that equity interest to his key managers, because otherwise he would have had to cough that up as part of his promise to them. Since they would be staying with Harlan's company after the acquisition by ICIP, it made sense that they had a piece of the action, and Harlan certainly had no interest in holding the bag while his company had a $25 million ball and chain around its neck.

With the acquisition now completed, Harlan was able to convince ICIP that they didn't want his company's cedar-products operation. It detracted from their core business and adversely affected their profit margins. Instead, Harlan formed his own cedar-products company, which then entered into supply contracts with ICIP to put cedar in each one of Harlan's former company's boxes as a value-added item, thus locking in guaranteed sales for his newly owned cedar operation. This side deal for the cedar-products operation added about a million dollars of present value to Harlan's purchase price, since he was keeping that asset but not being docked for it.

It's a good thing the deal closed when it did because the way things were going it seemed like Harlan could have gotten $50 million from these guys and still owned half the company. As it was, Harlan didn't do too badly. The $25 million would have been split equally with his partner, yet his partner had agreed to sell his share for $5 million, or half of the $10 million expected purchase price. Harlan would also have had to share a portion of his price with his key managers had he not arranged at the end for the managers to have a small piece of the new highly leveraged company instead of a piece of the cash Harlan was taking out. Add the million dollars of asset value from the cedar operation that he was able to withhold from the transaction, and Harlan walked away with $21 million before taxes for his half of a dinky distribution business in the housewares industry doing three million bucks pretax in a good year.

God bless America!

LESSONS FROM HARLAN BAXTER

Harlan's story is a great example of mobilizing when an opportunity is upon you.

Had he lingered until his cedar business was up and running as he was tempted to do, it might have been three, four, or five quarters before Harlan could focus on an acquisition. ICIP and its affiliated venture fund might have been out of money by then, or maybe by then their core companies would have been bought and they would have stopped paying eight times pretax earnings, or maybe ICIP's investors would have yanked the money back because they hadn't employed any of it. Had Harlan not sprung into action when he did, he probably would not have gotten any of that money that was just lying around looking for a big, juicy company like his.

What Harlan did to his 50 percent partner was somewhat ruthless, but one could argue that had Harlan not had his partner's proxy and an option to sell his partner's shares at a set price, his partner might have insisted on a full 50 percent share all the way up to $25 million. In any event, $5 million is not exactly chicken feed, so please don't cry for Harlan's partner too much.

Had Harlan botched the presentation, ICIP would not have felt the pressure to do the deal and might have thought itself in an "only game in town" situation. An auction with only one bidder usually gets a lower price. Harlan went the distance with the pitch and put the heat on, prompting ICIP to make a preemptive bid before he could shop his company to another investor (something Harlan never really intended to do).

Finally, because Harlan cut his managers into the deal, albeit through sleight of hand, promising them one thing but changing course and convincing them their new position was better, he was able to keep their interest throughout and avoid having them feel overtaxed and underloved at a crucial time.

Harlan landed the big prize because he was willing to give it his all when the target was overhead. As he sensed how badly ICIP really wanted to buy his company, he was able to keep reloading and shooting and landing more value.

So take a lesson from Harlan . . . shoot ducks when they're flying, and for God's sake, don't leave any rounds in the chamber.

Appendices

APPENDIX A

The *MoneyHunt* Story

Since this is a book of "war stories" involving entrepreneurs who have either appeared on MoneyHunt or been screened for an appearance on the show, it is only appropriate that we tell our own story of how we founded MoneyHunt.

The idea for MoneyHunt was born in a middle school classroom in Fairfield, Connecticut, in early 1995. Cliff Ennico, a former Wall Street lawyer who was building a small business practice in southern Connecticut and teaching adult-education courses on business law and management in the hopes of attracting new clients, had invited his friend Miles Spencer to join him in a presentation on "Raising Capital for Your New Business." The room was designated to hold twenty-five middle school students in those teeny tiny little plastic chairs we all remember painfully from our childhood; over two hundred adult entrepreneurs showed up for the presentation and squeezed into the chairs, spilling out into the hallways and into adjoining rooms. No strangers to last-minute changes in plans, we moved the presentation to a larger room where it was "standing room only."

Midway through the program, the school fire marshal interrupted to say that there were too many people in the room and that we would have to cut the program short. Accepting this verdict, we stopped our back-and-forth banter and opened the floor to questions. A hand went up, and a person stood up and asked a question that has haunted us now for several years: "You two guys are great together—you are like the Siskel and Ebert of small business. Why don't you turn this into a radio or TV show?" It is rare that you can identify the precise moment when a successful business takes root, but for *MoneyHunt*, that was it. We hope someday to find the person who asked that question. We owe him or her (we don't remember which) a bouquet of flowers at the very least. It was all we could talk or think about for weeks afterwards: Why not do a television show about entrepreneurs on the firing line?

It wasn't the first time that we had given a joint presentation. In fact, we met for the first time on the public-speaking circuit. Every year one of our local entrepreneurs organizations has a luncheon honoring the most promising new "players" in the Fairfield County, Connecticut, small-business community. We had both been selected as honorees and sat next to each other on the dais. Despite significant differences in background, style, and temperament, we hit it off and soon became fast friends. Shortly after the venture-club luncheon, Miles called Cliff and asked for legal help on a number of his investments in private companies, while Cliff asked Miles for help in drafting a magazine article on small-business-financing techniques.

Whenever Miles needed a speaker to talk about legal issues during one of his entrepreneurial talks, he invited Cliff along. Whenever Cliff needed someone to talk about raising money and dealing with investors, he invited Miles along. Pretty soon we both stopped asking and did all our small-business programs together. We became a "team" and were soon invited to give joint presentations for entrepreneurial associations, venture-capital clubs, chapters of the Service Corps of Retired Executives (SCORE—an association of retired businesspeople who donate their time to give advice to struggling small-business owners in their communities), colleges, and business schools throughout the northeastern United States. Which eventually led us to that middle school classroom, and to *MoneyHunt*.

We knew right away how we were going to structure our entrepreneurial television show (as yet unnamed). We would bring on two entrepreneurs, critique their business plans, and then (this was the initial idea) rate the business plans on a scale of 1 to 10, just like the Olympics. We even had little plaques printed with the numbers 1 through 10 on them so we could hold them up like the Olympic referees do. The show would end with the two of us critiquing each other's judgment and rating of the entrepreneurs, just like we did in our live presentations. "Cliff, you're out of your mind; as usual you're thinking like a lawyer, not a businessperson." "Miles, as usual you've got your head so far up your rear end that you can see daylight. The guy's got a great story, and you're a sucker for great stories, but there are some details that are going to present some real problems for him down the road." Remember, we're very close friends. Watching the show or listening to one of our live presentations, you may not believe that, but it's true. Trust us.

Within a few weeks of our middle school enlightenment, we had booked studio time at our local cable television station in Norwalk, Connecticut, and had signed an agreement to produce thirteen episodes of our new show for public-access cable TV—the same place where you find the crazy preachers, the teenagers talking about their favorite rock bands, and the call-in show for people who are into ancient Greek coins. Nonetheless, it was a start. Miles commissioned a local carpenter to build an "interview table" that looked vaguely like the Superman insignia with three legs, two of which maybe were the same length (we learned to support the table with our knees during the show so it wouldn't wobble). Miles's wife, a leading graphic designer in our area, designed a logo for our show which we still use—a coin, a clock, and a compass—representing the money, time, and strategic direction (i.e., a terrific idea) that one must have to build a successful business.

We had only two problems: Neither of us had appeared before a TV camera in our entire lives, and we didn't have a name for the show. Miles bought a video camcorder, and we began practicing around a conference table in Miles's office, with Miles's mother holding the camera and various of our personal friends pretending to be entrepreneurs. We recognized that this would not be enough.

Our "not ready for TV" problem was solved when we hired a producer for our foray into the netherworld of public-access TV—a beautiful local grandmother named Joyce Fischman—who taught us when (and when not) to look at the cameras, how to sit at a table (we had thought we knew how to do that, but we were wrong), how we can't wear the same color sports jackets on the set, and so forth. We became Joyce's surrogate children, and believe us, we obeyed. Joyce was also brilliant at dealing with (read: disciplining) the technical people that were assigned to us. You must know, if you are thinking of doing a TV show on public-access cable, that public-access cable does not attract the world's greatest technical talent. The camerapeople and floor managers would show up for the tapings a half an hour late after a three-martini dinner at the Italian bistro next door to the studios, forget to give us our cues, let us get through a full fifteen-minute segment with an entrepreneur only to tell us afterwards there was a technical glitch and we had to do the whole thing over, and ask Cliff for free legal advice during the (all too frequent) production delays. We recall one early episode where Cliff was explaining how the show worked, and the camera angle cut him off at the nose so that all you could see was his mouth moving.

Despite the obstacles, the show happened, and began to build a local following. We held a contest among our friends to name the show, and some of the names that were actually volunteered (these people are still our friends) were:

Quest for Capital (or Capital Quest—try saying it five times fast).

The Entrepreneur's Information Exchange.

So You Think You Can Run a Business?

The Small Business Gong Show.

Your Business, the World, and You.

The Patron Saint of All Entrepreneurs.

We settled on MoneyHunt, partly because we liked the sound of it and partly because we felt it would be easily remembered. Every once in a while Cliff can be counted on to introduce the show as "Monkey Hunt," but otherwise it works.

During our twelve months on public-access cable TV, we made a few changes to the show. We got rid of the Olympic-style ratings, for one thing. Not that it didn't work on TV—it actually worked quite well. Viewers would sit on the edge of their seats waiting to see what numbers Miles and Cliff would come up with. The problem was that even though Miles and Cliff look at the world of entrepreneurship from entirely different angles, their gut instincts were (and still are) perfectly in tune, as if they were part of the same organism. We can't tell you how many times it happened that, after a knock-down-drag-out "analysis section" where Miles and Cliff vigorously disagreed over the merits of a particular business plan, the following dialogue occurred:

"So what did you rate the business plan, Cliff?"

"I gave it a seven. What did you give it, Miles?"

"Uh, seven."

The most important change was the addition of a third panelist. By removing the Olympic-style rating system, we now no longer had a "hook" at the end of the show to keep viewers interested. So we developed the concept of having a "famous name" act as a guest panelist—someone who would be a "household word" in the guest entrepreneurs' industry. At the end of our analysis section, when the three of us would debate the merits of each entrepreneur's business plan, the guest panelist (who quickly became dubbed the "MoneyHunt Mentor") would offer to give one of the entrepreneurs some free consulting time to help them overcome the problems we identified during the show.

At the same time as we were putting together a unique and original TV show, we were also building a business, with all of the problems and headaches that our entrepreneurial guests were facing every day. We formed a limited liability company, MoneyHunt Properties, LLC, to own all rights to the "MoneyHunt" name (it is now a registered trademark), produce the TV show, and build a brand identity within the small-business community for advice and resources about raising capital. Miles manages the day-to-day operations of the business, with assistance from Capital Express, LLC, a New Jersey–based venture-capital firm that was our first investor.

At the same time we launched *MoneyHunt* on public-access cable TV, we set up a World Wide Web site at www.moneyhunter.com as a clearing-house of information, resources, and advice for entrepreneurs nation-wide. In less than two years, our moneyhunter.com site has become one of the most popular Internet venues for small-business financing. Among the services we've added to the site over the years are:

The MoneyHunt Business Plan Template: an interactive "form" that walks you step by step through the process of writing a business plan for consideration by investors, which to date has been used by more than 500,000 entrepreneurs throughout the world.

The MoneyHunt Mentors: offering bullet-form tips for raising capital from Cliff, Miles, the MoneyHunt Mentors (past and present), the MoneyHunt Brain Trust, and other entrepreneurs who have done it before and succeeded.

The MoneyHunt "How to Hunt" Newsletter: articles and advice on raising capital for a growing business from some of the leading people in the venture-capital industry, which is delivered by e-mail twice a month to more than 100,000 entrepreneurs throughout the world.

On-line Auditions: allowing entrepreneurs to volunteer as guests for our TV show for a fee, which is currently $35 (most of our current guests are first introduced to us through the on-line audition).

The MoneyHunt Community Page: featuring on-line chat rooms, seminars, and other interactive information resources for entrepreneurs and investors.

In our first year of operations we raised private capital from a number of individual investors, including some major "players" in the television industry who could furnish contacts and introductions to the "powers that be" in television as well as their money. These investors were asked to join an advisory board, which quickly became known as the "MoneyHunt Brain Trust." As a result of the Brain Trust's activities and Miles's active solicitation of television executives throughout the country, we approached WHYY Channel 12 in Philadelphia, Pennsylvania, and soon returned with an offer to bring MoneyHunt to public television.

The rest, as they say, is history. Adjusting to public television and a nationwide audience has taken time, effort, and money. Among some of the changes we've made since our first public television show two years ago:

The addition of a "feedback session" where the entrepreneurs appearing on the show can tell us what they thought of our analysis of their business plan (we felt it was only fair to give them the last word). This part of the show is hosted by Margot Lee, a television "natural" who first became known to us when she e-mailed a question to our Web site.

The construction of a world-class set, which one of our management team describes as a cross between the Temple of Dendur and the bridge of the Starship *Enterprise*, but which has been nominated for a number of design awards.

The addition of a world-class production team including our producer Deb Ely and our personal trainer and coach Wellington "Tad" Jones (producer of off-Broadway shows and world-class Washington, D.C., fund-raising events).

The addition of a "letter from our fans" section where Cliff reads and answers a question that was posted by a viewer to our Web site.

The addition of one or two "anniversary" shows each season, where we bring back entrepreneurs who had appeared on the show in prior seasons and give them the opportunity to tell us "what really happened" and whether our analysis was on target or not (this usually gives Miles or Cliff, whoever was right, the chance to gloat at the other's expense on nationwide TV).

As MoneyHunt continues to grow in popularity, we are pursuing a number of business opportunities to expand the MoneyHunt franchise globally and establish MoneyHunt as the resource for entrepreneurs worldwide. These efforts include:

Extending MoneyHunt worldwide (the show is currently broadcast in Japan over BBT Tokyo, in conjunction with SkyPerfect TV, and plans are under way for syndicating MoneyHunt in several European, Middle Eastern, and Asian countries).

Developing a syndicated MoneyHunt radio show offering advice, business plan critiques, and interviews with successful entrepreneurs around the world.

Developing a syndicated MoneyHunt column for newspapers and small-business magazines.

Developing information resources for entrepreneurs, such as our CD-ROM venture-capital directory.

Dare we say it in print? MoneyHunt tchotchkes—T-shirts, watches (with coin, clock, and compass logo), coffee mugs, and brand merchandise. Maybe Miles and Cliff plush voodoo dolls for entrepreneurs who get trashed on the show?

But as MoneyHunt grows, we know that some things will never change:

"Miles, once again, you're totally off base. You have no appreciation of this industry and what it really takes to generate revenue."

"Cliff, once again your head is in the law library, not in the real world. You're right when you say our guest has underestimated her competition, but hey, every dog has its day."

We are still friends . . . trust us.

APPENDIX B

Business Plan Template

The first step toward starting or growing a business is having a business plan that maps out your course. The document can serve two masters: As an internal piece, it can be a compass for your company's goals and directions. As an external piece, it is used to solicit interest from potential partners, key employees, and key business alliances. Both versions should be living documents, updated and improved as the business and its market evolves.

Miles spent ten years raising money for growing companies and eventually developed this template as a starting point for every plan he wrote. It was used to write the business plan for MoneyHunt Properties, LLC, and became the first item offered on www.moneyhunter.com. The template's popularity in the small-business community helped launch MoneyHunt and helped hundreds of thousands of entrepreneurs write their first business plans.

This entire template can be downloaded from our Web site at www.moneyhunter.com.

THE MONEYHUNTER
Business Plan Template

TITLE PAGE

Here's your sample Title Page. It's a great idea to put a color picture of your product right on the front. But leave room for the following information.

[Your Company Name]

Month, Year
[month and year issued]

Business Plan Copy Number [x]

This document is confidential. It is not for redistribution.

[Name of point man in financing]
[Title]
[Address]
[City, State, Zip]
[Phone]
[e-mail]
[company home page URL]

This is a business plan. It does not imply an offering of securities.

TABLE OF CONTENTS

Here's a sample Table of Contents. Be sure to modify the page numbers when you've finished your Business Plan.

EXECUTIVE SUMMARY

If the executive summary doesn't succeed, your business plan will never sell investors. We recommend that you write the summary first and use it as a template for the plan as a whole. Since one of its primary functions is to capture the investor's attention, the summary should be no longer than two pages. The shorter the better.

Want to see what the pros think about raising money? Tune into The MoneyHunt Show (for info on showtimes, etc., go to http://www.moneyhunter.com/htm/show/show.htm).

Mission

Our company's mission is to [describe your ultimate goal, or insert your mission statement].

Company

[The Company] was founded in [date] and [describe what your business does, such as baby products manufacturer, distributor of pencils, provider of medical services]. It is a [legal form of your company, such as LLC, S-Corporation, C-Corporation, Partnership, Proprietorship]. Our principal offices are located at [x].

Business

We make [describe product, or service that you make or provide].

Our company is at the [seed, start-up, growth] stage of business, having just [developed our first product, hired our first salesman, booked our first national order].

In the most recent [period], our company achieved sales of [x], and showed a [profit, loss, break-even]. With the financing contemplated herein, our company expects to achieve [x] in sales and [x] in pretax profits in [year] and achieve [x] in sales and [x] in pretax profits in [year+1]. We can achieve this because the funds will allow us to [describe what you will do with the funds, such as (a) marketing for your new product, (b) build or expand facilities to meet increased demand, (c) add retail locations or others means of distribution, (d) increase research and development for new products or to improve existing ones.

Product or Service

Tell us about your product or service in terms we can understand.

[The company] produces the following products: [list products here briefly, in order of highest sales or significance in product line].

Alternatively,

[The company] delivers the following services: [list services here briefly, in order of highest sales or significance in product line].

Presently, our [product or service] is in the [introductory, growth, maturity] stage. We plan to follow this [product or service] with extensions to our line which include [x, y, and z].

Critical factors in the [production of our product or delivery of our service] are [x and y]. Our [product or service] is unique because [x, y, or z] and/or we have an advantage in the marketplace because of our [patent, speed to market, brand name].

The Market

We define our market as [manufacture and sale of writing and drawing instruments, low-fat cheese, oral-care products]. This market was approximately [$x] at [wholesale or retail] last [period available], according to [cite resource], and is expected to grow to [$x] by the year [x], according to [cite resource].

Competition

Who are your customers? Where are they, and how do you reach them? Are they buying your product/service from someone else?

How will you educate customers to buy from you? Why will they care?

We compete directly with [name competition]. *Or,* We have no direct competition, but there are alternatives to our [product or service] in the marketplace. Our [product or service] is unique because of [x] and/or we have a competitive advantage because of our [speed to market, established brand name, low-cost producer status].

Risk/Opportunity

The greatest risks we have in our business today are [market risk, pricing risk, product risk, management risk]. We feel we can overcome these risks because of [x].

The opportunities before us are significant; we have the opportunity to [dominate a niche in the marketplace, become a major force in the industry] if we can [x].

Management Team

Our team has the following members to achieve our plan. [x] men and women who have a combined [x] years of experience; [y] years in marketing, [y] years in product development, and [y] years in [other disciplines].

Capital Requirements

We seek [$] of additional [equity, sub-debt, or senior financing], which will enable us to [describe why you need the funds, and why the opportunity is exciting]. We can provide an exit for this [loan, investment] within [x] years by [a dividend of excess profits, recapitalizations, sale of company, or public offering].

Financial Plan

At this point the investor must have a clear idea of where your business stands today. If you bore him or make the information he needs hard to find, you get canned. You must provide a snapshot, however sparse, of your financial position.

Sales Summary

	Last Year	This Year	Next Year	Year Two
Sales:	_____	_____	_____	_____
Gross profit:	_____	_____	_____	_____
Pre-tax:	_____	_____	_____	_____

Balance Sheet Summary

Assets:	_____
Liabilities:	_____
Book Value:	_____

In [x] years we will provide an exit, which we expect to be in the form of [sale to a competitor, initial public offering, distribution of profits] or perhaps [z]. We expect to be able to achieve this in [b months/years].

MISSION

No one understands a successful company's mission like entrepreneurs who have built success-ful companies themselves. See MoneyHunter's mentors at http://www.moneyhunter.com/htm/mentor/mentors.htm.

Mission Statement

Our goal is to become [describe your ultimate goal, or insert your mission statement; example: the leading manufacturer and marketer of branded in-line skate replacement wheels or the first name in low-fat cheese].

We aspire to carry a reputation in the marketplace for developing and delivering [time saving, better-way products sold at a fair price for uses in the (x) market]. We can achieve this by [cutting-edge product development, close understanding of market trends and needs, innovative and profitable merchandising and packaging].

To accomplish our goal, [your company name] needs [capital, management talent, larger, more efficient facilities].

In pursuit of our goal, we resolve to treat stakeholders, customers, and the community with [description of the reputation your company seeks]. These groups see our company as providing [describe benefits to each group of being associated with your company].

THE COMPANY

[The Company] was founded in [date] and [describe what your business does, such as baby products manufacturer, distributor of pencils, provider of medical services]. The legal name of the business is [x]. *Include d.b.a. in the legal name.*

It is a [legal form of your company, such as LLC, S-Corporation, C-Corporation, Partnership, Proprietorship]. Our principal offices are located at [list primary address as well as any other facilities]. We have approximately [x] square feet of office space and [x] square feet of [factory or warehouse]. Our current capacity is [x] units per month. If we exceed [x] units per month, we will need additional space. We expect this facility to be adequate for the company's needs for [two years, a year, a week] after funding.

Regulations and Permits *(cut now if inappropriate)*

[Your Company Name] operates in the [toxic waste, weapons and armaments, genetic engineering, explosives] industry, or [uses controlled substances in the manufacturing process or delivery of service], and falls under the jurisdiction of the [name government agency].

[Your Company Name] has all necessary permits to operate, and has an up-to-date record of inspections. These permits include: [list briefly here]. These agencies regulate our business in the following manner: [we must document and account for uses and disposal of all toxic materials or we must document and background check all employees with access to the launch codes for our missiles].

Strategic Alliances

The leverage from relationships can be appealing to investors. Explain how you work with others to improve your performance.

[Your Company Name] has developed important and profitable strategic alliances with the following larger, more established business: [describe each company, its position in the marketplace, the details of the alliance, and what risks are involved in the alliance]. For example, we have developed marketing agreements with [x], the [market leader in gummed erasers] which will enable us to sell, alongside them, our [extramessy children's pencils].

The side-by-side positioning at retail, as well as the ability to share wholesale sales leads with their established customer base, can help us penetrate the market more quickly.

The risk in the relationship is that they may [decide to sell pencils themselves] and cut us out of the process.

Another type of strategic relationship that benefits the company is our development joint venture with [x]. We would never be able to fund the research of the new [low-fat Swiss cheese that melts smoothly], but with access to their prior research in [smooth-melting cheddar] we cut our development time in half. By using some of their [equipment, or people] who were not being utilized fully, we were able to avoid the expense of [major capital expenditures, additions to the payroll]. We have agreed to pay a royalty of [x] to this development partner for their role in this product's ultimate success.

We have a strategic relationship with a number of suppliers. In exchange for a blanket commitment to purchase [more than 80 percent of our supply of a specific raw material from them], they have agreed to [not make it available to the market at large for six months, or to give us a preferential price].

[Your Company Name] also has strategic Original Equipment Manufacturer relationships with a number of customers. This allows us to sell a large and steady volume of [in-line skate wheels] to [boot manufacturers, who use them to sell complete skate sets]. This gets many units of our product out into the marketplace; however, it provides little or no brand awareness for us.

THE BUSINESS

[Your Company Name] is a [manufacturer, distributor, marketer, service provider] of [describe your product or service].

Our company is at the [seed, start-up, growth] stage of business, having just [developed our first product, hired our first salesman, booked our first national order].

Product or Service

Explain how your product works or how the service is used. What burning marketplace needs are addressed by your product? What value do you add to the product?

The Mentors also have a wealth of experience when it comes to positioning their products. See http://www.moneyhunter.com/htm/mentor/mentors.htm.

[The company] produces the following products: [list products here, in order of highest sales or significance in product line].

Be sure to refer readers to product pictures, diagrams, patents, and other descriptive material.

Or, alternatively:

[The company] delivers the following services: [list services here briefly, in order of highest sales or significance in product line].

Be sure to refer readers to brochures and material describing your service.

Presently, our [product or service] is in the [introductory, growth, maturity] stage. We first developed our [product or service] in [year] and have made [x] improvements and redesigns since then.

Provide a history of product developments, introductions, and improvements leading up to the present day. Table form may be appropriate.

Unique Features or Proprietary Aspects of Product

This is a crucial paragraph. Investors must see something unique, proprietary, or protected about your product or service.

Our products are unique because of [secret ingredient, our patented process, our proprietary manufacturing process].

Others in the market are able to provide somewhat similar [products or services], but we are able to differentiate ourselves in the market because of [x].

We have [applied, been granted, licensed] a patent for [x], an abstract of which can be found in appendix [x]. We have integrated this into our process, which others will not be able to duplicate. Our lead product, [x], addresses the following customer needs [x] and delivers [x] benefits to customers.

Tell us about the unique value-added characteristics your product line or process provides to customers and how these characteristics translate into a competitive advantage for your company.

Research and Development

Our research and development is headed by [name of person or contractor] whose major objective is to use market input to [develop products that solve problems or provide superior benefits to customers]. Last [period], our R&D yielded the following products and innovations: [list products or innovations]. [Your Company name] has spent [% of revenues, or absolute $] in the past year in R&D, and plans to spend [% or $] in the next [period].

Our R&D occasionally yields innovation without input from customers or the marketplace. Our product selection criteria in this case is as follows: [relatively low investment requirements, positive return on investment, fit with present strategy, feasibility of development and production, relatively low risk, time to see intended results, buyer in common]. Our R&D will require additional resources in the future. These will include [people, capital expenditures] to [speed up development process, test results more efficiently].

New and Follow-on Products

Responding to market needs, we plan to follow [product or service] with extensions to our line which include [x, y, and z].

Our target introduction dates for these products are [x, y, and z], which corresponds with [a major trade show, industry event]. In addition, we plan to introduce the following new products in the upcoming season: [x, y, and z].

Production

Our [product, service] is [manufactured in-house, assembled in-house from components from various vendors, (service) provided by our staff, or subcontracted to field consultants]. [Raw materials, subassemblies, components] used in our products are readily available from a variety of manufacturers who can meet our quality standards.

Critical factors in the [production of our product, or delivery of our service] are [x and y].

Enumerate and explain capital-equipment, material, and labor requirements. Are the above items readily available? Do you have multiple supply sources? List inventory requirements, quality and technical specifications, hazardous materials.

Uniqueness

Our [product or service] is unique because [x, y, or z] and/or we have an advantage in the marketplace because of our [patent, speed to market, brand name].

THE MARKET

Sad fact: This is the most crucial but worst-prepared section of most business plans.

Market Definition

What markets are you competing in? If you make glove-compartment hinges, don't gush about the $80 billion automobile market. You make hinges—not cars—for that market, so tell us how many hinges were sold last year. Are there other markets where you sell your products?

For specific information on understanding your market, see "How to Hunt," http://www.moneyhunter.com/htm/hunt.htm.

We [expect to compete, are competing] in the [define niche] of the [define industry]. This market was approximately [$x] at [wholesale or retail] last [period available], according to [cite resource]. We believe, the major future trend in the industry will be toward [environmentally-oriented, miniaturized, high-quality, value-oriented] product offerings.

Market research [cite source] suggests this market will [grow/shrink] to [$x] by the year [year]. We expect the niche in which we compete to [grow, shrink, remain stagnant] during this time. The major forces affecting this change will be [falling cost of computers, explosion of home-based businesses, tendency for baby boomers to have fewer kids—and pamper their pets]. The area of greatest growth within the industry will be [x].

Identify where you got this information, and how up to date it is.

Market Segment

We define our market segment as [the writing and drawing instrument segment of the school/home/office products industry, the low-fat dairy products segment of the food industry]. This segment has been [volatile, steady] in the last few years. Industry experts [name them] forecast [x] for the industry in the next few years.

The major market segments are [segment a, segment b, segment c]. List, in general, the types of customers you are likely to reach (retailers, electrical contractors, catalog buyers, etc.) The [a] segment of the market is based on [product type] that retail in the [x to y] price range. Most of the sales in the segment are delivered through the [catalogs, retailers, manufacturers reps, OEMs].

A typical customer for our product is a person who currently may use [alternative product or service] for [what purpose]. They are motivated to buy our product because of [its value, its quality, its usefulness]. We know this from [customer responses, trade-show input, ad inquiries] and feel our customers perceive our products as [good value, superior performance, great taste].

Our product does, however, have the following weaknesses: [higher price point than most other cheeses, weak brand identity in a commodity market]. We are working to position our product as [x] in order to reduce this vulnerability.

Marketing

Our marketing plan is based on the following fundamentals:

We expect to penetrate the [x] segment of the market[s] and achieve this by using the [retail, mail order, multilevel marketing, Internet] as our primary distribution channel[s]. In time, we plan to capture [%] share of the market.

Position

We will position our product as [good value for price, top quality, cheap and fun], which is a position not presently being addressed by the competition. One demographic group in particular, the [elderly, Hispanic, generation X, techies] has a particular need for this product, and we tailor our positioning accordingly.

Pricing

Our pricing strategy is [describe policy, or at least philosophy].

Is this pricing based on cost? Gross margin objectives? Market?

We arrive at our pricing based on [cost, gross margin objectives, market prices, perceived value].

We review this pricing [monthly, quarterly, annually] to ensure that potential profits are not squandered. Customers seem willing to pay as much as [x] because of [explain reasoning].

Distribution Channels

The distribution channels we use for our product are [wholesalers, catalogers, mass-merchant retailers, consolidators]. These make sense for delivering our product to the end user because [customer profile, geography, seasonal swings]. The competition uses the [wholesalers, catalogers, mass-merchant retailers, consolidators] channel. Our channel will prove more advantageous because [x].

Our major current customers include: [list top five, with one- or two-sentence descriptions]. The attached chart [see appendix z] demonstrates how our product reaches the customer.

Advertising, Promotion, Trade Shows

Your purpose is to introduce, promote, and support your products in the marketplace. Although considered a cost, a properly designed and executed campaign is an investment.

[Your Company Name] has developed a comprehensive advertising and promotion strategy, which will be implemented by the best possible firm when funding is completed. We expect to have a presence in several national magazines as well as the trade press. We will produce our own ads and be a part of ad campaigns of our JV partners or OEMs. Our publicity plan is to remain in constant contact with editors and writers of the [trade journals that serve our industry] and seek stories and coverage that will [enhance our reputation, introduce us to buyers].

We plan to promote our product through a variety of [on-site product sampling, demonstrations at high-profile events, give-aways at fundraisers] and other high-leverage events. The objective of all our promotions is to [expand the audience, position our product as a premium brand, strengthen our ties to the community].

[Your company name] participates in the following trade shows: [list trade shows, briefly describe organization that sponsors them and who attends, and describe presence there]. We have a regular [twenty-foot display booth of knockdown construction, which allows us to display our existing products and introduce new ones, or we prefer to attend trade shows as visitors and walk the show while displaying our wares only to prequalified buyers who will come to our nearby hospitality suite]. The following factors are taken into account when considering a trade show: Will this event help deliver our message to our target audience? Does the location of the show have significance? Is the time frame convenient? Is it a "must-go show"?

COMPETITION

Tell us about key competitors in regard to product, price, location, promotion, management, and financial position. False or incomplete information here translates as dishonesty and negligence to investors, bankers, etc. Do not delude yourself (or your investors) about your competition.

Look in your telephone book's yellow pages. Look in the industrial directories at your local library. Search on-line databases that provide competitive profiles of other companies. Read industry magazines and look for advertisers.

MoneyHunter can help you size up the competition: http://www.moneyhunter.com/htm/hunt.htm.

We have no direct competition, but there are alternatives to our [product or service] in the marketplace.

Or,

We compete directly with [name competitor a, b, and c].

Provide a sample of each . . .

[example . . . Acme Inc. is a $3 million sales manufacturer and marketer of pencils in the Northeast region. Acme Inc. is a division of Acme Corp., a public company with $800 million sales. The division sells pencils, pens, and other writing and drawing instruments. The recent trend for the division has been static, as the parent has not provided working capital to modernize machinery. Acme Inc. is managed by one Vice President who has been there for six months. The previous manager worked there for eleven months.]

The competition [does, doesn't] [use the same means of distribution as the company, advertise in the same trade journals]. *If the advertising is regular—it probably works!*

Our [product or service] is unique because of [x] and/or we have a competitive advantage because of our [speed to market, established brand name, low-cost producer status].

RISK/OPPORTUNITY

Business Risks

This is also a critically important part of the plan. Knowing your risks and having a strategy are a must for attracting an investor. There are several kinds of risk, especially among entrepreneurial, growing businesses. Be sure to address the following, and provide your strategy for dealing with them.

Moneyhunter's Mentors know a thing or two about taking risks. See http://www.moneyhunter.com/htm/mentor/mentors.htm.

Some of the major risks facing our development include [limited operating history, limited resources, market uncertainties, production uncertainties, limited management experience, dependence on key management].

Opportunities
This is also a critically important part of the plan. Use it to provide excitement and promise.

Although our business today has its share of risk, we feel we can overcome these risks because of [x]. We will address [market risk] by [doing a comprehensive study, partnering with a larger company who knows the market]. We feel we can address [pricing risk, product risk, management risk] by focusing on [x].

If we are able to overcome these risks, our company has the opportunity to [dominate a niche in the marketplace, become a major force in the industry]. We feel our brand could become known as the [place entrepreneurs look for financing help, the place people look for good-tasting, low-fat cheese]. We think we can achieve this goal in the next [x] years.

Specifically, our lead product [x], has the chance to [change the industry, affect many lives, improve performance in the (x) field]. This would also enable us to tap markets we have not yet begun to approach, such as [international sales, ethnic market, gen X].

MANAGEMENT TEAM

It is clichéd but true: Investing is a people business. Tell us not only about your managers but how they work together as a team.

Our team has the following members to achieve our plan. [x] men and women who have a combined [x] years of experience, [y] years in marketing, [y] years in product development, and [y] years in [other disciplines].

Frankly, if you have more than a few people filling these positions, you're lucky. Tell us who you have, how much they have aged, and how much of the company they own.

Officers and Key Employees	Age	Stock
[A], President	_____	_____
[B], Vice President of Marketing	_____	_____

[C], Vice President of Sales   _____   _____
[D], Vice President of Finance   _____   _____
[E], Vice President of R&D   _____   _____
[F], Vice President of Operations   _____   _____
[G], Controller   _____   _____
[H], Corporate Attorney   _____   _____

Ownership

The company has authorized [x] shares of common stock, of which [100] are issued and outstanding. The following persons or organizations are significant owners of the company:

Name	# Shares Held	% Ownership
[A. B. Founder]	52	[52%]
[C. R. Inventor]	22	[22%]
Management Team	10	[10%]
[Seed Ventures]	10	[10%]

Professional Support

We have strung together a team of professionals, including:
   [Corporate Attorney]
   [Accounting Firm]
   [Other Consultants]

Board of [Advisers, Directors]

We have also secured the assistance and support of the following business and industry experts to help in the decision making, strategizing, and opportunity pouncing process.

Highlight your board members, detailing where and why they add strategic importance, what experience they have, and what contacts they can contribute.

CAPITAL REQUIREMENTS

Needless to say, this is important—state what your capital requirements are.

MoneyHunter's Golden Rolodex can help you find investors to back you. Go to Footprints at http://www.moneyhunter.com/cfm/grolodex.htm.

We seek [$] of additional [equity, sub-debt, or senior financing] to fund our growth for the next [two years, year, month]. At that time, we will need an additional [$x] to reach a positive cash-flow position.

The initial stage of funding will be used to [complete development, purchase equipment, introduce and market our new/next product line, fund working capital, acquire a competitor]. Here is a breakdown of how the funds will be spent:

Complete development	[$x]
Purchase equipment	[$x]
Market our new/next product line	[$x]
Fund working capital	[$x]

We can provide an exit for this [loan, investment] within [x] years by [a dividend of excess profits, recapitalizations, sale of company, or public offering].

Define how much time you will require to pay back the loan or provide a return to investors. And tell us how the repayment will be accomplished, and what strategy will be used to achieve that exit.

Conclusion
Be bold, amigo(a). This is the finale of the entire document.

Based on our projections, we feel an [investment in, loan to] our Company is a sound business investment. In order to proceed, we are requesting an [investment, loan] of $[x] by [date].

FINANCIAL PLAN

Assumptions
The attached projections assume the following:

Income Statements
We recommend that financial statements be monthly for the first year or two, then quarterly thereafter. Incorporate year-to-date figures if they exist.

Sales will increase with the introduction of the [new line, improved line]. We plan to introduce these products roughly on the following schedule: [detail here]. And we expect to be able to sell at the rate of [x] units per month within [x] months of introduction.

Cost of goods sold will [decrease as a percentage] as we are able to buy more efficiently in the marketplace and use our new equipment to produce more units at lower cost.

Gross profit will remain static as [new introductions will be at higher margins, while we expect margins of older lines to erode].

Selling and administration expense will increase in absolute dollars, but decrease as a percentage because while expense is increasing, [name largest items here, or items that will change most significantly] our sales will be growing faster.

Research and development, which will appear as a high percentage of sales early, will be reduced as a percentage over time.

Our head count will increase after funding to [x], which will include a [VP-Sales, paid on commission; VP-R&D, $[x], VP-Finance, $[x]; VP-Operations, $[x].

Keep in mind that projections do not stand on their own. The rationale of how you prepared the numbers—and how sober you were when you did them—is important to investors. Expect the discussions you made about market size, time to market, market acceptance, and competitive pressures to tie into these numbers.

Discuss any large numbers or numbers that change significantly from period to period. Include discussion of sales growth rationale, expense growth, etc.

Balance Sheet Summary

Comment on any large or unusual items, such as other current assets, other accounts payable, or accrued liabilities.

Cash Flow and Break-even Analysis

These are critical statements, even more so than the Balance Sheets and Income Statements. Cash, and how much you have at the end of the day, is everything to investors.

We have assumed that our suppliers will be willing to grant us terms of [x] until we reach monthly purchases of [x]. At that time, we have assumed that our terms will be stretched to [x] days.

We have also assumed that we can collect our billings within [x] days because of [special programs with large customers, factoring arrangement, credit-card and COD sales].

We have assumed that the first part of our [loan, investment] will be made in [month], and the balance in [month].

We can reach break even by the [x] month. Sales are expected to be at the [$x] level by that date.

EXHIBITS

A common rookie error is mucking up the body of a plan with too much detail. That's what the exhibits are for.

Exhibits give an investor a better feel for the company behind the numbers. Be sure to include illustrative material such as:

- Product literature and brochures

- *Sales sheets*

- Media coverage

- Clips from industry publications

- *Relevant patents*

- Market research data

- *Past advertising campaigns*

- Useful photographs of facilities, warehouses, etc.

APPENDIX C

On-Line Audition for *MoneyHunt*

Once upon a time, we booked guests for our show based on people we knew in the market for capital, and the occasional plan that would come in from people that heard about MoneyHunt through the grapevine.

When we achieved national distribution for our show and our Web site grew dramatically, something had to give. With more and more entrepreneurs clamoring to be on TV, we saw the opportunity to create a fully relational database of business ideas and opportunities through a simple process we called on-line audition. The multiple-choice questions allow us to segment shows by theme and match entrepreneurs with mentors who have experience and contacts in their field. Our producers can select from a very large group of qualified entrepreneurs for each season, making the quality of our shows all the better.

For any entrepreneur who buys this book, we make the following promise. Miles or Cliff will personally review every on-line audition submission that comes through from anyone that reads the book. Just mention this book in the comment section of your audition.

If you would like to try, here is what the on-line audition looks like. It can be accessed on-line at www.moneyhunter.com.

COMPANY SUMMARY

Please include all of the following: A 100-word description that includes product and service description, market, competition, management team, sales level, the amount of capital you have raised to date, the amount of capital you are seeking, and the uses for this capital. The only way you can be eligible for the show is if you include ALL of this information.

Do you have a current business plan?
(Y/N)

What category best describes your business?
Consumer Products
Housewares
Hardware
Pets
Franchise
Finance
Insurance
Energy
Machinery
Sports
Construction & Materials
Internet
Info Technology
Communication
Entertainment
Education
Agriculture
Food
Beauty/Fashion/Textile
Travel & Leisure
Environmental Services
Health Care
Other

Enterprise Age
Less than one year
Greater than one year
Greater than five years

What type of funding do you seek?
  First Stage
  Second Stage
  Mezzanine
  Leveraged Buyout
  Seed
  Research and Development
  Special Situations
  Factoring
  Start-Up
  Control Block Purchase
  Buyout or Acquisition
  Management Buyout

How much funding do you seek?
  under $250,000
  $250,000–$500,000
  $500,000–$1M
  $1M–$5M
  over $5M

Do you have a tangible product that can be demonstrated on camera?
  (Y/N)

Have you ever been on television, radio, or made a public appearance?
  (Y/N)

Do you have an unshakable belief in the viability of your business?
  (Y/N)

Can you discuss every element of your business plan?
  (Y/N)

Are you prepared for criticism of your idea or plan?
  (Y/N)

APPENDIX D

Legal Dos and Don'ts of Raising Capital

Do Your Homework Before You Go Out into the Marketplace

BY CLIFF ENNICO

Most legal hassles in raising capital can be avoided if you do a little homework before you start "beating the bushes" for investors. The questions your lawyer will want answered at the initial meeting ("What? We have to deal with *lawyers*?" You betcha, and darn good ones too) include the following:

How many investors do you plan to have? Who are they (individuals, trusts, pension plans, corporations, limited liability companies)? In what states or foreign countries are they located? What type of company do you have (Delaware corporation, New York LLC, etc.)? What kind of security are you offering (debt, equity, warrants, some combination of the above)? How much capital are you trying to raise (the rules for financings of $1,000,000 or less are generally less strict than those for more than $1,000,000)? How much of the company are you offering?

What is the market capitalization (100 percent valuation) of your company? Do you have a preexisting relationship with each of the people to whom you will offer your securities? Will your offering be limited to "accredited investors"? If so, how will you determine if someone is "accredited" or not? N.B.: If you don't know what an "accredited investor" is, stop reading this outline, go directly to a securities lawyer, do not pass go, do not collect any money from anyone, don't do ANY-THING until you get the competent legal advice you need.

DON'T Try This Without Help

You will need to build a "transaction team" to put the offering together and run the selling effort. In addition to your core management team, you will need, at the very least:

- A good lawyer who specializes in securities regulation and carries the necessary malpractice insurance for this type of work (securities work carries the highest malpractice premiums in the legal profession, and many qualified corporate lawyers do not carry sufficient insurance to do securities work),

- A good accountant familiar with the Securities and Exchange Commission's accounting rules (known as "Regulation S-X") and the financial disclosures required for private offerings (known as "Rule 502(b)"), and

- A financial adviser or "placement agent" with a strong database of investors whom he or she has prequalified as "accredited."

Unlike some areas of the law, which can be mastered by nonlawyers in a reasonable period of time, securities law is fraught with "traps for the unwary" and it's easy to make mistakes. Be prepared to spend money on professional fees; while painful in the short term, the cost of making and correcting mistakes in this area is prohibitive and may cost you your company.

DON'T Offer Your Company's Securities to People You Do Not Know

Under federal securities regulations, you are not allowed to make a "general solicitation" of company securities unless:

- The offering is less than $1,000,000, or

- You file a prospectus with the Securities and Exchange Commission and distribute it to prospective investors when offering your securities to them.

What is a "general solicitation"? Basically, it's offering securities to people you do not know. SEC regulations require that you or someone on your management team (including your financial adviser or "placement agent") have a preexisting relationship with each prospective investor before you start offering securities to them. Even if you make an offer to a stranger, he buys your security, and he turns out to be an "accredited investor," your offer is still illegal if there was no preexisting relationship between you and the investor.

DON'T RAISE CAPITAL ON THE INTERNET

Contrary to recent press releases, the Securities and Exchange Commission has not yet sanctioned private offerings on the Internet. All the SEC has said is that if you registered your prospectus with the SEC in a "public offering," and the prospectus has been declared effective by the SEC, the SEC does not care where you advertise. As far as they are concerned, you can staple your prospectus to telephone poles, drop them from airplanes during the Super Bowl, or post them on the Internet, whatever you like, because you have complied with their rules for a "public offering." At the time I am writing this, the technology does not exist that will enable you safely to make a private offering of securities on the Internet. We're working on it.

DO COMPLY WITH THE "BLUE SKY" LAWS OF THE STATES WHERE YOUR INVESTORS RESIDE

So you've hired the best securities lawyer in the United States, you've written a three-hundred-page offering memorandum with financial statements and projections out the wazoo, and you have complied with every rule the Securities and Exchange Commission has for private offerings. Are you ready to start selling now? Not yet, chucko. First you have to know the states where your investors reside and be sure you have complied with the state securities, or "blue sky," laws of each state where your investors reside. The states have the power to regulate sales of securities to their residents, and most states have complicated rules for certain types of offerings (such as limited partnerships and other "tax shelters"). Some states require that you file your offering materials with a state government agency and have them approved in writing before you can accept money from in-state investors. In a few states (Connecticut comes to mind), you have to file certain documents with the state securities agency before you can even make offers to state residents.

Because the rules vary widely from state to state, "blue-skying" an offering of securities is an expensive, time-consuming process, best accomplished by lawyers who lack social lives. So what if you don't comply—you let Aunt Irma in Iowa buy into your company without filing the proper papers with the Iowa Securities Division. What can happen? If your investment heads south, or if Aunt Irma is dissatisfied with her investment for any reason (real or imagined), Aunt Irma has the right at any time to demand her money back, you may be prosecuted in the state of Iowa for selling unregistered securities, and you may be barred from ever selling securities in any state ever again. That's all.

DO KNOW UP FRONT IF YOU ARE A "DIRECT PARTICIPATION PROGRAM"

Over the years, a lot of people have been defrauded in oil and gas, timber, mining, commodities and real estate "tax shelters." Most states require specific disclosures to investors in these types of securities, which they call "direct participation programs," or DPPs. Even though you do not look upon your company as a "tax shelter" in the classic sense, any company (such as a Subchapter S corporation or a limited liability company) that offers "pass-through" tax treatment for its investors (i.e., the company itself does not pay taxes but the investors report their pro rata share of profit and loss on their personal tax returns) may potentially fall within the DPP regulations of some states. As always, seek competent tax and legal advice before offering securities in a tax-favored entity.

DO CHECK TO MAKE SURE YOU ARE NOT A FRANCHISE OR "BUSINESS OPPORTUNITY"

In some offerings, what you're offering is not technically a "security" but rather the right to act as an agent of the company in marketing, selling, and distributing the company's products or performing the company's services. If you do not structure such an offering carefully, you may fall within the franchise or "business opportunity" regulations in many states. Do not assume that because you are not licensing a trademark or asking for a big up-front fee from the "investor" that you are not a franchise operation. As with the "blue sky" laws, the definition of a franchise or "business opportunity" varies from state to state, and what is okay in one state may shut you down in another.

DO LET YOUR INVESTORS KNOW UP FRONT WHAT THEIR MANAGEMENT RIGHTS ARE

In small offerings to so-called angels, the investor may expect to be your business partner, helping to conduct the company's business or otherwise having a say in the management of your business. If this is not your intent, you need to let investors know before they put money on the table. And keep in mind that anyone who owns 20 percent or more of your company is a "six-hundred-pound gorilla" who will need to be kept happy no matter what you tell them up front. The best advice: Don't give a significant chunk of your company to someone who isn't going to stick around for the long haul.

DO KNOW THE TAX CONSEQUENCES OF AN INVESTMENT IN YOUR COMPANY

Certain types of investments can have adverse tax consequences for your investors. An offering of "in the money" warrants, for example, may be regarded as income to the recipient even though he or she doesn't immediately exercise the warrant. Be sure to get good tax advice when structuring an investment, and don't assume that the investor is aware of the tax consequences. Tell him or her in writing what the tax consequences will be, and if they have questions refer them to your tax professionals before they commit funds.

DO BE CAREFUL WHEN DEALING WITH IRAs AND PENSION/RETIREMENT PLANS

Often an investor will sign up for a big investment in your company, walk into your office on the closing date, and say, "You know, I've decided that I really want my IRA to hold this investment. Will that be a problem?" Under the rules governing pension and retirement plans such as IRAs and 401(k) plans, an investment in speculative securities (such as yours) may be a "prohibited transaction" that cannot legally be made by the plan's trustee. Do not allow investors using their IRAs, pension, or retirement plans to become stakeholders in your company without making sure they have received competent tax advice.

DO NOT LET LEGAL RESTRICTIONS PREVENT YOU FROM RAISING CAPITAL

The American legal system does not make it easy or inexpensive for start-up or small companies to raise capital. If you are planning a private offering of your company's securities, the cost of complying with the federal and state securities laws alone may cost anywhere from $10,000 to $50,000 depending on the firm you use and the amount of time they take in preparing the necessary documentation. Unfortunately, the cost of not complying or (worse yet) launching an offering that only partially complies with applicable laws is far greater—for most small companies, it will probably cost you the ranch. The best advice is to build a team of competent experts and work closely with them to make sure the "t's" are crossed, the "i's" are dotted, and the investors are prequalified.

The good news? The cost of doing the second offering is a lot cheaper when the first one is done right.

APPENDIX E

Demystifying the Business Organization, or, Partnerships, Corporations, S-Corporations, and Limited Liability Companies (Oh, My!)

BY CLIFF ENNICO

There are five "flavors" of business organization currently allowed under the laws of most states: the sole proprietorship, the general partnership, the limited partnership, the regular (or "C") corporation, the "S" corporation (or "Subchapter-S Corporation"), and the limited liability company, or "LLC." Some states also allow limited liability partnerships or "LLPs."

There is no one "perfect" way to organize your business; each "flavor" involves certain tradeoffs and only you can weigh the pros and cons to determine which "flavor" is right for you.

THE SOLE PROPRIETORSHIP

This is what you are right now—a solitary human being engaged in a trade or business.

What's Good About a Sole Proprietorship?
1. You don't need a lawyer to set up a sole proprietorship; no start-up costs.

2. The only piece of legal paperwork is a "trade name" or "fictitious name" certificate—and this only if you are doing business using a

name other than your own name (you file this in the city clerk's or town clerk's office in each town or city in which you maintain an office).

3. Taxes are easy too—you fill out Schedule "C" on your Form 1040 and pay taxes at your individual rate.

What's Bad About a Sole Proprietorship?

1. Unlimited personal liability for every business mistake you make—you breach a contract, you lose your house; you get into a traffic accident (that's not covered by insurance), you lose your house; you bake cookies that get people sick, you lose your house.

2. You can limit this risk by buying an umbrella liability policy, but this can get expensive depending on the nature of your business.

THE GENERAL PARTNERSHIP

A general partnership is formed when two or more "sole proprietors" agree to pool their resources and—this is the key—share profits and losses from the business (i.e., if two or more lawyers share office space and refer clients to each other but render separate bills for their services and keep what the client pays them, this is not a partnership; if they render a joint bill for their services and split the profits fifty-fifty, that's a partnership).

What's Good About a General Partnership?

1. Easy to form and no start-up costs; you don't need a written partnership agreement (legally) to form a general partnership—you can do it with a handshake (of course, if you do so there will be a lot of unresolved questions that may have to be resolved in the courts, which is why most people have a written partnership agreement even if the law does not specifically require one).

2. Taxes are easy, too—the partnership files an information return on Form 1065 but pays no taxes—each partner pays taxes on his/her "pro rata share" of the partnership's profits at his/her individual tax rate.

What's Bad About a General Partnership?

1. Unlimited personal liability, the same as a sole proprietorship, but with a twist—if A and B are partners, and B runs someone over

with his car while on partnership business, both A and B lose their houses even though A had nothing to do with the accident. Lawyers call this "joint and several" liability.

2. Partnerships have what tax lawyers call a "phantom income" problem, in that the partners have to pay taxes on their "pro rata shares" of the partnership's profits even though the partnership did not pay them cash to pay the taxes with.

THE LIMITED PARTNERSHIP

A limited partnership is a partnership with two tiers or classes of partners—general partners, who have unlimited personal liability for the things they do (or don't do) while on partnership business; and "limited partners," who are liable only for the money they contribute (or pledge to contribute) to the partnership.

Because relatively few "operating" businesses—businesses that provide products or services—use the limited partnership form, this outline won't go into the details (the limited partnership is, however, an excellent vehicle for certain "passive investment" types of business, such as real estate investment or oil and gas exploration).

Basically the "what's good" and "what's bad" aspects of limited partnerships are the same as they are for general partnerships, with the differences that (1) only the general partners have unlimited personal liability, (2) limited partners cannot participate in the management or operation of the limited partnership's business without becoming a general partner (and therefore "going naked" for anything bad that happens), and (3) limited partnerships are more complex than general partnerships and require more paperwork and legal expense. Lawyers like limited partnerships.

THE REGULAR OR "C" CORPORATION

A corporation, unlike a partnership, is a taxable entity—when you form a corporation it is as if you have had a baby, with the difference that the baby pays taxes from the day it's born.

It's called a "C" corporation because it is taxed under Subchapter C of the Internal Revenue Code of 1986 (you had to ask).

What's Good About a "C" Corporation?

1. Limited Liability—generally, the owners of a "C" corporation (called "shareholders" or "stockholders") are liable only for the

amounts which they contribute (or agree to contribute) as capital to the corporation, but will still be liable for their own negligence or stupidity.

EXAMPLE 1: A and B are shareholders of ABC Corporation. A runs over someone with his car while on the corporation's business. The injured party may sue the corporation and win a judgment up to the amount of the corporation's assets (because that's all it has). The injured party may sue A in his/her individual capacity and take A's house away. But the injured party cannot sue B in any way unless it can be shown that B contributed actively in some way to his/her injury (for example, by serving A too much liquor which caused A to be intoxicated at the wheel).

EXAMPLE 2: A and B are shareholders of ABC Corporation. ABC Corporation enters into a contract with a supplier to buy 10,000 widgets, and then discovers that it doesn't have enough money to pay for the 10,000 widgets. ABC Corporation breaches the contract, and the supplier sues. The supplier may sue the corporation and win a judgment up to the amount of the corporation's assets, but the supplier cannot sue either A or B, even if A or B actually signed the contract as an officer or employee of ABC Corporation.

What's Bad About a "C" Corporation?

1. Expensive to form—legal expenses and filing fees are usually between $1,000 and $1,500 to form a corporation in most states.

2. Expensive to keep alive—if a corporation fails to pay taxes for X consecutive years or fails to file a report (and pay a fee) every Y years with the secretary of state's office, the attorney general comes along and "dissolves" the corporation (and your limited liability along with it). To add insult to injury, you are not informed that this has been done, so you continue blissfully in business thinking you have a corporation when you really don't.

3. If you don't use the corporation and treat it with respect, you lose the corporation; people suing you for something your corporation did will always try to argue they didn't know they were dealing with a corporation—if you conducted business in your own name, writing checks from your own checking account and accepting money in your own name that should have gone to the corporation, you can't argue it was really the corporation that should be sued and not you personally. Lawyers call this "piercing the corporate veil."

4. Lots of paperwork—when you have a corporation, you don't do anything; the corporation does everything. This means that for a corporation to do anything the shareholders (that's you) have to prepare written documents (called resolutions or "minutes") authorizing the directors of the corporation (again, that's you) to do the thing, and the directors have to prepare written documents authorizing the officers of the corporation (again, that's you) to do the thing. Resolutions are a pain in the neck, but if you don't do them you will be tempting the courts to say that you didn't treat your corporation with the proper respect so that creditors are allowed to get at your personal assets.

5. Taxes—because corporations are taxable entities, they pay taxes (albeit at a lower rate than you do yourself, in most cases); this means that any income a corporation earns is taxed twice.

    EXAMPLE: XYZ Corporation has two stockholders—A and B—and makes $100 in net income for a particular year. The corporation pays 15% to Uncle Sam as federal income tax, and books the remaining $85 as "net after-tax earnings." XYZ Corporation then resolves (remember those minutes?) to pay A and B the $85 in the form of a dividend, and distributes $42.50 to each of A and B. A and B each has to report that $42.50 as income on their Form 1040 for the year and pay taxes on that $42.50 at their individual rate. The result? If A and B are in the top tax bracket, that $100 in corporate income has dwindled down to about $26 in each of A's and B's hands after federal income taxes. Add state and local taxes to this calculation, and the tax "bite" becomes much larger.

The "S" Corporation

An "S" corporation is the same as a regular or "C" corporation with one important difference: it is not taxed by the federal government. This means that the "S" corporation is taxed just like a general partnership, but with the powerful advantage that stockholders in an "S" corporation have limited liability.

Some states, however, do not recognize "S" corporations. This means that "S" corporations with offices in such states are taxed twice at the state level.

What's Good About an "S" Corporation? The same things that are good about a regular or "C" corporation.

What's Bad About an "S" Corporation? The same things that are bad about a regular or "C" corporation (except the tax part), with a couple of additions:

1. Because "S" corporations are taxed like partnerships, "S" corporations have the "phantom income" problem (if you've forgotten what this was, look under "What's Bad About General Partnerships" in the "General Partnerships" section of this outline).

2. "S" corporations have lots of icky little rules that you have to comply with if you don't want to be taxed as a regular or "C" corporation (note: If the IRS takes away your "S" corporation status you don't—repeat don't—lose your limited liability; the worst thing that happens is that you're taxed as a regular or "C" corporation). For example, you can't have anything but natural human beings as stockholders in an "S" corporation (forget parent-subsidiary arrangements), you can't have more than 35 stockholders, and so forth.

3. "S" corporations file different forms with the IRS than regular or "C" corporations do, and have to report certain items of income differently; it is virtually impossible to operate as an "S" corporation without a darned good accountant. Accountants and lawyers both like "S" corporations.

THE LIMITED LIABILITY COMPANY

The limited liability company, or LLC, has become the most popular alternative for small business formations since the IRS approved it in 1988. Virtually all states except Vermont and Hawaii allow LLCs in some form.

What is an LLC? Well, it's basically an "S" corporation without all of the icky little rules that make "S" corporations unattractive for a lot of folks.

What's Good About LLCs?
1. Owners of an LLC (called "members") have limited liability—if A and B are members of an LLC and B runs someone over with his car while on LLC business, B may lose his/her house, but A will not lose his/her house unless A actively contributed to the injury.

2. Like partnerships, LLCs are simple to operate—there is no need to prepare resolutions or minutes to authorize people to do things (although banks and some other folks may still require you to do

resolutions because they haven't gotten the idea yet); they just do them.

3. The costs of starting up an LLC are likely to be much less than forming a "C" corporation or an "S" corporation.

4. LLCs are taxed like partnerships, so there is no "double taxation" of an LLC's income.

5. If you are doing a lot of overseas business, the LLC format may give you an edge on your competition. Most foreign business organizations (such as the German GmbH and the Italian S.r.l.) are a lot closer in structure to an LLC than they are to a partnership or corporation; with an LLC you can give your managers the same titles as their European or Asian counterparts (Europeans especially cannot understand that in America one can be a "director" of a corporation and have absolutely no power to bind the corporation; in Europe business organizations are managed by their "directors," not by officers or mere employees).

What's Bad About LLCs?

1. Really not a lot—while not perfect, LLCs are the closest thing to a "perfect" business organization the law has come up with to date.

2. Because LLCs are taxed like partnerships, they have the "phantom income" problem.

3. Watch out if you do business in Vermont or Hawaii, as those states have not yet passed LLC legislation and you do not know if you will enjoy limited liability if something goes wrong in those states.

4. It may be difficult for existing businesses to convert to LLC's— corporations and their shareholders incur "double taxation" upon liquidation, while general and limited partnerships formed to acquire or hold title to real estate (as many are) may incur transfer taxes and other fees upon converting to an LLC.

LIMITED LIABILITY PARTNERSHIPS

Limited liability partnerships, or "LLPs," are allowed in a growing number of states; while theoretically any business can operate as an LLP, this form of organization is best suited to lawyers, doctors, accountants, and other professional practices, and to existing general partnerships that wish to achieve limited liability status with a minimum of legal expense.

An LLP is a general partnership in which the partners have limited liability for the acts and omissions of the other LLP partners; an LLP partner is always liable for his or her own negligence or willful misconduct.

An LLP partner also enjoys limited liability for contracts he or she signs on behalf of the LLP.

An existing general partnership that converts into an LLP can continue to use its existing partnership agreement, usually without significant modification. This is an advantage for older partnerships that may have lengthy, detailed partnership agreements that the partners do not wish to renegotiate at the present time.

In practice, LLPs are best suited to professional practices, particularly those with offices in two or more states (such as the so-called "Big 6" accounting firms). In some states, professionals are not allowed to conduct business in corporate or LLC form. By reorganizing as an LLP in each state where it does business, a multistate professional practice complies with local laws, ensures consistent accounting and tax treatment in all states where it does business, and provides at least some limited liability protection for its partners.

CONCLUSION

Like we said at the beginning, there is no "perfect" way to organize your business activities. Each of the "flavors" discussed in this outline has pros and cons, and most lawyers will want to spend some time learning about your business plans before recommending that you consider one or the other.

Generally, the less you are concerned about limiting your liability, the less legal complexity and hassle you will be forced to live with. The more you are concerned about limiting your liability, the more complexity and hassle you will live with, and will have to learn to live with.

A good lawyer is someone who doesn't just "form the corporation" and then leave you to figure out the rest; a good lawyer is a good "teacher" who helps you figure out how to do the paperwork, keep the records, and otherwise avoid making the dumb mistakes that can get you into trouble.

Index